# THEIR LAST BATTLE

## ALSO BY NICOLAUS MILLS

*American and English Fiction in the Nineteenth Century*

*The Crowd in American Literature*

*Like a Holy Crusade: Mississippi 1964—*
*The Turning of the Civil Rights Movement in America*

*The Triumph of Meanness: America's War Against Its Better Self*

## EDITOR

*Comparisons:*
*A Short Story Anthology*

*The Great School Bus Controversy*

*The New Journalism*

*Busing USA*

*Culture in an Age of Money:*
*The Legacy of the 1980s in America*

*Debating Affirmative Action:*
*Race, Gender, Ethnicity, and the Politics of Inclusion*

*Arguing Immigration:*
*The Debate over the Changing Face of America*

*Legacy of Dissent: 40 Years of Writing from Dissent Magazine*

*The New Killing Fields: Massacre and the Politics of Intervention*
(with Kira Brunner)

# THEIR LAST BATTLE

The Fight for the National
World War II Memorial

NICOLAUS MILLS

BASIC
BOOKS

A Member of the Perseus Books Group
New York

Published by Basic Books,
A Member of the Perseus Books Group

Books published by Basic Books are available at special discounts for bulk purchases in the United States by corporations, institutions, and other organizations. For more information, please contact the Special Markets Department at the Perseus Books Group, 11 Cambridge Center, Cambridge MA 02142, or call (617) 252–5298, (800) 255–1514 or e-mail special.markets@perseusbooks.com.

Library of Congress Cataloging-in-Publication Data

Mills, Nicolaus.
    Their last battle : the fight for the national World War II memorial /
Nicolaus Mills.—1st ed.
        p. cm.
    Includes bibliographical references.
    ISBN 0-465-04582-0
    1. World War II Memorial (Washington, D.C.)   2. Mall, The (Washington,
D.C.)   3. Memorials—Washington (D.C.)   I. Title.

D836.W37M55 2004
940.54'6573—dc22

                                                                2003025543

*Text design by Jeff Williams*
Set in 12-point Adobe Garamond by Perseus Books Group

First Edition

1 2 3 4 5 6 7 8 9 10—06 05 04

*For*
*The Reverend John Hall*
*and*
*Judy Serafini-Sauli*

# CONTENTS

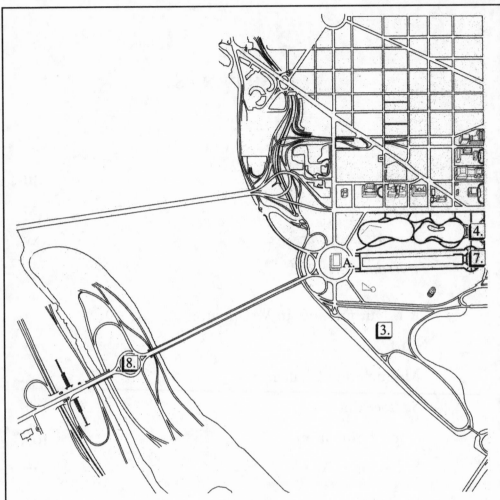

## MEMORIAL SITES UNDER

1. CAPITOL REFLECTING POOL
2. TIDAL BASIN
3. WEST POTOMAC PARK
4. CONSTITUTION GARDENS

A. THE LINCOLN MEMORIAL    B. THE WHITE HOUSE

### DAVIS BUCKLEY
A PROFESSIONAL CORPORATION
### ARCHITECTS AND PLANNERS
1612 K STREET, NW SUITE 900
WASHINGTON, D.C. 20006

# MEMORIAL
## DISTRICT OF COLUMBIA

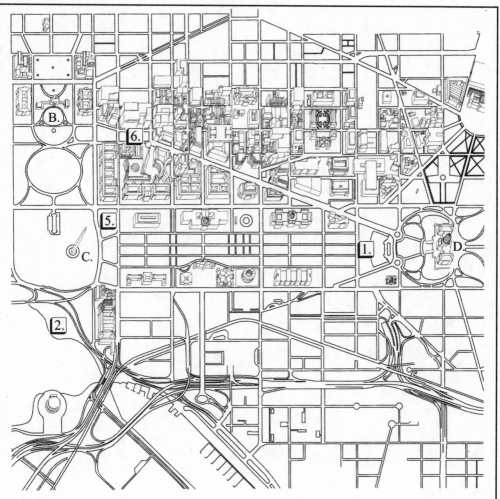

# CONSIDERATION IN 1995

5. WASHINGTON MONUMENT GROUNDS
6. FREEDOM PLAZA
7. THE RAINBOW POOL
8. COLUMBIA ISLAND/ARLINGTON NATIONAL CEMETARY

C. WASHINGTON MONUMENT      D. THE CAPITOL

AMERICAN BATTLE MONUMENTS COMMISSION

COURTHOUSE PLAZAJ II, SUITE 500

2300 CLARENDON BOULEVARD

ARLINGTON, VA 22201

# PREFACE

This book is the story of the National World War II Memorial—the struggle to bring it into existence, the battles over where it should go, what it should symbolize, and how it should look. As a result, it is a book that is as much about political process as architecture, as much about how Americans see themselves today as how they remember World War II. For a writer, the chance to be the biographer of the National World War II Memorial is a once-in-a-lifetime opportunity. But as soon as friends learned that I was writing a book about the National World War II Memorial being built in Washington, the first question they asked was, "Why?"

It was the kind of question that I was never asked when I wrote about affirmative action or immigration or the Reagan money culture of the 1980s. When I took on these subjects, friends always felt sure about the conclusions they believed that I would reach. But the National World War II Memorial was a different story. It did not seem to matter when I said that the National World War II Memorial would soon be joining the Washington Monument and the Lincoln Memorial on the most important piece of political real estate in America. It was as if the only kind of war memorial that a liberal could take seriously after the 1960s was one like Maya Lin's Vietnam Veterans Memorial, which architecturally and politically went against the historical grain.

What lay behind such thinking was the assumption that the Vietnam Veterans Memorial represents what we have become as a nation and that any memorial that projects a benign view of the uses of American power at this time in history is misleading. Not surprisingly, long before it was completed, the National World War II Memorial ran into trouble in the media. To be sure, the memorial did acquire some important defenders—among them the architectural critics Benjamin Forgey and Witold Rybczynski. But in the country's leading newspapers the praise of the memorial's defenders was continually overshadowed by the harsh attacks of the memorial's detractors. To the *Washington Post* columnist Jonathan Yardley, the National World War II Memorial was "ponderous and pompous." To the *New York Times* architecture critic Herbert Muschamp, it was "well-designed propaganda." To the *New Yorker* architecture critic Paul Goldberger, it was "a bureaucrat's idea of classical grandeur." To the *Los Angeles Times* art critic Christopher Knight, it was a memorial that threatened to "disfigure the memory of the war."

Would critics, even those who disliked the design of the National World War II Memorial, have written so harshly at the end of 1945 with the memory of Franklin Roosevelt still fresh and the task of rebuilding the postwar world lying ahead? I doubt it. But that difference, along with the fact that by being built after the Vietnam Veterans Memorial and Korean War Veterans Memorial, the National World War II Memorial came to life out of sequence, is central to the National World War II Memorial story. The National World War II Memorial pays homage to the sacrifices that were made on the home front and the war front during the 1940s, but it is also a memorial that belongs to the period in which it was constructed.

Our reactions to the National World War II Memorial, particularly our quarrels over it, reflect both our current distrust of government as well as the need we have had since the September 11 attacks to come together as a nation. Honoring the World War II generation has seemed the right thing to do as far as most Americans are concerned, but what has been much harder for us to determine is whether honoring the World War II generation with a memorial is more than grateful remembering, more than a tribute to beliefs that we are no longer confident that we share.

As someone who was a teenager in the 1950s, I found the 1960s a period of welcome change. I was part of the civil rights movement in Mississippi for one summer. Later I worked in California as an organizer for the United Farm Workers, and like virtually everyone my age I know, I took part in teach-ins and anti-war marches while the Vietnam War was going on. But then, as now, I viewed the political positions I took in the sixties and seventies as extensions of an argument that said that from Mississippi to Vietnam we were violating what we stood for as a nation. I was not skeptical about the values I was defending or the history behind them.

In my judgment these same values go to the core of our involvement in World War II. While too young to have a vivid memory of that war, I have a vivid memory of the men who fought it. They included two uncles, the son of our next-door neighbor, and the headmaster of my boarding school. There was in my mind nothing inconsistent about opposing the war in Vietnam and believing World War II was our "good war." Nowadays it seems to me a sign of how estranged from ordinary life many who regard themselves as liberals or progressives have become when they cannot imagine a National World War II Memorial that speaks to what is best about us as a nation.

In writing *Their Last Battle,* I never felt that I had chosen the wrong subject, but what did worry me initially was writing a biography of the National World War II Memorial as it was still being built. While working on *Their Last Battle,* I read Christopher Thomas's masterful book, *The Lincoln Memorial and American Life.* The publication of his study in 2002, eighty years after the dedication of the Lincoln Memorial, seemed to me to be perfect timing. Thomas not only mined archival sources to perfection; he captured how America's changing view of the Lincoln Memorial reflected the nation's changing thinking on race.

I envy Thomas his perspective, and I expect that eighty years from now, if not sooner, we will get a similarly expansive book on the National World War II Memorial and American life. The absence of such a perspective on the National World War II Memorial should not, however, be an excuse for failing to write about the memorial now. Journalism may be history on the run, but it is also history rooted in the living. In writing about the National World War II Memorial, I have had a chance to speak with, among others, its design architect, Friedrich St.Florian; its most important public defender, former senator and presidential candidate, Bob Dole; its principal artist, Ray Kaskey; and its chief congressional sponsor, Representative Marcy Kaptur. The value of such opportunities seems to me more than enough to offset the disadvantages of being so close to the events I describe.

In the end, my great concern in writing about the National World War II Memorial at this time does not come from worrying that I jumped the gun. It comes from worrying that I did not always do justice to the passionate feelings that the memorial elicited during its approval and construction period. These feelings, for all their differences in motivation, reflect something that nobody associated with the debate over the National World War II Memorial ever doubted: For centuries to come, the National World War II Memorial, like the Washington Monument and the Lincoln Memorial, will be viewed as a symbol for who we are as a people.

# Cast of Characters

**James Aylward:** Executive director of the National World War II Memorial Project and the insider most responsible for the successful organization of the American Battle Monuments Commission's fund-raising efforts.

**Nick Benson:** A third-generation stonecarver and, like his father and grandfather, head of the John Stevens Shop in Newport, Rhode Island, who created a special, hand-drawn form for the letters of the National World War II Memorial inscriptions.

**J. Carter Brown:** From 1971 until his death in 2002, the chairman of the Commission of Fine Arts and by far the most influential figure in the Washington art and architecture community. Championed the National World War II Memorial and its placement on the center line of the Mall.

**David Childs:** Senior partner, Skidmore, Owings, and Merrill and designer of Constitution Gardens. Headed the Design Jury for the National World War II Memorial competition and later made a video defending the National World War II Memorial site and design.

**Leo A. Daly III:** Chairman and president of Leo A Daly, the powerful international firm responsible for architect-engineer design services for the National World War II Memorial Project. As architect-engineer, Leo

A Daly had a wide range of supervisory authority and primary responsibility for the production of architectural construction documents, as well as contract administration and engineering.

**Bob Dole:** Former senator and 1996 Republican presidential candidate. Served as chairman of the National World War II Memorial Campaign and along with co-chairman Fred Smith, CEO of Federal Express, turned the campaign into a stunning success.

**Roger Durbin:** Battle of the Bulge veteran whose belief that there should be a National World War II Memorial set in motion the events that resulted in that memorial. Durbin died before the memorial was completed.

**Ed Feiner:** Chief architect for the General Services Administration. Responsible for managing the National World War II Memorial design competition.

**Judy Scott Feldman:** Leader of the opposition to the National World War II Memorial Project. Founder and chair of the National Coalition to Save Our Mall.

**Andrea Ferster:** Environmental lawyer who led the legal effort to stop the National World War II Memorial from being built on the Mall.

**Benjamin Forgey:** Architecture critic of the *Washington Post* who became by far the most influential writer on the National World War II Memorial and who was in the end a memorial supporter.

**Harvey Gantt:** Chairman of the National Capital Planning Commission during the crucial approval phase of the National World War II Memorial. Became the subject of a controversy when it was learned that he had inadvertently cast votes he should not by law have made on memorial decisions after his term as chairman had run out.

**Tom Hanks:** The star of *Saving Private Ryan* and a two-time Academy Award winner whose public service announcements on behalf of the National World War II Memorial brought it tremendous popularity and financial support.

**Hugh Hardy:** Leading American architect and partner in Hardy Holzman Pfeiffer Associates. Hardy chaired the National World War II Memorial Architect-Engineer Evaluation Board and served on the Design Jury as well. He was an important public defender of the National World War II Memorial during its approval phase.

**George Hartman:** Partner in the Washington architecture firm of Hartman-Cox and associate architect for the National World War II Memorial.

**Marcy Kaptur:** Democratic representative from Toledo, Ohio, who led the congressional fight to build the National World War II Memorial. It was Kaptur whom Roger Durbin first approached about building a National World War II Memorial.

**Ray Kaskey:** Sculptor responsible for the art work of the National World War II Memorial. Played a crucial role in blending his vision of the memorial with that of its design architect, Friedrich St. Florian.

**P. X. Kelley:** Retired commandant of the U.S. Marine Corps, appointed by President George W. Bush to a second term on the American Battle Monuments Commission in 2001. Served as the ABMC chairman during the National World War II Memorial's construction and final resolution of its artwork and inscriptions.

**Bob Kerrey:** Veteran of the Vietnam War, Congressional Medal of Honor winner, and former senator from Nebraska whose early opposition to the design of the National World War II Memorial gained national attention.

**Bill Lacy:** Former president of the State University of New York at Purchase. Lacy, in his role as professional advisor, brought order to the National World War II Memorial design competition by requiring anonymous submissions for the initial entries.

**Richard Longstreth:** Professor of American Studies at George Washington University and leading authority on the Mall. Went from a key academic critic of the National World War II Memorial in 1997 to a key supporter in 2000.

**Eleanor Holmes Norton:** Delegate to the House of Representatives from Washington, D.C. and longtime civil rights activist, who argued that locating the National World War II Memorial at the Rainbow Pool trespassed upon the Lincoln Memorial and its historic civil rights associations.

**John Parsons:** Associate regional director for land, resources, and planning for the National Park Service's National Capital Region. Parsons played a crucial role in the National World War II Memorial site selection and approval process.

**Friedrich St.Florian:** Former dean of architecture at the Rhode Island School of Design. St.Florian was declared winner of the National World War II Memorial design competition in 1997 and then endured years of approval hearings before gaining final acceptance for his classically inspired design.

**Bob Stump:** Arizona congressman and World War II navy veteran who in 2001 led the fight in the House of Representatives for legislation to expedite construction of the National World War II Memorial.

**James van Sweden:** Partner in the Washington landscape architecture firm of Oehme, van Sweden & Associates. Landscape architect responsible for the plantings and the area of contemplation at the National World War II Memorial.

**John Warner:** Virginia senator and World War II navy veteran who in 2001 led the fight in the Senate for legislation to expedite construction of the National World War II Memorial.

**Haydn Williams:** Member of the American Battle Monuments Commission who took the lead role in promoting the National World War II Memorial. A former ambassador and World War II navy veteran, Williams was involved in every phase of the National World War II Memorial development as chairman of the World War II Memorial Site and Design Committee.

**Fred Woerner:** Retired four-star U.S. Army general appointed by President Clinton to serve as chairman of the American Battle Monuments Commission. During his chairmanship, which lasted from 1994 to 2001, the National World War II Memorial won its important approval battles.

# Introduction:
# The Power of Dog Tags

In the 1825 address he delivered at the laying of the cornerstone for the Bunker Hill Monument, Daniel Webster made no effort to hide how moved he was by the sight of the Revolutionary War veterans at the head of the crowd of fifteen thousand, which, after a procession through the streets of Boston, gathered at Bunker Hill. It was fifty years to the day since the battle of Bunker Hill was fought, and the aging Revolutionary War veterans, including the frail Marquis de Lafayette, nearing the end of his farewell tour of America, had made an enormous effort to be present for the ceremony.

The keynote of Webster's speech was America's progress, but two centuries later what is most memorable about his speech is its poignancy. Time and again Webster voiced his concern that the Revolutionary War veterans, most of them in their seventies and eighties, were a vanishing generation. "Those who established our liberty and our government are daily dropping from among us," he observed. "The great trust now descends to new hands." Behind Webster's description of the disappearing Revolutionary War generation was not just sadness, but generational envy, a belief that the "venerable men" whom the Bunker Hill Monument honored were superior to those of his own time. "We can win no laurels in a war for independence. Earlier and worthier hands have gathered them all." Webster concluded his speech by declaring, "Our proper business is improvement."[1]

Today the language we use to describe the veterans of the World War II generation is strikingly similar to Webster's language in 1825. We have as a nation come to accept NBC anchor Tom Brokaw's designation of the World War II generation as "the greatest generation," and their accomplishments have left us feeling unequal to their patriotism and their capacity for sacrifice. As the historian Stephen Ambrose wrote in a 1998 essay describing the citizen-soldiers of World War II, "They were the sons of democracy, and they saved democracy. We owe them a debt we can never repay." Most of all, with the veterans who won World War II now in their mortality years, we are aware that more will soon be leaving us. As one of their own, former senator and Republican presidential candidate Bob Dole noted during his speech at the November 11, 2000, groundbreaking ceremony for the National World War II Memorial, "Our generation has gone from the shade to the shadows. . . . our dwindling ranks will soon belong to the history books."[2]

Why it took us, as it did Daniel Webster and his peers, so long to honor a war generation we admire is a complicated story. When it comes to healing memorials, those designed to deal with a war that went badly or a national trauma, we have in recent years managed to build in less than a decade memorials that give us comfort. In 1982, seven years after the end of the Vietnam War, construction on the Vietnam Veterans Memorial began, and within the year, the memorial opened to the public. In 1998, just three years after the bombing of the Alfred P. Murrah Federal Building in Oklahoma City, groundbreaking on the Oklahoma City National Memorial began, and two years later on April 19, 2000, the memorial officially opened. By contrast, with the exception of the Jefferson Memorial, on which work began more than one hundred years after Jefferson's death, work on the great presidential memorials on the National Mall typically gets started around a half century after a president's death, a time when the last generation with living memory of that president is itself passing from the scene. Construction on the Washington Monument began in 1848, forty-nine years after Washington's death, and the Washington Monument opened to the public in 1885. Groundbreaking, followed by work on the subfoundation, on the Lincoln Memorial began in 1914, forty-nine years after Lincoln's assassination, and the Lincoln Memorial opened to the public in 1922. Construction on the Franklin D. Roosevelt Memorial began in 1994, forty-nine years after Roosevelt's death, and the FDR Memorial opened to the public in 1997.[3]

In the case of the World War II veterans, in the period after the war there were efforts made to honor those who had died, as well as those returning, with traditional memorials. A plaster sculptural replica of Joe Rosenthal's famous February 23, 1945, photograph of five marines and a navy corpsman raising the American flag on Mt. Suribachi during the bloody battle for Iwo Jima quickly assumed iconic status. The replica by sculptor Felix de Weldon was used to help sell war bonds in 1945 and was briefly installed in Times Square on May 11, 1945, for the Treasury Department's "Mighty Seventh" bond drive. Later that year on Veterans Day, de Weldon's statue was given a more dignified home on Constitution Avenue within sight of the White House, where it remained until 1947, when it was moved to make room for the new Pan American Union Annex. Then seven years later, as a gigantic, 78-foot-high bronze sculpture, de Weldon's statue, today known as the Marine Corps War Memorial, was given a permanent home in Arlington, Virginia, just north of Arlington Cemetery at the junction of Arlington Boulevard and Ridge Road, in a highly publicized November 10, 1954, dedication ceremony attended by President Dwight Eisenhower.[4]

At almost the same time a parallel effort to honor the veterans of World War II with a local memorial was taking place across the country in Omaha, Nebraska. In July 1944, just a month after D-Day, the Omaha World War II Memorial Park Association was formed and began making plans to erect a World War II Memorial on 65 acres of rolling grassland on what had been the Dundee Golf Course. The price for the undertaking was just over $262,000, but with fund-raising drives in the greater Omaha area, the park association was able to raise enough money from individual contributors to start construction on the memorial by October 1, 1945.

Everything else went equally quickly. By 1947 work was completed on the centerpiece of the memorial, a semi-circular, granite colonnade, 32 feet high, with reliefs of the various branches of the armed services along its top and bronze plates inscribed with the names of the nearly eight hundred Douglas County, Nebraska, World War II dead on its colonnades. Designed by Leo A. Daly, the father of Leo A. Daly III, the head of the firm (which continues to bear his family's name) with the responsibility for the architect-engineer design services for the National World War II Memorial Project in Washington, the Omaha World War II Memorial won immediate acceptance. In 1946 the memorial was made part of the Omaha City park system by a unanimous vote of the Omaha City Council, and two years later at a June 5, 1948, ceremony presided over by President Harry Truman, the memorial was officially dedicated, following a parade through downtown Omaha that drew a crowd estimated at 160,000 people.[5]

In the years after World War II, the Marine Corps War Memorial and the Omaha World War II Memorial were, however, exceptions. There was great resistance at this time to creating World War II memorials that had the look of a traditional war memorial. A community might add the names of its World War II dead to an honor roll containing the names of its World War I dead, but that was usually as far as most cities and towns were prepared to go when it came to conventional memorials. Communities were, moreover, under no pressure from the returning veterans to do otherwise. Backed by the 1944 G.I. Bill of Rights, which promised government aid for higher education and home-buying, most vets were anxious to get back to "normal life" as soon as possible. Treated as heroes and helped by the $3.7 billion the G.I. Bill invested in them between 1945 and 1949, the returning vets of World War II did not see a national World War II memorial as a priority.[6]

In a 1945 *Art News* article, "War Memorials: What Aesthetic Price Glory?" Philip Johnson, whose own architecture—from his additions to the Museum of Modern Art to his work with John Burgee on the AT&T

Building—would over the course of the next half century change the skyline of New York, captured the post–World War II attitude toward war memorials that would prevail for years. "Today the climate of opinion in this country is unfavorable to the concept of the traditional war memorial," Johnson wrote. "One college president has suggested that we endow hospital beds instead. The Dean of Architecture at Harvard urges that we build playgrounds, schoolhouses, parks, anything rather than 'to increase the dreadful population' of our monuments 'by so much as a single increment.' Even returning GI's are quoted as taking a stand against cast iron soldiers."[7]

The postwar alternative to the traditional memorial was the useful memorial or the living memorial, and as Andrew Shanken observed in a recent *Art Bulletin* essay summarizing the subject, the postwar living memorial could range from a building as large as the Onondaga County War Memorial in Syracuse, a multipurpose auditorium and exhibition space for which planning began in November 1944, to a building as small as a local recreation center. The political support for living memorials during the late 1940s reflected the continuing New Deal belief that government money should be used to rebuild the country, and in the postwar years the Federal Security Agency, a New Deal agency created by the Reorganization Act of 1939, was able to mount a successful campaign for living memorials through its own publications and films as well as through its sponsorship of the American Commission for Living War Memorials.[8]

The living memorial movement of the late 1940s was, however, anything but a New Deal carryover that was rammed down the nation's throat. The living memorial movement not only had the support of local politicians anxious to rebuild their communities; it had the support of serious thinkers in and out of the architecture community. They saw the utilitarianism of the living memorial as embodying America's belief in the future in the way that no "dead" memorial could. "Let us then take as our first theme for memorials, destruction. Let us destroy the slum," architect and city planner Percival Goodman wrote in a *New York Herald Tribune* article, in which he quoted with approval New York

City Park Commissioner Robert Moses' call for memorials with year-round value. "Living trees and parks, lakes and clean streams," not "dead stones and cast iron," was what America needed, insisted Pulitzer Prize–winning novelist Louis Bromfield in an essay for *Recreation* that he titled, "Let's Have Living Memorials." Bromfield concluded his essay by observing of the returning vets, "All of them would prefer to be remembered by a forest or a game sanctuary or a lake than by some useless and possibly ugly cast iron statue." For a nation anxious to put behind it the images of war, especially those revealed by newsreels of the Nazi death camps and the devastation caused by the atomic bomb, the living memorial also had the advantage of leaving out any references to the horrors of World War II. As painter John Scott Williams asked in the October 1945 *Art Digest* article that cited gyms, lakes, and bridges as worthy memorials, "Why should there be War Memorials when most people wish to forget the tragedies of war and turn to the more hopeful occupation of peace and prosperity?"[9]

The virtues of the living memorial movement that, beginning in the middle 1940s, had such a powerful influence on America over the next decade were also its limitations. In focusing so much attention on the practical issues of community and the future, the living memorial avoided directly dealing with death and sacrifice as well as the task of commemorating the individual lives lost in World War II.

With the dedication of the National World War II Memorial on Memorial Day weekend 2004, we have at last begun to make up for not honoring our World War II veterans with a memorial fifty-nine years ago. That by itself is a historic act, and its significance is heightened still further by the placement of the National World War II Memorial on the central spine of the Mall between the Washington Monument and the Lincoln Memorial. No other place in the country more dramatically symbolizes who we believe ourselves to be as a people.

How the National World War II Memorial came into being is inescapably a story of art and architecture. Just as we cannot understand the Washington Monument and the Lincoln Memorial without understanding their designers, Robert Mills and Henry Bacon, we cannot hope to make sense of the National World War II Memorial without understanding its designer, Friedrich St.Florian. But as a series of contemporary memorial historians have made clear in recent years, the story of a memorial is not only about art and architecture. The origins of a memorial, the political and cultural battles that bring a memorial into being, are as central to its meaning as its stone and marble.[10]

As James E. Young has argued in his study of Holocaust memorials, *The Texture of Memory,* we do not come to a memorial, as we come to the art in a museum or a gallery, primarily because it is novel or fascinating. We may be enthralled or repelled by the design of a memorial, but we do not visit a memorial to engage in a critique of it. Instead, we bring a sense of history with us when we come to a memorial, and we expect that as public art, the memorial will lead us beyond its own materiality and back in time to the persons or events it commemorates.[11]

In this regard the National World War II Memorial is no different from other memorials. Not only does its biography involve a fifty-nine-year delay between the war it commemorates and its dedication, but it also entails the history of the land on which the memorial rests. We need to remember that the Mall on which the National World War II Memorial sits has its eighteenth-century roots in the decision of Pierre Charles L'Enfant, a Frenchman who fought in the American Revolution, to adapt the landscape schemes of Versailles and Paris, designed for the benefit of French royalty, to the New World. The specific acreage on which the National World War II Memorial now sits, West Potomac Park, did not exist when Washington was made the nation's capital; in fact the Potomac River then flowed very close to the present site of the Washington Monument. West Potomac Park was created through a massive Army Corps of Engineers project that between 1882 and 1900 added more than 700 acres to the Mall by reclaiming the tidal flats of the Potomac River that lay to the west and south of the Washington Monument.[12]

The beauty of the landscape and the two memorials surrounding the National World War II Memorial have a similarly complex history. As the architectural historian Richard Guy Wilson has noted, during its early years the Mall was "an unkempt gardenesque park, with no particular symbolic value." For much of the nineteenth century the Mall was burdened with a smelly canal—"a dirty, stinking, filthy ditch," in the words of President Andrew Jackson—along its northern border, and after the canal was removed in 1872, there were still unsightly railroad tracks and a train station, which remained until 1907. Even the memorials and monuments on the Mall that we now regard as sacred were not always seen in that light. After construction on the Washington Monument came to a halt in 1854 as a result of political and financial problems encountered by the Washington Monument Society, the unfinished Washington Monument shaft was allowed to stand for decades, looking like nothing so much as a factory chimney, until in 1876 Congress finally appropriated enough money for the monument to be completed eight years later. As for the landfill on which the Lincoln Memorial rests, its marshy origins and its distance from the Washington Monument prompted Joe Cannon, the powerful Speaker of the House, to deride it as a "God damned swamp" in his campaign to get the Lincoln Memorial built elsewhere.[13]

Only with this background in mind can we gain historic perspective on the public battles that arose over the National World War II Memorial during the seventeen years between 1987, when the first legislation to build the National World War II Memorial was proposed, and 2004, when the memorial officially opened to the public. And even this historic perspective stops short of revealing all we need to know before we look at the memorial itself. When we think of the National World War II Memorial, we constantly need to bear in mind its birth order. Logically, the National World War II Memorial should have been built before, not after, the memorials to the veterans of the Vietnam and Korean Wars. As a consequence, comparisons were inevitable. From the start, the question surrounding the National World War II Memorial was, Did it not have to be more architecturally significant and more centrally located than the memorials to the two lesser wars that came after World War II?

As for the history of the National World War II Memorial, not only does it span four presidencies, the fall of the Berlin Wall, and the September 11 bombings of the World Trade Center and the Pentagon, but it has all the twists and turns of a movie plot and more than fulfills the observation of *Washington Post* architecture critic Benjamin Forgey that "creating major national memorials is always tricky, often messy, and sometimes ugly."[14]

The men and women who dominated the media coverage of the battle over the National World War II Memorial reflect the scope of the struggle to build it. The initial proponent of a National World War II Memorial, Roger Durbin, was a rural mail carrier and a veteran of the Battle of the Bulge, who, except for a Frank Capra-like faith in the American political system, had no reason to believe that his wish for a World War II Memorial in Washington would ever become a reality. The politician who from 1987 to 1993 led the congressional fight for a National World War II Memorial was not, as we would expect, a good old boy from the South with years of political seniority. She was Marcy Kaptur, a liberal Democrat from Toledo, Ohio, who was first elected to Congress in 1982. The designer of the National World War II Memorial, Friedrich St.Florian, was not in 1997, the year he was announced as the winner of the National World War II Memorial design competition, a famous architect with an international reputation. He was a former dean of architecture at the Rhode Island School of Design, known mostly in academic circles for his avant-garde work.[15]

The political figure most linked in the public's mind with the National World War II Memorial, Bob Dole, was present at the White House for the unveiling of the winning design for the memorial because the president, who had just defeated him in the 1996 election, decided to use the ceremony to award Dole the Medal of Freedom. The movie star and two-time Academy Award winner, Tom Hanks, who became the spokesman for the National World War II Memorial public-service advertising campaign, was born long after World War II ended. It was his role in the 1998 hit film about World War II, *Saving Private Ryan,* that gave him the credibility to be an advocate for the memorial. Senator Bob Kerrey, the figure most closely associated with the early opposition to the National World War II Memorial, was an effective memorial critic because of his service as a U.S. Navy SEAL in the Vietnam War, for which he was awarded the Congressional Medal of Honor. The Washington insider and chairman of the Commission of Fine Arts, J. Carter Brown, who until his death in 2002 was the most influential advocate for the National World War II Memorial within the Washington art establishment, had a decade earlier put his reputation on the line to champion Maya Lin's untraditional Vietnam Veterans Memorial.[16]

The group that mounted the most effective opposition to the National World War II Memorial, the National Coalition to Save Our Mall, did not even exist at the time the memorial was being proposed, but under the leadership of Judy Scott Feldman it quickly surpassed the traditional Washington preservationist organizations in influence and has become a permanent force in the capital today. Congress, not the arts and planning commissions whose primary business includes approving memorials on federal land in Washington, is the institution responsible for the fact that construction on the National World War II Memorial began in August 2001 rather than years later. Exasperated by the opponents of the memorial, the members of the House and the Senate took matters into their own hands in May 2001 and passed special legislation stating that the memorial site and design approvals granted to the National World War II Memorial by the Commission of Fine Arts and the National Capital Planning Commission by the end of 2000 were final and not subject to judicial review.[17]

What follows from this biography of the National World War II Memorial is, however, not only the story of how the memorial went from an idea to a reality. The biography of the National World War II Memorial also forces us to re-examine a series of prevailing assumptions about the Mall and its memorials.

*The Mall is a completed urban work of art that should have its cross-axis protected by a no-build zone.* Now officially the law of the land as a result of a 2003 amendment to the Commemorative Works Act of 1986, this idea was first explored in 1996 by the Memorials Task Force of the National Capital Planning Commission. By January 2000 a Joint Task Force on Memorials, composed of representatives from the National Capital Planning Commission, the Commission of Fine Arts, and the National Capital Memorial Commission, reached the conclusion that the area on the Mall formed by the cross-axis that links the Capitol and the Lincoln Memorial in one direction and the White House and the Jefferson Memorial in the other should be a no-build reserve. The theory behind this thinking—namely, that proliferation of memorials on the Mall is certain to create a theme-park effect that will undermine the Mall's existing memorials—is impossible to deny. The space around any memorial is crucial to its uniqueness and its capacity to elicit awe, as the Lincoln Memorial Commission argued at the turn of the last century. But as the National World War II Memorial shows, strict enforcement of a no-build policy for the Mall's great cross-axis exacts an enormous price. Without meaning to, such a policy forever locks the Mall into the past. It implicitly says that no contemporary figure or future event in American life can ever be as worthy of commemoration on the Mall as those of the past.[18]

*Preservation of the Mall's existing spaces and structures should control decisions over future building on it.* For any number of Washington preservationist groups, "protecting the historic and scenic integrity of the Mall" is, to quote Richard Moe, the president of the National Trust for Historic Preservation, a "high priority." The difficulty comes when this priority is combined with the belief that the Mall is, in the words of Eleanor Holmes Norton, Washington's congressional delegate and a persistent critic of the National World War II Memorial, "the urban equivalent of the Grand Canyon." What follows, as the battle over whether to build the National World War II Memorial at the site of the historic Rainbow Pool showed, is the notion that virtually nothing on the Mall should be modified, because the Mall itself is a timeless natural wonder. When such thinking is applied, it does not matter that the original Rainbow Pool, architecturally problematic from the start, was for years generally ignored and allowed to fall into a state of disrepair. Nor does it matter that the history of the Mall is a history of dramatic change. The controversy surrounding the National World War II Memorial demonstrates that such preservationist fundamentalism puts the entire Mall at risk. It turns historic preservation from a process of controlling change and dealing with competing claims into what J. Carter Brown, the longtime head of the Commission of Fine Arts, called an excuse for "freezing and embalming everything."[19]

*A memorial's design should reflect the architecture of its time, not that from a bygone period.* In the 1930s this conviction was at the center of the attacks on John Russell Pope's Pantheon-like Jefferson Memorial. Pope's detractors, from Frank Lloyd Wright to the faculty at Columbia's School of Architecture, which called Pope's design a "lamentable misfit in time and space," saw the classical design of the Jefferson Memorial paying false homage to Roman architecture in an age of modernism. Today, parallel arguments have surfaced with regard to the National World War II Memorial. These arguments were stated bluntly by a letter writer to the *Washington Post* who asked, "Cannot our memorial take advantage of contemporary vision, contemporary taste, contemporary design?" But in subtler form these same arguments were also made by the *New York Times* architecture critic Herbert Muschamp in a front-page article, written before construction began, in which he attacked the memorial's design architect, Friedrich St.Florian, for "copying period styles" and criticized the memorial for being unequal to the innovative work done in postwar Washington by I. M. Pei on the East Wing of the National Galley, Maya Lin on the Vietnam Veterans Memorial, and James Ingo Freed on the United States Holocaust Museum that "developed abstract geometry into complex formal vocabularies." What the completed National World War II Memorial suggests, by contrast, are the virtues of taking a more pluralistic approach to contemporary memorial design. By its use of an aesthetic borrowed from the 1930s and 1940s, the National World War II Memorial is not only able to allude to the period it commemorates but to extend rather than ignore the historic neoclassicism of the Mall's architecture.[20]

*The most important audience for a memorial will be drawn from future generations.* This is certainly true of any memorial that is going to endure, but it is a view that is typically advanced, as with the National World War II Memorial, in order to criticize a memorial for being too tied to the generation associated with it. In the case of the National World War II Memorial, this generational view was put forward both by architect Roger Lewis, in a highly critical *Washington Post* essay he subtitled "Trying to See the World War II Memorial from a Future Perspective," and a year later by *New York Times* art critic Michael Kimmelman, in a lengthy feature article in which, after dismissing the National World War II Memorial as high kitsch, he asserted that "great art outlasts historical memory" and that the National World War II Memorial was unfortunately a "forgettable memorial." Nothing about the National World War II Memorial contradicts the certitude that within a few decades none of its visitors will either have fought in World War II or have been alive during the 1940s. But what the National World War II Memorial design does do is make the point that there is much greater value than we now concede in building a memorial with deep generational roots. Just as the Lincoln Memorial is enhanced by its thirty-six columns representing the number of states reunited in 1865, so the National World War II Memorial is enhanced by its relief panels based on 1940s news photos and its Field of Stars with its direct reference to the individual gold star that a family who had lost someone in the war hung on a banner in the window. Such time-bound references help us and future memorial visitors to see World War II, as we ordinarily would not, through the eyes of those who experienced it.[21]

*A memorial should be privately financed.* In recent decades this thinking has become the conventional wisdom, despite the fact that it was money from the federal government, not the private sector, that was either the only source or most important source of funding for the Washington Monument, the Lincoln Memorial, the Jefferson Memorial, and the Franklin D. Roosevelt Memorial. In the case of the National World War II Memorial, money was from the start a deep worry for

Fred Woerner, the retired four-star U.S. Army general, who during the crucial fund-raising years served as chairman of the American Battle Monuments Commission (ABMC), the agency Congress made responsible for establishing the National World War II Memorial. The startup funds that the government supplied the American Battle Monuments Commission were minimal, and only after the ABMC was able to put together a financial team that, in addition to its own staff, included Bob Dole, Federal Express CEO Fred Smith, and actor Tom Hanks, was the commission able to get the donations it needed (in the end, over $194 million). The example of the American Battle Monuments Commission's success in raising money does not, however, settle the memorial economics question so much as make it more imperative than ever for us to find a way of making sure all federal memorials, especially those that may be less appealing to corporate donors, receive the support they need and are not forced to have their architecture determined by the ability of their backers to pay for it.[22]

In telling the story of the National World War II Memorial, it is essential for a book like *Their Last Battle* to look at the big picture. At the same time it is crucial to remember that this big picture is composed of numerous small pictures, often no more than snapshots, and that these small pictures contain a life of their own. Their importance was driven home to me time and again when I did interviews with the men and women working on the National World War II Memorial, but at no point so deeply as on a spring day in 2002 when I walked through a muddy memorial site with Jim McCloskey, the general superintendent for the project. As we got near the spot where the northern arch of the National World War II Memorial was going to be built, McCloskey asked me to turn off my tape recorder, and he began telling me about the World War II veteran who had come by his office trailer earlier in the week.

"He wanted me to bury his dog tags in the foundation," McCloskey said. "He was the third vet who asked me this year, and I didn't tell him, like I didn't tell the others, that it was against government rules. I just took the dog tags and said I'd bury them under one of the arches." McCloskey, who had started out in the construction business forty years earlier as a carpenter's apprentice, was not impressed with his own willingness to break the rules. What impressed him was the significance that the memorial had taken on for the vet, who had spent two days driving on his own just to get to Washington.

In succeeding years, when the significance of the National World War II Memorial in American life is debated, I do not imagine those buried dog tags will figure in many discussions. Jim McCloskey, who died of an aneurysm before the National World War II Memorial was completed, was not much of a talker, and he did not think that it was his business to ask the veteran his name or to find out if the veteran had any family. Still those dog tags at the bottom of the memorial do speak to us, and what they say about the National World War II Memorial and its ability to reach across generations does matter—as much as anything we will ever learn from going to the Mall ourselves.[23]

# 1

## Mr. Durbin
## Goes to Washington

"Congresswoman Kaptur," Roger Durbin shouted, "how come there's no memorial to World War II in Washington?" It was not a question that Representative Marcy Kaptur was anticipating. On this cold February night she had driven from her office on Summit Street in the central business district of Toledo to the Lucas County Township Trustees Association fish fry in nearby Jerusalem Township, expecting to do nothing more than spend a pleasant evening with other elected officials from Ohio's Ninth District. Kaptur had been a Democratic representative since 1982, when she came into office by pulling off an upset of a pro-Reagan Republican incumbent who outspent her by a three-to-one margin during a campaign that became national news. As she drove herself past the corn and soybean farms that lined Route 2, the need for a national World War II memorial was not something she thought would be on voters' minds.[1]

Standing nearly six feet tall and weighing just a little more than he did when he entered the army in 1943, sixty-seven-year-old Roger Durbin was still a commanding presence. "I turned and faced a solidly built graying gentleman with a square jaw, twinkling eyes, and a churlish grin," Marcy Kaptur would recall years later. She would also remember answering Durbin's question about why there was no national World War II memorial in Washington by telling him that there was one.

"Well, there is," I said. "Iwo Jima."

"No," he corrected, "that's a monument to one service branch, the Marines."[2]

It was an answer that caught Kaptur by surprise, and as people crowded around her and Roger Durbin, she promised that she would get back to him after her staff researched the question.

Although neither Kaptur nor Durbin realized it at the time, the first step in the seventeen-year process of getting a national World War II memorial built on the Mall had just been taken. Kaptur's promise that she would get back to Durbin was not one that she had made in order to get out of an awkward situation. When the Smithsonian Institution informed Kaptur that there was no national memorial for World War II, her first step was to tell Durbin that he had been right after all. Then before 1987 was up, she introduced legislation to build a national World War II memorial. For Roger Durbin, the meeting with Kaptur was even more momentous. In a manner reminiscent of Jefferson Smith, the everyman hero played by Jimmy Stewart in Frank Capra's 1939 film classic, *Mr. Smith Goes to Washington,* Durbin had started down a road that would take him from local politics to the halls of Congress and the White House.[3]

For the next thirteen years, until his death from pancreatic cancer in February 2000, Durbin devoted all the time he could to making certain a national World War II memorial got built in Washington.[4] His decision to make the creation of the memorial his cause was not one that he suddenly reached in 1987. It was a decision that reflected how his thinking—and by extension, that of countless other World War II veterans—had evolved in the decades following the 1940s, finally peaking shortly after the fiftieth anniversary of the war.

When Roger Durbin enlisted in the army in 1943, he did not doubt that the time had come for him to do his duty. But he was also unwilling to romanticize what lay ahead. He did not imagine a glorious war, filled with adventure, awaiting him. Like so many men who did not graduate from high school during the Great Depression, Durbin had built his life around the idea of making the best he could of the tough choices that he was given. Growing up in Sylvania, Ohio, he had left Burnham High School in 1938, his senior year, to take a job. Then just over a year later in 1940, he and his high school sweetheart, Marian Sanderson, married and, unable to afford a house of their own, moved in with Marian's parents on their farm.

It was not an ideal situation for a young couple starting out in life, but in the final years of the Depression, it was a welcome alternative to struggling to get by on their own. Durbin, whose first job out of high school was working as a groundskeeper for Highland Meadows golf course, was now working for the Spicer Manufacturing Company in nearby Toledo, making automobile transmissions, and with a roof over their heads and a steady factory job, he and Marian were better off than most of their friends. A year later in May 1941, when their son Peter was born, they had the consolation of knowing Marian could stay home and take care of him.

It was a feeling of security that became even more important when, realizing that he would soon be drafted, Durbin enlisted in the army and left Ohio for Fort Benning, Georgia, to begin training with the Ninetieth Cavalry Reconnaissance Squadron of the newly activated Tenth Armored Division. He did not have to fear, as so many men his age did, that all his wife and son could rely on when he was gone was his meager army pay. Like so many army wives, Marian went south to see her husband during training camp, but these rushed visits, with stays in boardinghouses, were difficult for both. It was the farm in Ohio, where Marian's father and youngest brother continued to live after Marian's mother died in 1940, that gave Roger Durbin the sense that his young family could weather the worst of times.[5]

The best early indication of how Roger Durbin felt about the war—and how those feelings would over time become the basis for his belief in the need for a national World War II memorial—is contained in a letter he mailed to his son on August 15, 1944, from Camp Gordon, Georgia, just as he and the Tenth Armored Division were about to leave for France. It is not a letter that Durbin expected three-year-old Peter to read. Rather it is a letter written by a father who, fearing he may be killed in combat, wants his son (who over half a century later would grant me access to his father's papers) to have something to remember him by. As such, much of the letter is devoted to telling Peter how proud he is of him and assuring him that as a father he will be looking out for Peter, no matter what happens during the war.

But what is politically telling about the letter is that long before he entered combat, Roger Durbin saw neglect of the soldier as an accepted part of war. It is an idea he develops in the letter by describing war as fought by "common people like myself and like all the other people I know" and then contrasting soldiers like them with those who "don't realize what the men in the service have to go through." The American troops who entered World War I in the belief that they were fighting a war to end wars "died for nothing," he tells Peter, and he worries that World War II may produce the same result. What Durbin asks his son to do—and what he himself will do years later—is try to make sure history does not repeat itself. "If I don't come back from this war," he tells Peter, "I want you to look after your mother and do all in your power to make sure the thousands of men who have died in this war haven't died for nothing."[6]

Later, as the Tenth Armored Division moved through France and as part of George Patton's Third Army had its worst experience of the war at the Battle of the Bulge, Roger Durbin did not return to these themes again. He was too busy staying alive. Years afterward, when he talked about the war, his most vivid memories were always about the death and winter. He would remember lying on the transmission of his half-track to keep warm during the Battle of the Bulge, and he would recall how in the December cold a dead body froze in place in less than two hours.

By the conclusion of the war Durbin was amazed that he had survived and grateful that the fighting in the Pacific ended before he and his division could be shipped off to Japan. As he observed in a speech he delivered on the subject of remembering 1945 to the Tenth Armored Division at their 1990 reunion, "None of us felt that we were heroes. I was just plain glad to be alive and home in one piece."[7]

The Roger Durbin who returned to Ohio after three years in the army was, nonetheless, a very different man from the one who had left home in 1943. Like the majority of veterans at that time, he did not want memorials. He wanted to get back to leading a normal life as soon as possible. Peter, then five, remembers his father arriving in Toledo early one morning on the train and the family having a pancake breakfast together in the dining room when they got home. But the Durbins kept their celebrating to a minimum. In a once-again prosperous America, Roger Durbin was anxious to settle into the kind of routine that had been impossible in the seven years since he had left high school.

In 1947 he and Marian moved into their first home of their own, and when he got a chance to spend more time with his family and work as a rural letter carrier in Berkey, Ohio, Roger Durbin willingly took a pay cut and quit his job making transmissions with the Spicer Company. Soon he was coaching a team in the Berkey Little League, and later, when he got the chance, he entered local politics, serving ten years as a Richfield Township Trustee. But the war was never forgotten. The American Legion post in Sylvania and the vets in it became a very important part of Durbin's life and so did his memories of the horrors he had witnessed in Europe, even if he did not dwell on them. Peter would remain the Durbins' only child. After returning from the war, Roger had decided against adding to the family. He had concluded, "No child should be brought into a civilization that would act like that."[8]

It was not, however, until 1962, when the Durbins took a family trip to Washington, D.C., that the idea of memorializing the war began to take shape for Roger Durbin. Since the end of the war, he had remained in close contact with two of his buddies, Harold "Shorty"

O'Neill and Lemuel "Bud" Patraw. The three vets and their families had continued to get together over the years, and their time in the Tenth Armored Division had always been a topic of conversation. But in Washington the meaning of the war took on new significance for Roger Durbin. It was the first time he had visited the nation's capital, and as he and Marian walked from monument to monument, Durbin was astonished to find that there was no single memorial commemorating World War II.

It was not a discovery that soured Roger Durbin on Washington or on the country. Back home he continued to make sure that on Memorial Day there were flags on graves of the vets buried in the cemeteries around Berkey, and he regularly attended the meetings of his American Legion post. But it gnawed on him that in a city like Washington, where it appeared to him that every major war since the American Revolution was honored, nothing marked World War II.[9]

Four years later, however, the memory of that Washington visit took on a very different meaning for Roger Durbin when he went to Europe for a Tenth Armored Division reunion. Durbin had never been so sick in his life as on the Liberty Ship he took to cross the Atlantic in 1943, and he had vowed never to board a ship again if he could help it. But flying to Europe in September 1966 was a different story and so was visiting Bastogne for the first time in over ten years. There he discovered what he had not been able to find on his trip to Washington—a World War II memorial that said to men like himself that the war had not been forgotten.[10]

The memorial Durbin saw was nothing elaborate. It was the Mardasson Monument, a star-shaped memorial located two kilometers from Bastogne on a hill overlooking the city. Built in 1950 by the Belgian-American Association as Europe was still recovering from the ravages of war, the monument, designed by the architect Georges Dedoyard, makes a point of being as direct as possible in the feelings it conveys. Standing twelve meters high and built out of sandstone and limestone, Mardasson tries to console rather than overwhelm. The points on its five stars radiate from a central atrium that, in conjunction with its supporting columns, gives Mardasson a feeling of solemnity, as does its crypt, with separate areas for Catholics, Jews, and Protestants to worship in.

The names of all the American states in 1945 are engraved in bronze along the crown of the monument. On the outside of the pillars supporting the memorial is a list of the American armies that participated in the Battle of the Bulge, and on the inside of the same pillars in gold leaf is a history of the battle, which notes, "Seldom has more American blood been spilled in the course of a single battle." A tourist can take in Mardasson in a matter of minutes. But in 1966 what the Mardasson Monument offered a returning vet like Roger Durbin was a hilltop view of Bastogne and a reminder that the town, with a Sherman tank in its square and the turrets from Sherman tanks flanking the roads leading into it, had not forgotten the Battle of the Bulge or the 33,000 Americans who died fighting in it.[11]

Thirty-two years later, in campaigning for congressional support for the National World War II Memorial, Durbin would refer back to his 1966 European trip and its meaning for him. "Five years after the end of World War II the small liberated nation of Belgium had a memorial built and paid for in memory of the American Army that liberated their nation," he wrote. "After seeing that memorial, I thought, Why can't the greatest nation in the world do that for their 16 million men and women who served America during World War II?"[12]

In turning to Marcy Kaptur for an answer to his question, Roger Durbin had chosen someone who would not in 1987 have seemed in the best position to lead a congressional fight for a national World War II memorial. Kaptur was not a veteran. She had not been in Congress long. And she was anything but a good old boy. Yet in turning to Kaptur, Durbin had done more than choose someone with whom he would build a friendship that would last until his death. He had chosen someone who on a political and personal level brought exactly the resolve that was needed to win the six-year legislative battle for a national World War II memorial.

Since coming to the House in 1982, Kaptur had established herself as a Democrat who even during the Reagan years showed that she was capable of winning elections by wide margins in the blue-collar district she represented. On the economy, Kaptur was an old-fashioned liberal, constantly fighting to preserve jobs and raise the minimum wage, and on cultural issues she was a Midwestern traditionalist, opposed to government funding for abortion and willing to break ranks with her party on issues that she regarded as matters of principle. On a visit to Japan she had handed the Japanese prime minister a bag of Toledo-manufactured spark plugs to drive home the point that Japanese auto imports were hurting the American job market, and at a Jeep plant in her district, she had confronted a campaigning President Clinton over the consequences of his free-trade policy. Equally important, Kaptur's own background made a fight over a national World War II memorial second nature for her. With a degree in public planning and graduate work at the University of Michigan and MIT, she was able to talk about architecture and the National Mall with as much authority as anyone in Congress, and on the question of World War II, she brought the kinds of feelings that came from growing up in a family in which Franklin Roosevelt was a "saint" and military service was honored. Of her three uncles, one served in World War I and two in World War II.[13]

With this background, it was only natural for Kaptur to seek a seat on the Committee on Veterans' Affairs shortly after arriving in Congress and to have the kind of friendships in the House and Senate that allowed her to gather support across party lines when it came to her memorial legislation. In the House she would benefit from a network of powerful supporters, including Chairman Sonny Montgomery of the Veterans' Affairs Committee as well as conservative Republican Bob Stump, and in the Senate she could count on similarly well-placed allies, among them Ohio Democrat John Glenn and Republicans Bob Dole and Strom Thurmond.

"It was, I felt, my generation's job to thank them," Kaptur would say of her desire to see the World War II veterans get a memorial in Washington. What Kaptur had not counted on was the difficulty of actually getting memorial legislation passed. At the start she told herself, "This legislation is so worthy. No one could object. This should just go through Congress like white lightning." A few years later she remembered thinking, "I must not be a very good lawmaker, because, if I were, I could have gotten this through in one session."[14]

What made Kaptur's job so difficult were in part the times. In the late 1980s honoring the World War II vets was on few people's minds. The veneration that peaked a decade later with Tom Brokaw's bestseller *The Greatest Generation* and Steven Spielberg's film *Saving Private Ryan* had not yet begun, and in introducing legislation both to build a national memorial and to help pay for it through the sale of commemorative coins, Kaptur had, without realizing it, made extra trouble for herself. Keeping track of two bills, each designed to be a companion to the other, forced Kaptur into a constant balancing act. As she later put it, "You would have to get one foot on the accelerator and another foot on the brake at the same time just to get the car to move."[15]

Kaptur was not exaggerating. How the National World War II Memorial finally won congressional approval and initial funding is a story of six years of legislative stops and starts that makes one wonder how any bill ever becomes law. In her speeches and congressional testimony, Kaptur continually emphasized the need for quick passage of her legislation if the surviving veterans of World War II were ever to see the memorial within their lifetimes. But even this emotional issue did not speed her legislation through the House and Senate, nor did it seem to matter that what she proposed was an enormously straightforward bill that declared: "The American Battle Monuments Commission shall establish a memorial and museum on Federal land in the District of Columbia or its environs to honor members of the Armed Forces who served in World War II and to commemorate the United States' participation in that conflict." On December 10, 1987, when Kaptur first proposed H.R. 3742, authorizing the erection of a World War II memorial, Ronald Reagan was president. By the time her legislation was law, George Bush had lost his re-election bid, and Bill Clinton was in his second year in the White House.[16]

The process of getting memorial legislation passed would in the end take longer than it took to win the war. On December 10, 1987, Kaptur's memorial bill, H.R. 3742, was referred both to the House Committee on House Administration and the House Committee on Veterans' Affairs, and in the spring its progress continued when on April 21, 1988, it was sent to the House Subcommittee on Housing and Memorial Affairs. By June 21 the subcommittee sent the bill back to the full Committee on Veterans' Affairs, and in July 1988, after receiving favorable comment from the Commission of Fine Arts and the National Capitol Planning Commission, the amended bill was reported to the full House. But there its luck ran out. No further action was taken on H.R. 3742 during the 100th Congress, nor on S. 2734, a companion bill introduced in the Senate on August 11, 1988, by Strom Thurmond.[17]

In 1989, as the 101st Congress began, Kaptur began the process all over again. On January 19, 1989, she introduced memorial legislation in the form of H.R. 537. On that same date H.R. 537 was referred to the House Committee on House Administration and its Subcommittee on Libraries and Memorials as well as to the House Committee on Veterans' Affairs. Then six months later, on June 15, H.R. 537 was sent on to the Subcommittee on Housing and Memorial Affairs, but there it died. In the meantime S. 160, a parallel memorial bill again introduced in the Senate by Strom Thurmond, was meeting the same fate. Thurmond's bill was referred to the Senate Committee on Energy and Natural Resources on January 25, 1989, and then on January 26 to its Subcommittee on Public Lands, National Parks before it wound up with no action being taken on it.[18]

It was a discouraging start for Kaptur, but on June 29, 1989, she began the process a third time with H.R. 2807. This time her bill got further than its two predecessors before failing to win House approval. On June 29, H.R. 2807 was referred to the House Committee on House Administration. On July 10, it went to its Subcommittee on Libraries and Memorials, and on September 19 it was discharged by the subcommittee and ordered by the full committee to be reported to the House. A similar process with H.R. 2807 was also happening in the House Committee on Veterans' Affairs. H.R. 2807 was referred to it on June 29. On September 12, it went to its Subcommittee on Housing and Memorial Affairs, which then forwarded the bill back to the full committee, which sent it on to the House on September 26 for action that was never taken for the remainder of the congressional session.[19]

Kaptur did not take the time to feel sorry for herself. In 1990 she took on the equally difficult task of trying to get the startup money the memorial would need. On March 22, 1990, three years after she first proposed building a national World War II memorial, Kaptur introduced in the 101st Congress H.R. 4365 requiring the Secretary of the Treasury to mint coins in honor of the fiftieth anniversary of America's involvement in World War II. Her bill, which quickly gathered two hundred and eighteen cosponsors, was referred to the House Committee on Banking, Finance, and Urban Affairs, and from there it was sent on to the Subcommittee on Consumer Affairs and Coinage on April 16, 1990. With Roger Durbin at her side, Kaptur made a dramatic appeal for quick passage of H.R. 4365 during the April subcommittee hearings, but to no avail. No further action on H.R. 4365 was taken during the 101st Congress.[20]

A year later in the 102nd Congress, Kaptur restarted the funding process. On March 22, 1991, she introduced a new coin bill, H.R. 1623, and once again her coin bill was sent to the House Committee on Banking, Financing, and Urban Affairs and from there to the Subcommittee on Consumer Affairs and Coinage. But this time the results were much better than before. On June 18, 1992, the coin bill was discharged by the subcommittee and ordered to be reported out as amended. On June 30, 1992, the amended version of the bill was called up by the full House and, despite strong objections by veteran Republican Congressmen William Dickinson of Alabama and Al McCandless of California, who wanted only private financing of the National World War II Memorial, Kaptur's coin bill passed by voice vote. Kaptur's greatest fears about the initial financing of the National World War II Memorial were now over. She had worried that in the hands of a private, nonprofit group, rather than a governmental agency like the American Battle Monuments Commission, the

National World War II Memorial would be vulnerable to the kinds of financial problems that had plagued the private Battle of Normandy Foundation, which since its founding in the 1980s had become mired in debt while failing to complete the Wall of Liberty it promised contributors it would build on the coast of France at a 25-acre site near Utah Beach.[21]

1991 and the 102nd Congress would also provide Kaptur with a breakthrough on the legislation authorizing the memorial itself. As she pushed her new National World War II Memorial bill, H.R. 1624, Kaptur was able to make far more headway than in the past. In the House, H.R. 1624, which started out by being sent to the House Committee on House Administration and subsequently to its Subcommittee on Libraries and Memorials, actually got passed. On March 22, 1991, H.R. 1624 went to the House Committee on Veterans' Affairs and then on July 11 to its Subcommittee on Housing and Memorial Affairs. On July 18 the subcommittee held a markup session, and the bill as amended was forwarded to the Committee on Veterans' Affairs, which on July 23, 1991 then sent H.R. 1624 on to the full House. Eleven months later, on June 22, 1992, the bill was considered by the full House and passed by voice vote.[22]

It was the best position Kaptur had been in since she introduced her National World War II Memorial legislation in 1987. Now, however, she needed help with companion legislation in the Senate for both her bills. This time she did not have to wait long. On August 12, 1992, the help she needed with the coin bill arrived when her fellow Ohio Democrat, John Glenn, introduced S. 3195, directing the Secretary of the Treasury to mint coins in commemoration of the fiftieth anniversary of World War II, the Battle of Normandy, and D-Day. With Glenn's weight behind it, his bill was referred to the Committee on Banking on the same day it was introduced, and immediately a big push was made by veterans' groups to gain cosponsors for the bill. By September 18, Glenn's coin bill had forty-four Senate cosponsors, and by unanimous consent it was discharged by the Committee on Banking and passed by the Senate on a voice vote. The coin bill battle was at last over for Kaptur. On September 22, 1992, a message on the Senate action on S. 3195 was sent to the House, and a week later, after some stylistic differences with the House version of the bill were ironed out, the House passed S. 3195 by voice vote, clearing the way for approval by President Clinton, who quickly signed the bill into law on October 14, 1992.[23]

As Public Law 102–414, the World War II 50th Anniversary Commemorative Coins Act did not promise to solve the budget problems that lay ahead for the National World War II Memorial. But the Commemorative Coins Act did get the memorial's funding off to a strong start. The first $3 million from the sale of the coins were earmarked for the struggling Battle of Normandy Foundation, but the next $7 million (only $4.8 million would actually result) were committed to the American Battle Monuments Commission, and thereafter the money taken in would be split on a 30 percent, 70 percent basis.[24]

Kaptur was now free to turn her attention to getting a version of H.R. 1624, her House National World War II Memorial bill, passed in the Senate. There Senator Strom Thurmond was working, as before, on parallel legislation, but this time in Senator Thurmond's bill, S. 2244, there was a key difference with Kaptur's bill. Senator Thurmond's bill authorized the National World War II Memorial Fund, a private nonprofit organization with conservative backing, rather than the American Battle Monuments Commission, to establish the National World War II Memorial, and it was necessary to rework S. 2244 so that it placed, as all previous legislation had, the American Battle Monuments Commission in charge of the memorial. By the fall, however, the differences in the two bills had been reconciled in favor of the American Battle Monuments Commission, and on October 7, 1992, the Senate Committee on Rules discharged the bill to the full Senate, where it passed by voice vote. On October 8, 1992, a message of the Senate's action was sent to the House, and the long struggle to get the memorial legislation approved seemed at an end. But on the next day, before S. 2244 could be considered, the House, anxious to begin its fall recess, adjourned.[25]

It was another frustrating end for Kaptur's efforts to get a national World War II memorial built, but this time the last-minute defeat of her and Senator Thurmond's memorial legislation would pay off. In 1993, as the 103rd Congress began, there was finally widespread agreement that the memorial legislation should not be subjected to more delays for any reason. On January 26, 1993, Thurmond introduced legislation in the form of S. 214, and Kaptur did the same on January 27 with H.R. 682. In the Senate, S. 214 quickly sailed through the Committee on Energy and Natural Resources and was passed by voice vote on March 17, 1993. H.R. 682 moved with similar speed through the House Committee on House Administration, and on May 4, 1993, it passed the House by voice vote. On May 5, the message on the House action was received by the Senate, and on May 12, 1993, the Senate agreed to the amended House version of the bill. After six years the legislative battle to authorize the building and funding of a World War II memorial was over.[26]

The bill that President Clinton signed into law on May 25, 1993, provided essentially everything Marcy Kaptur had asked for in 1987, when with H.R. 3742 she introduced the first national World War II memorial legislation. Using language almost identical to that in Kaptur's original bill, Public Law 103–32 authorized the American Battle Monuments Commission to construct a memorial, but without a museum as H.R. 3742 had proposed, on federal land in Washington, D.C., or its environs to honor the veterans of World War II and commemorate American participation in the war. It established a twelve-member World War II Memorial Advisory Board, appointed by the president, to assist in the process, and it created in the U.S. Treasury a fund to help the American Battle Monuments Commission establish the memorial.[27]

For Roger Durbin, a new era was also beginning. Since 1987 he had sought to move the House and the Senate to authorize a national World War II memorial. Now the challenge facing the national World War II memorial involved questions of site, design, and environmental safety, and there was much less Durbin could do to influence decisions in these areas. Still, he persisted in doing whatever he could to get the memorial built as quickly as possible. By this time Durbin had become, as he well knew, a familiar face in the World War II Memorial campaign, and he was happy to be used in any kind of memorial promotion. "They need some more publicity in Washington. They're rolling me out again," was a refrain his family heard with increasing frequency during this period.[28]

In 1993 Durbin went to Washington to present the first set of World War II commemorative coins to President Clinton in a ceremony in the White House East Room, and in 1995 he returned for the dedication ceremonies for the National World War II Memorial site on a Veterans Day that exceeded anything he could have imagined when he began his quest for a memorial. Early in the day Durbin was for the second time a guest of President Clinton at the White House, and in the afternoon the president honored him in his National World War II Memorial dedication speech, observing, "I want to thank Roger Durbin for his idea and for the triumph of his idea today, and the triumph of the idea that an American citizen can have a good idea and take it to the proper authorities and actually get something done." The next day, much to his and his family's surprise, Durbin appeared in a front-page photograph in the *Washington Post* helping President Clinton unveil the plaque marking the site where the National World War II Memorial would go.

In 1998 Durbin returned to Washington for still another official ceremony, this one for the unveiling of three stamps commemorating World War II. This time Durbin had a chance to speak at length, and in his talk he put forward a theme that, in the years following congressional approval of the National World War II Memorial, would increasingly dominate his thinking—time was running out for the World War II veterans still alive. It was a theme Durbin emphasized first by talking about the casualties sustained by the Tenth Armored Division with which he served. "The Tenth seized more than 450 towns and cities and earned more than 3,000 medals. But it was achieved at a terrible cost. When finished, the Tenth Armored had 8,381 killed, wounded, and missing. There was a 78.5 percent turnover of personnel." Then at the conclusion of his speech, Durbin linked what had happened to the men he served with to what was happening to vets all across the country. "An average of 30,000 World War II vets now die each month. Only 7 million remain," he reminded his audience. "For most of those now remaining, this stamp will be the nation's tribute to their service."[29]

In Durbin's mind his generation had become "an endangered species," and he could not rid himself of the fear that "at the rate our memorial is progressing, there will not be enough of us still living to make a large crowd at the dedication." Any delay on the memorial worried him, and when in 1997 both Senator Bob Kerrey and Revolutionary War historian Joseph Ellis came out with public criticism of the site chosen on the National Mall for the World War II Memorial, it was more than Durbin could take. "He just went bonkers," his wife would remember.[30]

"My answer to Senator Kerrey is, if we had lost World War II, he would not have a Congressional Medal of Honor," Durbin wrote. "TAKE ANOTHER LOOK!" he told Kerrey. "I stood at the site of the memorial November 10, 1995, watching the activity thereon. Touch football, stick ball, Frisbee, picnicking. The next day November 11, 1995, Veterans Day, I stood with President Clinton at the end of the glorious site dedication ceremony and scattered soil gathered from fourteen World War II cemeteries from around the world upon the sparse and worn grass. That is when it became the most sacred, revered, beautiful spot in America."[31]

His deepest anger was, however, reserved for Joseph Ellis, the National Book Award-winning historian, who in a March 24, 1997, *New York Times* op-ed opposed the location of the National World War II Memorial on the Mall because it "would break the line of vision between the Founding Father of the union and the President who saved it." As far as Durbin was concerned, Ellis had a poor eye for history. Rather than believing that what Ellis called the "conversation" between the founder of the country and the savior of the country was being interrupted by the National World War II Memorial, Durbin saw the conversation as being extended. "I say," he declared, "Washington and Lincoln would be saying THANK GOD for the gallant men and women of World War II who fought and gave their lives to preserve this great country as they did in the Revolutionary and Civil Wars."[32]

Nobody, however, was safe from Durbin's anger at this time. His files are filled with letter after letter that he wrote to those he thought were slowing down the memorial approval process. Even his granddaughter, Melissa Growden, an art historian and educator at Siena Heights University and a member of the World War II Memorial Advisory Board, found herself dreading the questioning she received from her grandfather if she returned from a meeting in Washington and could not explain to his satisfaction a decision that the advisory board had made.[33]

Neither Melissa Growden nor anyone in the Durbin family expected that Roger would ease up or mute his criticism. "I want to live long enough to visit a World War II memorial in my nation's capital" had become such a refrain in his speeches that it seemed like a point he would be making up until the National World War II Memorial opened to the public. But in 1999, less than a year after his Veterans Day trip to Washington for the unveiling of the World War II stamps, all that changed. Durbin was diagnosed with pancreatic cancer. He was never again able to wage the kind of campaign that he had been carrying on for the past twelve years. As much as his strength allowed, he continued to follow the bumpy approval process the National World War II Memorial was going through and continued to insist that he and Marcy Kaptur had won a great political victory. Visiting him in his home just two weeks before he died, Kaptur found that Durbin, despite his fatigue, insisted on telling her that if she ever needed them, in his footlocker were the scrapbooks that he had kept of the battle to get the National World War II Memorial built.[34]

It was the last time Marcy Kaptur and Roger Durbin saw each other. The trip they had planned to make together for the opening of the National World War II Memorial in 2004 would never take place. It would be another year before work crews and bulldozers started digging up the grass on the National Mall where the president and Durbin had stood for the dedication of the memorial site. At the gravesite he chose for himself and his wife at Wolfinger Cemetery, just a few miles from their home, Roger Durbin would, however, leave behind a reminder of how he wanted to be remembered and how so much of what he did in the last decade of his life depended on memories that nothing could change. There, at the Durbin gravesite, chiseled on a blue-granite tombstone would be his rank, Tech 4 U.S. Army, his birth and death dates, April 18, 1920—February 6, 2000, and the distinct lightning bolt and tank tread insignia of the Tenth Armored (Tiger) Division.

# 2

# TURF WARS

Shortly before Thanksgiving in 2002, the American Battle Monuments Commission project executive for design and construction, hung up two pictures in the hall outside his office in the trailer he worked from at the construction site of the National World War II Memorial. The pictures, both archival photos, showed the area around the Washington Monument and the Lincoln Memorial during the 1940s. What was most striking about the pictures was not the breathtaking view they offered of the monument or the memorial but the view they offered of the unsightly "tempos"—the barracks-like buildings for military office workers that stretched from the base of the Washington Monument down to Seventeenth Street and along both sides of the Lincoln Memorial Reflecting Pool, where they were linked by two footbridges.

For Owenby, a 1973 Citadel graduate and an army veteran dedicated to making sure the National World War II Memorial got built with as few construction delays as possible, the point of hanging the photographs outside his office was not to demean the space around the National World War II Memorial. It was to put the space in historic perspective, to remind himself and others that the Mall and its landscape were a work in progress, not a static achievement unchanged since 1800.[1]

Owenby's point cannot be emphasized enough. When in 1995 approval was finally granted to build the National World War II Memorial on the main axis of the Mall between the Washington Monument and the Lincoln Memorial, it meant not only that the memorial would be sitting on the most important civic real estate in America but that the National World War II Memorial was inheriting two centuries of thinking about how the Mall should look and what it should signify. The ferocious site and design battles over the National World War II Memorial are inseparable from the view, voiced throughout the 1990s, that the Mall is an endangered landscape.

The story of the National Mall begins at the end of the eighteenth century with the decision of Pierre Charles L'Enfant, the planner of Washington, to make what he called a "public walk from under the Federal House to the Potomac and connected with the palace" that "will give to the city from the very beginning a superior charm over most of those of the world." In the battle over the site of the National World War II Memorial, critics of the memorial's placement continually portrayed themselves as defenders of L'Enfant's vision of the Mall. It was an assertion that required an imaginative leap. In L'Enfant's time the grounds that the National World War II Memorial and the Lincoln Memorial now occupy did not exist. They were the Potomac River. There is, however, no disputing L'Enfant's vision of a vast L-shaped open space going from the Capitol to the current site of the Washington Monument to the White House, and in recent years anyone who favors keeping the central axis of the Mall as close as possible to an uncluttered greensward may at least claim kinship with L'Enfant.[2]

What put L'Enfant in a position to design the Mall as he did was his success in persuading George Washington that he was the right person to plan the new capital. In a September 11, 1789, letter to Washington, L'Enfant did not hesitate to spell out the magnitude of the opportunity that he believed was at hand. "The late determination of Congress to lay the Foundation of a city which is to become the Capital of this vast Empire," he wrote the president, "offers so great an occasion of acquiring reputation to whoever may be appointed to conduct the execution of the business, that Your Excellency will not be surprised that my Ambition and the desire I have of becoming a useful citizen should lead me to wish a share in the undertaking."[3]

The son of a painter who was elected a member of the Royal Academy of Painting and Sculpture in 1754 and who for eight years held a commission to aid in the decoration of the Ministry of War building at Versailles, L'Enfant was a twenty-three-year-old lieutenant in the French army when he came to America in 1777 to aid in the Revolution. During the war he achieved notice for doing eight drawings for Baron von Steuben's army manual, and at Valley Forge in the winter of 1777–1778, he met Washington when he was commissioned by Lafayette to draw the general's portrait. Following the war, L'Enfant, now a major, began an architecture career in New York, when he was commissioned to remodel Federal Hall so that it could hold meetings of the Continental Congress. L'Enfant's application to plan America's first capital was thus not a presumption, despite his youth. There were indeed few others Washington might have chosen for this task.[4]

In his enthusiasm for the opportunity to design the nation's capital, L'Enfant more than repaid Washington's confidence. Article I, Section 8 of the Constitution authorized Congress to create a "district" not exceeding ten miles square to become the "seat of the government of the United States." But the location of the district was a more open matter. All the Residence Act of 1790 said was that within ten years the federal government was to be built somewhere on the Potomac. The location described covered eighty miles, and it was left for President Washington to choose precisely where the new capital would go. The decision to locate the capital in the South was one that Thomas Jefferson had facilitated by persuading a series of Southern congressmen to support Alexander Hamilton's plan for funding the national debt, which would benefit the North, and the great fear on Jefferson's and Washington's part was that the victory they had won for the South with the Residence Act would be snatched away from them by new legislation sponsored by the North if they did not find a way to get the capital financed and built quickly.[5]

Undeterred by these fears, L'Enfant emphasized the unique opportunity that building the new federal city presented and how important it was to avoid the "restraint of petty saving." As he wrote Washington, "No nation perhaps had ever before the opportunity offered them of deliberately deciding on the spot where their Capital city should be fixed or of combining every necessary consideration in the choice of situation." Jefferson's plans for Washington, which are visible in sketches he did, show a city that is laid out in grids and is roughly the size of Williamsburg, Virginia. By contrast L'Enfant's plan was for a capital of more than eleven square miles, and instead of being built exclusively on a grid, L'Enfant's federal city used both a radial and a grid system with broad avenues, such as Pennsylvania Avenue, cutting through the city on diagonals to give it grandeur as well as room for expansion.[6]

On his ideas for the Mall, L'Enfant was even more daring. In 1791, he asked Jefferson, who also favored locating "public grounds in the center" of the buildings of government, for his maps of the great cities of Europe, and soon the influence of eighteenth-century France became part of the plans L'Enfant produced for America. At Versailles the architect André Le Nôtre had used a series of formal gardens to create a central axis that emphasized the royal château, and in Paris, there was a similar use of space in the axis that went from the Gardens of the Tuileries, which Le Nôtre also designed, to Place Louis XV (renamed Place de la Concorde in 1795) and then took a ninety-degree right turn at the equestrian statue of Louis XV and went to the Madeleine church.[7]

L'Enfant did not, however, simply transpose what he knew of France to America and the National Mall. The last thing he wanted to be accused of was duplicating the Old World in the New World. As he observed to Jefferson in the same letter in which he asked to borrow his European maps, "I would reprobate the Idea of Imitating and that contrary of Having this intention it is my wish and shall be my endeavor to delineate on a new and original way the plan the contrivance of which the President has left to me without any restriction soever." What L'Enfant did on the Mall, as both historian Pamela Scott and architect Allan Greenberg have argued, was transform landscape concepts previously used to assert the power of kings to express the beliefs of American democracy.[8]

At the heart of L'Enfant's plan was the space that we now think of as the central axis of the mall. But in L'Enfant's hands this central axis, which he described as a "Grand Avenue 400 feet in breadth, and about a mile in length, bordered with gardens," was not merely a pathway. At Jenkins Heights, the highest point in Washington, L'Enfant placed "the congressional building" on a piece of land he called "a pedestal waiting for a monument." Then from Jenkins Heights, L'Enfant ran his central axis west, rather than east, extending it to the banks of the Potomac in a gesture that reflected the direction in which America was expanding.[9]

L'Enfant was, however, only getting started at this point. On the western end of his central axis, he created a crucial cross-axis. On a ridge that Washington had noticed when the two of them inspected the new capital together, L'Enfant placed a second key building, the "President's palace," and then connected it through a field "1800 feet in breadth and three-quarters of a mile in length" to a proposed equestrian statue of George Washington that he placed on a right angle with the central axis of the mall. The two most important branches of government, the executive and legislative, were now linked, but significantly in L'Enfant's plan, they did not directly face each other. They existed in a mediated relationship in which, as L'Enfant put it, "no message to nor from the president is to be made without a sort of decorum." The separation of powers that the Constitution decreed now was embodied in the open space of the National Mall.[10]

At a time when L'Enfant knew that funds for building the White House and Capitol were going to be limited, the result was a visual statement that insisted on respect for the American government and the Constitution. Citizen and politician alike were asked to put the country in perspective and accept a view "serving to give a grand idea of the whole" that, L'Enfant believed, would acquire a new sweetness "being laid over the green of a field well level and made brilliant by shade of few trees artfully planted."[11]

To achieve these results L'Enfant had worked at a feverish pace for most of 1791, and there is no telling what he might have accomplished if he had been allowed to continue revising his plans over the next nine years before the capital officially moved from Philadelphia to Washington. L'Enfant did not, however, get the time or the money that he needed to transform the 227-acre National Mall he had designed into a reality. On February 27, 1792, L'Enfant was informed by Thomas Jefferson that, on orders from President Washington, he was to cease work on the federal city.[12]

It was not a decision Washington made lightly. He was enormously appreciative of what L'Enfant had done "to change a wilderness into a city," and in his correspondence with L'Enfant, Washington constantly strove to keep L'Enfant from being his own worst enemy when it came to "having the beauty and regularity of your plan only in view." But by 1792 L'Enfant had become more trouble than he was worth for a president desperately worried about funding for the capital. Washington was constantly being called upon to settle quarrels that L'Enfant had gotten himself into, and the quarrels seemed to have no end. In October 1791 L'Enfant delayed arranging for a printed map of the city to be available at the time its first land sales were occurring, and as a result only thirty-five lots, worth a disappointing $2,000, got sold. L'Enfant then continued to refuse to submit to the authority of Daniel Carroll, Thomas Johnson, and David Stuart, the three commissioners appointed by President Washington under the provisions of the Residence Act to supervise the development of the capital, and finally L'Enfant made his conflict with the commissioners still worse by tearing down the house of the largest property holder among them, Daniel Carroll, because the house Carroll was building stood in the path of a proposed street. When on February 26, 1792, L'Enfant, smarting from criticism for his actions, wrote Jefferson that he refused to remain in his job if it meant "my continuance shall depend upon an appointment from the Commissioners," he sealed his own fate. L'Enfant's letter was the last straw for President Washington, and in an apologetic letter to Daniel Carroll, Jefferson made clear how exasperated he and the president had become in "endeavoring to induce Major L'Enfant to continue the business he was engaged in, in proper subordination to the commissioners."[13]

In 1800, as the new capital became the official seat of government, the Mall, like the city itself, thus began its existence without the man responsible for planning it in charge. It was an enormous handicap, and it would bring to a halt any chance of the Mall developing with a continuity that reflected L'Enfant's original vision. Over the course of the nineteenth century—as a result of both economic and aesthetic decisions—the Mall would stray from the elegantly balanced civic space that L'Enfant had designed to a space in which neither the values of the Republic nor the Mall's original sightlines would dominate.

In a capital starved for public money, neglect was the first source of the Mall's problems. Essentially unoccupied as the new century began, the Mall quickly came to seem ordinary rather than sacred territory for many. Private use of the Mall began as early as 1804, and as the decade progressed, individual Washingtonians did not hesitate to cultivate their own gardens on the Mall as well as use it as a storage place for lumber and a dumping ground for rubbish.[14]

But what is most revealing about the way in which the Mall was viewed in the post-L'Enfant era are the plans, both realized and unrealized, that were offered for its development and that gained national attention. The first serious plan was put forward in 1816, when in response to President James Madison's recommendations for a national university, Benjamin Latrobe, the Capitol architect for more than a decade, proposed building a university at the western end of the Mall on a 34-acre site between Thirteenth and Fifteenth Streets. Latrobe's design, similar to that which Thomas Jefferson employed in 1817 in designing the University of Virginia, was brilliant, but if built, Latrobe's national university would have been a disaster, closing off future western development on the Mall and eliminating the open vista L'Enfant had worked so hard to establish.[15]

Latrobe's plan was deferred, then forgotten, but the sensibility it reflected survived. The idea of developing the Mall without regard to the overall vision of L'Enfant gained new impetus a few years later when in

1820 Congress granted the Columbian Institute, Washington's first important intellectual society, 5 acres on the eastern end of the Mall to cultivate gardens that included two oval ponds, an island, and gravel walks. Then in 1832, Congress approved still another intrusion, when it passed legislation allowing the canal that was on the Mall's north side to expand from 80 to 150 feet in width. The Mall's center, already out of balance because of the original canal, designed by Benjamin Latrobe, was now pushed still farther off the axis that L'Enfant had planned for it to have with the Capitol.[16]

The most significant change in the post–L'Enfant era would follow from the decision, made in 1847, to build the Smithsonian Institution 300 feet from the center line of the Mall rather than on its southern border. The decision, reached twenty years after the English scientist James Smithson left America a bequest of more than $500,000 to create an institution "for the increase and diffusion of knowledge," ran directly contrary to L'Enfant's plans for placing buildings along the northern and southern perimeters of the Mall, and once again narrowed the center of the Mall and the visual ties it established between the executive and legislative branches of government. In conjunction with the start of the Washington Monument in 1848, the start of architect James Renwick's Smithsonian Institution also reopened the question, How was the Mall going to be seen in the future?[17]

The most ambitious attempt to answer that question in the pre–Civil War era came in 1850 when President Millard Fillmore retained horticulturalist and landscape gardener (the term landscape architect had not yet come into use) Andrew Jackson Downing to design the Mall and the White House grounds. Downing had been consulted by the Washington Monument Society and Building Committee of the Smithsonian in 1848, and he brought to his plans for the Mall the belief, expressed most fully in his *Treatise on the Theory and Practice of Landscape Gardening Adapted to North America,* that the essence of landscape gardening was a romantic process made visible in the "embellishment of nature."[18]

Downing had, as he told President Fillmore in his 1851 "Explanatory Notes," a threefold plan for the Mall: (1) "To form a national Park, which should be an ornament to the Capital of the United States"; (2) "To give an example of Landscape Gardening which may have an influence on the general taste of the Country"; (3) "To form a collection of all the trees that will grow in the climate of Washington." To achieve these objectives Downing proposed to divide the Mall into what he called "six different and distinct scenes." The scenes would consist of a President's Park south of the White House, a Monument Park between the Washington Monument and the Potomac River, an Evergreen Garden of 16 acres at Fourteenth Street, a Smithsonian Pleasure Grounds, a Fountain Park supplied from a basin at the Capitol, and a Botanic Garden on the east end of the Mall.

Downing's aim was to transform the Mall into a "public museum of living trees" built on "natural undulations of surface." The model for it would be, he explained to the president, bucolic Mount Auburn Cemetery built outside Boston in 1831. "The Public Grounds at Washington" treated in the manner of Mount Auburn would "become a Public School of Instruction in every thing that relates to the tasteful arrangement of parks and grounds." But Downing's plan for the Mall, save for the park around the Smithsonian, would never come to fruition. Congress refused to appropriate the $50,000 that Downing believed his landscaping required, and when he died in 1852, after the steamboat he was traveling on burned and sank in the Hudson, Downing's plan died with him.[19]

Downing's plan, with its roots in the romanticism of the rural cemetery movement did not turn out to be the alternative to L'Enfant's formalism. The next step was simply disorder. By midcentury the Mall had become a space that politicians as well as architects were willing to see fragmented, and not surprisingly, during the Civil War, when there was even less money available for civic improvements, the Mall was allowed to drift further into decay. In addition to the railroad tracks that were permitted to run across it at the foot of Capitol Hill, the Mall was marred by a canal that had become little more than a marshy sewer and a fenced-in Washington Monument grounds that housed cattle waiting to be taken to a nearby slaughterhouse serving the Union army. The

Mall's dreariness in the years following the Civil War was captured by Mark Twain and Charles Dudley Warner in *The Gilded Age* when they wrote of the uncompleted Washington Monument, "It has the aspect of a factory chimney with the top broken off," and then went on to note, "You can see the cow-sheds about its base" and "tired pigs dozing in the holy calm of its protecting shadow."[20]

In the years prior to the Civil War, visitors to Washington, especially those from Europe, had been highly critical of the appearance of the city. In his *American Notes* of 1842 Charles Dickens shrewdly observed of Washington that "it is only on taking a bird's-eye view of it from the top of the Capitol that one can at all comprehend the vast designs of its projector, an aspiring Frenchman," and in the years after the war, the criticism of Washington grew louder. There was even talk, led by Horace Greeley, the influential editor of the *New York Tribune,* of moving the capital west. During the Civil War, completion of the unfinished dome on the Capitol was given symbolic importance by President Lincoln, but Lincoln was not successful in improving the appearance of the Mall itself, and had the iron for the Capitol dome not already been on site, it is doubtful that work on the Capitol would have continued after 1861. At the war's end the Washington Monument, begun in 1848, was still incomplete, standing just a little over 150 feet high and looking like a modern ruin. The canal along the north side of the Mall remained what the former head of the Army Corps of Engineers called a "vast fermenting vat," and the Potomac River at the western shore of the Mall regularly overflowed its banks, providing a swampy breeding ground for the malaria-carrying mosquitoes that made Washington such an unhealthy place to live.[21]

In response to these problems the government embarked on three post–Civil War engineering projects that forever changed the look of the Mall and reflected the growing impact that technology would have on it. The first of these projects began in 1871 when the Washington Board of Public Works resolved to fill in the canal and convert it into a trunk sewer. The decision had an immediate effect on a number of fronts. It added an estimated 200,000 square feet to the Mall while widening its northern border. It removed the stench emanating from the canal, and it brought to a halt a situation in which, according to the District's Board of Health, at least 10,000 tons of excrement entered the canal annually.[22]

The second Mall project began in 1876 after Congress passed and President Grant signed a bill authorizing the government to complete the Washington Monument, on which no serious work had been done since the 1850s. Eight years would elapse before the Washington Monument was finished, but the resuming of construction had an immediate effect: The Washington Monument was transformed from a symbol of failure to a symbol of hope. The nation could now view the monument as a sign of the Mall's capacity for renewal.[23]

The third Mall project began in 1882 following the decision of Congress to provide a $400,000 appropriation for the Army Corps of Engineers to start reclaiming the Potomac River tidal flats south and west of the Washington Monument. The project, which had its immediate precedent in the successful reclamation of Boston's Back Bay, was an enormously ambitious one. It would take eighteen years before it was done, but its impact in the short and long term would be enormous. The kind of flooding that in 1881 had reached the base of the Washington Monument would come to a halt, and equally important, with the creation of West Potomac Park and East Potomac Park the Mall gained 739 new acres—room enough for the westward expansion that would allow for the building of the Lincoln Memorial.[24]

In a different era three such ambitious engineering projects might easily have provided the basis for a movement to rethink the meaning of the Mall. But in the decades after the Civil War, the Mall continued to be seen by most Americans as a space that had no need for special protection and no need for a unifying vision.

The train tracks that in 1854 had been allowed to cross the Mall near the Capitol had created a situation in which, as the head of the Army Corps of Engineers noted in his *Annual Report* for 1868, "The running of the trains is now distinctly heard within the halls of the Senate." But instead of providing an object lesson for what not to do in the future, the 1854 decision had the opposite effect. In 1872 Congress gave permission to the Baltimore and Potomac Railroad, a subsidiary of the Pennsylvania Railroad, to put tracks running north and south across the Mall along Sixth Street west of the Capitol. For thirty-five years, as Dian Olson Belanger notes in her essay, "The Railroad in the Park," protest over the "railroad-bemangled park" made little headway, despite the fact that in addition to its train tracks, the Baltimore and Ohio built a depot, with a 510-foot-long train shed at the site on Constitution Avenue, then called B Street, where the National Gallery of Art now sits. The railroad's defenders were able to beat back opponents by demeaning the importance of the Mall and insisting, as did Pennsylvania's powerful Republican senator, Simon Cameron, that anyone who wanted to see progress had only to compare "the difference between this little bit of park and the great benefits which a great railroad like this is going to bring into the city."[25]

A similar lack of concern for maintaining the openness of the Mall was also reflected in the government buildings Congress approved for construction on it at this time. The most important of these was the Department of Agriculture Building, which was built in 1867–1868 on a 35-acre site west of the Smithsonian. If placed along the perimeter of the Mall, as L'Enfant had wanted all the buildings on the Mall to be, the Department of Agriculture Building would have been a pleasant Victorian addition that, I-shaped and just 170 feet by 61 feet, modestly fit in. But instead of being located at the edge of the Mall, the Agriculture Department Building was aligned with the Smithsonian Institution at a location that lay within 300 feet of the Mall's center line. The decision was one that would be rectified in the early 1930s, when the Agriculture Department Building and its formal gardens were torn down. But for the rest of the nineteenth century, instead of having just one building crowding in on its central spine and limiting its open vista, the Mall had two. For years, it was not possible to think of the Smithsonian site as an exception to the rule when it came to L'Enfant's original plans for the Mall.[26]

Indeed, by the last decades of the nineteenth century, the challenge for anyone who cared about the Mall was to figure out by what standards it should be judged. Although it continued to provide a powerful visual link between the executive and legislative branches of the government, with its railroad tracks and train shed and separate parks, each controlled by a different congressional committee and professional staff, the Mall had, as Central Park planner Frederick Law Olmsted Sr. observed in 1874, deteriorated into a landscape "arranged in an absurd and wasteful way."[27]

As 1900, the year of Washington's centennial, approached, the Mall began to undergo new scrutiny. In response to a number of ill-advised proposals for changing Washington that grew out of meetings sponsored first by a committee of prominent Washingtonians and later by Congress, the American Institute of Architects, meeting in Washington in December 1900, made the city its focus and in a series of papers offered the most penetrating critique of the capital since L'Enfant's day.[28]

The key paper was that of Frederick Law Olmsted Jr., who, picking up where his father had left off a quarter century earlier, addressed the need to see the Mall in a comprehensive manner. "The Mall was not laid out on the main axis of the Capitol without a reason," Olmsted declared. "It was laid out there because it was meant to relate directly and visibly to the Capitol." The problem, he argued, was that over the years the Mall "has been planned and planted for the most part in utter disregard of this primary purpose. Its details, some good in themselves and some bad, instead of being subordinated to the considerations that fixed its position, have arrogated to themselves the control of the design."[29]

Olmsted's critique enjoyed widespread support within the American Institute of Architects, but what gave his ideas on the relationship between landscape and architecture the power to reshape the Mall was that at the end of the AIA convention on December 17, 1900, Michigan Senator James McMillan, the chairman of the Senate Committee on the District of Columbia, proposed the formation of a Senate Park Commission to report to the Senate on the development of the park system of Washington. The Park Commission, as it was finally constituted, included not only Olmsted but the architects Daniel Burnham and Charles McKim and the sculptor Augustus Saint-Gaudens, all of whom had worked together at the 1893 Chicago World's Fair, and it had the authority to explore in systematic fashion plans for changing Washington and the Mall.[30]

The result, one hundred years after Washington officially became the nation's capital, was a revival of L'Enfant's plan for the Mall by men who had come to embrace the idea of city planning. In his American Institute of Architects address, Olmsted had insisted that L'Enfant's vision of Washington offered a model for the future. "Here is a plan not hastily sketched, nor by a man of narrow views and little foresight. It is a plan with the authority of a century behind it, to which we can all demand undeviating adherence in the future," he declared. The Park Commission, which held its first meeting in April 1901, shared Olmsted's belief. Not only did the commission members make a point of immediately visiting the sites and towns in America with which L'Enfant was familiar, but in June they began a five-week tour of the European cities that L'Enfant, who had been given maps of Europe from Thomas Jefferson's library, had studied as models.[31]

What followed was a plan that paved the way for the Mall as we know it today. The full report, officially titled *The Improvement of the Park System of the District of Columbia,* was presented to the Senate on January 15, 1902, by Senator McMillan, and what it immediately revealed was not only how deeply the Park Commission had absorbed the spirit of L'Enfant's plan but how in bowing to the realities of a new century the Park Commission had chosen to "develop and supplement" rather than imitate L'Enfant's plan. The Park Commission plan, which quickly became known as the McMillan Plan, did not, for example, attempt to duplicate the 400-foot-wide Grand Avenue that L'Enfant had proposed for the Mall. Instead, it substituted a greensward for it. The Park Commission also did not keep the western side of the Mall open with an unobstructed view of the Potomac River, as L'Enfant had planned.

Instead, it proposed that a memorial to Abraham Lincoln be built at the end of the land that had been added to the central axis of the Mall during the nineteenth century.[32]

The effect of these changes was not to diminish L'Enfant's eighteenth-century vision but to tailor it to a twentieth-century Mall that with its new borders was now kite-shaped and much longer than in 1791. By sticking with the contention that over the nineteenth century "the great space known as the Mall, which was intended to form a unified connection between the Capitol and the White House, and to furnish sites for a certain class of public buildings, had been diverted from its original purpose and cut into fragments," the Park Commission put itself in a position to argue what should be done to the Mall. Yet it was careful not to appear overreaching when it maintained, "First, the railroad must be removed from the Mall, and, secondly, axial relations must be established between the Capitol, the Monument, and the White House."[33]

In its report to the Senate, the Park Commission was able both to argue that it had history on its side and to offer a plan that detailed how it believed the Mall, beginning at the Capitol and moving west, should look in the future. Indeed, to read the McMillan Plan in the order in which its sections are arranged is to walk the Mall much in the way the Park Commission envisioned a visitor to Washington would. At the American Institute of Architects Convention, Frederick Law Olmsted Jr. had complained of looking out from the Capitol and seeing dimly through the twigs a footpath and the water tank of the Pennsylvania Railroad. The Park Commission began by picturing Capitol grounds that would be much more awe inspiring. On the western side of the Capitol it proposed to emphasize the frontage that corresponded to the width of the Mall with a terrace and then add basins and fountains from which the water fell into a central pool at the level of First Street. Then, at the foot of the Mall, in the place occupied by the Botanic Gardens, the Park Commission proposed a broad thoroughfare with parterres of green that would further increase the organic connection between the Capitol and the Mall. In this same area a new Union Square with monuments to Generals Grant, Sherman, and Sheridan would also be proposed. With the railroad tracks that had once run across the Mall removed, this section of the Mall, in the Park Commission plans, would be more visually open than at any time in the past half century. Walled in by elm trees planted four abreast along its edges, it would offer a dramatic vista of the Washington Monument a mile and a half away.[34]

For the Park Commission, no place on the Mall was more important than the Washington Monument and the cross-axis formed by it, the Capitol, and the White House, and here the Park Commission, which spoke of the elms it wanted planted extending to the area around the Washington Monument, proposed doing nothing to change the relationship of these three structures. However, the Park Commission did believe that the area around the Washington Monument was badly in need of improvement if the monument was to retain the grandeur it inspired when viewed from a distance. Thus, the Park Commission proposed adding terraces and a sunken garden at the base of the Washington Monument and creating an area for recreation—the Washington Common, just south of the monument—which would also provide a link to the Tidal Basin that had been created from the dredging of the Potomac.[35]

The biggest change of all to this part of the Mall would take place west of the Washington Monument. There on the western end of the land reclaimed from the Potomac, the Park Commission proposed building a Lincoln Memorial, which it believed would dominate the site just as the Arc de Triomphe crowns the Place de l'Étoile in Paris. Equally significant, between the Lincoln Memorial and the Washington Monument, the Park Commission also proposed the construction of a canal 3,600 feet long and 200 feet wide with central arms and a border of trees. Thus, the Mall that the Park Commission was proposing was significantly different than the one envisioned by L'Enfant, and it would make a much broader political statement about the country. Instead of just being a tribute to America's revolutionary beginnings, the McMillan Plan was proposing a Mall that would acknowledge America's Civil War history and through its landscape and architecture explicitly link the president responsible for the country's foundation with the president responsible for its preservation.[36]

Implementing the McMillan Plan, however, was even more difficult than creating it. The report submitted by Burnham, Olmsted, McKim, and Saint-Gaudens was elegantly written and immediately drew favorable attention from journalists and architects. The timing of the McMillan Plan was opportune in a country just learning about city planning. On January 15, 1902, the day that Senator McMillan presented the Park Commission Report to the Senate, an exhibition of the McMillan Plan, complete with detailed models, opened in the afternoon at the Corcoran Gallery in Washington and was attended by President Theodore Roosevelt, and a month later, Charles Moore, secretary to Senator McMillan and later the chairman of the Commission of Fine Arts, who had been instrumental in the writing of the McMillan Plan, began a two-part series on the Park Commission Report in the widely read *Century Magazine*.[37]

On the other hand, there were problems facing the McMillan Plan that could not easily be bypassed, starting with the unexpected death of Senator McMillan in August 1902. Beyond that, there was the enormous expense of the plan. The Pennsylvania Railroad would ask for and receive $1.5 million just for moving its train station from the Mall, and the overall estimate for the McMillan Plan ranged from $200 million to $600 million. Furthermore, other projects, such as the elaborate terracing of the Washington Monument, would never be initiated because of the logistical problems they posed. Consequently, the ultimate significance of the McMillan Plan at the turn of the century was that it provided a standard for the Mall. In the future, those who wanted to build on the Mall or alter it would have to show that what they were proposing was consistent with the McMillan Plan. The idea of commercializing the Mall, as the railroad had done, was finished, and so too was the idea of blocking the Mall's axial vistas. Any new construction on the Mall was expected to fit in with a landscape in which the highest premium was on openness, and the Mall was seen as an organic whole.[38]

"Well over half a century passed before the Mall approached the state envisioned in the McMillan Plan," architecture historian Richard Longstreth would later write. When we look at the development of the Mall in the seventy-five years between the formation of the Park Commission in 1901 and the bicentennial dedication of Constitution Gardens in 1976, what we find is an era in which the opening up of the Mall was as crucial to its evolution as the unprecedented building along its borders. In 1927 Frederick Law Olmsted Jr. described the complexity of this add-and-subtract process when he observed that in order to keep the area of the Mall between the Capitol and the Washington Monument true to L'Enfant's vision and the McMillan Plan, three measures needed to be taken: (1) New buildings had to be designed to keep in place the Mall's longitudinal boundaries; (2) the "obstructive trees" on the central axis of the Mall had to be cut down; and (3) the Mall's length had to be graded and planted with formal rows of elms. But what Olmsted's memorandum does not anticipate is how contentious this add-and-subtract process would be, particularly in years when the budget for the Mall was meager as a result of the Great Depression and World War II.[39]

The first big test of the McMillan Plan came with the battle over the location of the Lincoln Memorial. In the years following the report of the Park Commission, its wishes had been followed. Congress acted promptly to remove the Pennsylvania Railroad tracks and train shed from the Mall, and when Daniel Burnham's Union Station opened in late 1907, the Mall was officially safe from the greatest immediate threat to its landscape. Indeed, in the wake of the McMillan Plan, even small attempted intrusions on the Mall's central axis were quickly beaten back. When in 1904 officials at the Department of Agriculture proposed placing the new Agriculture Department Building closer to the Mall's central axis than the McMillan Plan allowed, they were stopped by a coalition of architects led by Daniel Burnham and Charles McKim, who succeeded in getting President Theodore Roosevelt to take their side.[40]

The question of where to locate the Lincoln Memorial was, however, one that dwarfed all other concerns about the Mall's future. At stake was how the central spine of the Mall would be extended and anchored. Opposition to locating the Lincoln Memorial at the western end of the Mall, as proposed by the Park Commission, came from a number of powerful sources. There were those in Congress who saw the site as too isolated—a "God damned swamp" in the words of Speaker of the House Joe Cannon. Others wanted the Lincoln Memorial located at a different site within Washington, such as the plaza of the new Union Station or the grounds of the U.S. Soldiers' home at the head of North Capitol Street. Finally, there were powerful real estate and automobile lobbies that argued that the best tribute to Lincoln would be a "Lincoln Way" or "Lincoln Road" from Washington to Gettysburg.[41]

It took the new Commission of Fine Arts, created in 1910 with Daniel Burnham as it chairman, and the new Lincoln Memorial Commission, formed in 1911, with President William Howard Taft as its chairman, to thwart these alternative plans for the Lincoln Memorial, but once they did, and after Congress in 1913 approved construction of the Lincoln Memorial at the western end of the Mall, the first great challenge to the McMillan Plan was over. The sightlines on the central axis of the Mall were now firmly secured, and with the dedication of the Lincoln Memorial in 1922 and completion of the Reflecting Pool several months later in 1923, the principle of making sure that the Mall's major memorials had adequate space was also established for all to see.[42]

It was a victory for the McMillan Plan that would be reinforced in the 1920s on two fronts. Beginning with the Freer Gallery of Art, which opened to the public in 1923, all the new museums on the Mall would be located on its northern and southern borders and thus would not intrude on its central axis. In addition, the implementation of the McMillan Plan would receive legislative reinforcement from Congress. The creation in 1926 of the National Capital and Park Commission, the predecessor of today's National Capital Planning Commission, brought into being an independent body authorized to help implement the McMillan Plan's park proposals throughout Washington. In 1929 Congress went a step further, formally authorizing the development of

Washington and the Mall "in accordance with the plans of Major L'Enfant and the so-called McMillan Commission."[43]

The McMillan Commission's landscape plans for the Mall would not be seriously tested again until 1934, when the Jefferson Memorial Commission was created. This time the dictates of the McMillan Plan were not followed as dutifully as they had with the Lincoln Memorial. The spit of land on which the Jefferson Memorial would be sited was one that formed an axis with the White House and the Washington Monument. The Park Commission had at one time proposed erecting a Pantheon on that site that would contain "statues of the illustrious men of the nation" and be linked to the rest of the Mall through an elaborate landscaping scheme that included filling in at least part of the Tidal Basin. But for aesthetic and financial reasons, neither of these axis-enhancing proposals was implemented during the Great Depression. Reports by the Commission of Fine Arts calling attention to the need to develop the grounds of the Washington Monument were ignored, and when the Jefferson Memorial was finally dedicated by President Franklin Roosevelt in 1943, that portion of the Mall appeared essentially as it does today, without the Tidal Basin being in any way filled as the McMillan Commission had hoped.[44]

Nonetheless, this setback for the McMillan Plan was far from being a defeat of its principles. If, like the Lincoln Memorial, the Jefferson Memorial was at a distance from the original Mall, it was strongly linked to it visually and located on a site that reinforced the idea that the great memorials of the Mall should not crowd each other. Moreover, as the thirties and forties progressed, the new construction, which added not only the Jefferson Memorial but the National Gallery of Art to the Mall, reinforced the principle that the Mall's open space must be guarded at all costs. In 1934 the greenhouses of the old Botanic Gardens at the eastern end of the Mall were torn down to create more open space, and at nearly the same time the original Department of Agriculture Building, which in 1868 had been built too close to the Mall's central line, was also removed. Indeed, by the end of World War II, the Mall, with its three presidential memorials in place, had a remarkably finished look. Never in its history had it been so filled and at the same time so defined as a landscape free from intrusions.[45]

This pattern would continue after the war as the number of museums along the Mall's borders slowly increased while the Mall itself became increasingly free from clutter. The 1965 Skidmore, Owings, and Merrill Master Plan for the Mall maintained this precedent for development with its redesign of Union Square at the east end of the Mall. Under the Skidmore, Owings, Merrill Plan the fountains and trees at the base of Capitol Hill were eliminated to improve the views down Pennsylvania and Maryland Avenues, but equally important, Henry Shrady's Grant Memorial at Union Square was given a chance to dominate its surroundings more fully than it ever had when a 6-acre water basin that acted as a reflecting pool was placed in front of it.[46]

More modest but parallel steps toward uncluttering the Mall were also taken in this same period with regard to automobile traffic. Twelfth Street was rerouted from its surface path across the Mall and placed beneath it, and then in the 1970s the parking along the Mall's inner drives was eliminated when the drives were torn up and walks, approximating in their composition those of Tuileries Gardens in Paris, were substituted for them.[47]

The biggest change of all in these postwar years came with the final elimination of the temporary government buildings that had been erected on the Mall in 1917 with America's entry into World War I and then increased in number during World War II when office space was at a premium. From the start the "tempos" had been an eyesore. "These temporary buildings are so factory-like in design," the Commission of Fine Arts wrote in 1921, "that the American people will not suffer them permanently to overawe and dwarf one of their greatest memorials." Decades later, journalist and television anchor David Brinkley wrote of the World War II tempos in his memoir of the capital in the 1940s, *Washington Goes to War:* "The buildings were hideous. And they were everywhere. They lined both sides of the Reflecting Pool east of the Lincoln Memorial; two covered bridges spanned the pool to connect the various complexes. They nearly surrounded the Washington Monument." But it was not until 1971, on orders from President Richard Nixon, that the last-standing tempos, a group of buildings occupying the area of the Mall north of the Lincoln Memorial Reflecting Pool, were destroyed, and the land they occupied became available for park use. Nixon's proposal for the new space, as Commission of Fine Arts chairman J. Carter Brown noted with horror, was an amusement park with two levels of parking underneath it. It was an idea that was quickly rejected by the Commission of Fine Arts as inappropriate for the Mall, but what was substituted for the proposed amusement park was a different story. The substitute was Constitution Gardens, a 50-acre park with a lake and a meadow as its central features, which was dedicated in 1976 in honor of the nation's bicentennial and which completed a seventy-five-year period in which the ideas embodied in the McMillan Plan explicitly or implicitly shaped every phase of the Mall's development.[48]

A decade later it would be easy to look back on these years, which ended symbolically in June 1976 with the re-creation on the Mall by the Ruggieri Brothers of the kind of eighteenth-century fireworks display that Thomas Jefferson so admired, as a period in which those who cared about the Mall were confident—even during their most bitter battles—that the Mall's past and present could be reconciled. But beginning in 1982, with the controversy over Maya Lin's Vietnam Veterans Memorial, a very different view of the Mall came to dominate its landscape wars. Increasingly, the new battles over the Mall were shaped by the belief that the Mall was a completed landscape and that new additions would harm its overall symmetry and spaciousness.[49]

In the case of the Vietnam Veterans Memorial, objections to its perceived anti-war content were initially far stronger than any worry over the memorial's impact on the Mall's landscape. But as the furor over the memorial's design subsided in the wake of the Vietnam veterans' enthusiastic response to it when they saw it, the question of the memorial's location rapidly assumed center stage. J. Carter Brown, the longtime chairman of the Commission of Fine Arts, who from the start regarded Lin's memorial as a "masterwork," put the location question in perspective when he looked back and recalled, "The greensward that we were hoping to protect in Constitution Gardens, however, could not remain completely open." After the Vietnam Veterans Memorial was dedicated in 1982 and Frederick Hart's statue, *Three Servicemen,* was installed at the entrance to the memorial and dedicated on Veterans Day in 1984, Congress reached the conclusion that when it came to memorials on the Mall, it had a space problem on its hands.[50]

In 1986, environmentalist and liberal Democratic Congressman Morris Udall of Arizona, the brother of President Kennedy's Secretary of the Interior Stewart Udall, introduced H.R. 4378, a bill to "provide standards for the placement of commemorative works" on land in the District of Columbia. The bill, which had companion legislation in the Senate from Senator Malcolm Wallop of Wyoming, reflected a desire to avoid the kind of bitter controversy Maya Lin's Vietnam Veterans Memorial had produced, but underlying H.R. 4378, as testimony before committees in the House and Senate revealed, was the belief that there was little or no room on the Mall for additional memorials.[51]

This time J. Carter Brown was much more outspoken in discussing his worry over the remaining open space on the Mall. "We strongly oppose the erection of any future memorials on the Mall, the Washington Monument Grounds, the White House Grounds, Arlington Cemetery, or Pennsylvania Avenue," he told a Senate subcommittee, and in November 1986, when H.R. 4378 became law as the Commemorative Works Act, it reflected the concerns that Brown had expressed. At the core of the Commemorative Works Act was the conviction that in the future it should be very hard to build on the Mall. In speaking of the need "to preserve the integrity of the comprehensive design of the L'Enfant and McMillan plans," the Commemorative Works Act not only made the erection of memorials on the Mall dependent on a lengthy approval process but emphasized in its opening section that "the limited amount of open space available" on the Mall should be zealously guarded in order "to preserve the integrity of the comprehensive design of the L'Enfant and McMillan plans."[52]

Nevertheless, the 1986 passage of the Commemorative Works Act did not calm fears about the threats to the remaining space on the Mall. The Franklin D. Roosevelt Memorial had won congressional approval for a place on land in the Tidal Basin near the Jefferson Memorial long before the Commemorative Works Act became law. In the early 1960s Congress had rejected the initial design for the FDR Memorial. Then in 1974 landscape architect Lawrence Halprin was brought in to prepare a revised design, and finally in 1981, Congress authorized construction of the FDR Memorial. But the new FDR Memorial that followed, while much more modest than the original (which had earned the name "instant Stonehenge" because of its eight huge free-standing steles), was still enormously invasive, covering 7.5 acres and containing enough granite to construct an eighty-story building.[53]

Similar fears about space were also aroused by the Korean War Veterans Memorial, which in 1988 became the first memorial authorized under the Commemorative Works Act. While smaller than the FDR Memorial, the Korean War Veterans Memorial was much closer to the central spine of the Mall, sitting just southwest of the Lincoln Memorial in an area called Ash Woods and taking up a huge amount of space with a 350-foot-long installation that includes nineteen 7-foot-tall soldiers marching toward an American flag.[54]

In 1990, two years after congressional approval of the Korean War Veterans Memorial, *Washington Post* architecture critic Benjamin Forgey summed up the fears that now existed for the Mall in a prophetic June 16, 1990, article that he titled "Washington's Monumental Excess." In his article Forgey put the worry about the overcrowding on the Mall in a framework that over the next decade would inspire a series of negative articles. Describing the FDR Memorial as a design "willfully out of sync" that will "forever alter a quiet, open glade" and the Korean War Veterans Memorial as "an enclosed system imposed on a beautiful swath of open ground," Forgey argued that the

Mall and Washington faced a dark future if we continued "peppering" them with new memorials.[55]

Five years later, writing in the September 10, 1995, *New York Times* as the approval process for the site for the National World War II Memorial was concluding, James Reston Jr. took up the same issue in an article titled, "The Monument Glut." Reston's particular target was the military memorials going up on the Mall, which he viewed as turning Washington into a "martial experience." But like Forgey his ultimate fear was for the future of the Mall's openness. "One wonders how the great Lincoln will breathe now, flanked as he is on both sides by two 'Books of the Dead' from two nasty, inconclusive, foreign wars," Reston wrote. "The remaining seventy acres of the Washington Mall may be on the road toward the cluttered look of the Gettysburg battlefield."[56]

The result for the American Battle Monuments Commission as it tried to conclude its search for a National World War II Memorial site was that it faced a no-win situation no matter what choice it made. If the American Battle Monuments Commission asked for a central place on the Mall, it was bound to be accused of thumbing its nose at the L'Enfant and McMillan plans, but if it opted for a site off the main axis of the Mall, it seemed to be accepting the idea that World War II was of no more significance than the Korean and Vietnam wars. For the American Battle Monuments Commission the only choice that finally made sense was for it to stick with its belief that World War II, like the Revolutionary War and the Civil War, was a defining event for America and deserved to be honored with a central place on the Mall that made that parallel clear.

The American Battle Monument Commission's decision to build the National World War II Memorial on a site between the Washington Monument and the Lincoln Memorial elicited a flurry of criticism that took the form of a series of articles on "memorial mania." Even more important, beginning in 1996, the Mall's watchdog agencies got started on a campaign to stop memorial building on the Mall that changed the atmosphere in Washington. That year in response to what it called memorial "overload" in the Monumental Core, the National Capital

Planning Commission formed a Memorials Task Force to examine planning issues related to commemoration in Washington. What followed was a September 4, 1997, National Capital Planning Commission draft resolution that called for a "no-build" zone within the Monumental Core. A month later, the National Capital Planning Commission invited the Commission of Fine Arts and the National Capital Memorial Commission to join it in studying memorial overload. The result was creation of the Joint Task Force on Memorials and three years later the issuance of an influential Joint Task Force on Memorials report describing as "a completed urban work of art" the area on the National Mall from the Capitol to the Lincoln Memorial and the White House to the Jefferson Memorial. "No new memorial sites should be allowed" on this "reserve," the Joint Task Force concluded, and in August 2000 the Joint Task Force recommendation won Senate approval. Only the failure of the House to pass similar legislation prevented the reserve from being established in law, as it now is as a result of 2003 legislation.[57]

For the American Battle Monuments Commission, the House of Representative's failure to act was a decision that provided scant relief. Although technically the National World War II Memorial would not have been affected by the proposed legislation, since the National World War II Memorial site was already approved, the American Battle Monuments Commission still had to operate in a climate that had become hostile to new memorials on the Mall. The only solace the ABMC could take was in knowing that the Mall's history was replete with bitter turf wars over where its memorials should go and that if any idea might be labeled ahistorical, it was the notion that the National Mall should be treated as a finished work of art, closed to future generations.

# 3

# Monumental Challenge

On May 28, 2001, the battle over the site and design of the National World War II Memorial effectively ended when, in a Memorial Day ceremony at the White House, President George W. Bush signed the congressional legislation that became Public Law 107–11. Designed to expedite construction of the National World War II Memorial in Washington, the new law's three paragraphs took up less than one full page. But what Public Law 107–11 authorized was a turning point in the battle over the National World War II Memorial. The new law locked into place the approval for the site and design of the National World War II Memorial that had already been given by the Commission of Fine Arts and the National Capital Planning Commission; then in its concluding section, Public Law 107–11 declared that there could be no judicial review of the decisions that had brought the memorial to near completion.[1]

What lay behind Public Law 107–11 was congressional anger over how long the National World War II Memorial approval process was taking as critics of the memorial mounted one time-consuming challenge after another. The turning point came on May 3, 2001, with the decision of the National Capital Planning Commission to go back and re-examine a series of its earlier memorial votes. As Arizona Congressman Bob Stump, who led the fight in the House of Representatives to expedite construction of the memorial, put it, "It was up to Congress to save the memorial" from a "mind-numbing bureaucracy" that was taking twice as long to approve the National World War II Memorial as it took to win World War II.[2]

With more than 1,000 World War II veterans dying each day according to the Department of Veterans Affairs, Congress's rush in 2001 to get the National World War II Memorial built as quickly as possible is easy to understand. But equally essential to understand, if the warfare over the memorial is to be seen in historical perspective, is that bitter and often lengthy battles over the Mall's memorials are nothing new. Controversy has been the rule rather than the exception when it comes to our most important Washington memorials.[3]

Nothing makes the depth of this controversy clearer than the struggle to build the Washington Monument, which lasted for decades, involved four government investigations, and cost more than $1 million. Frederick Gutheim in a 1951 address to the Society of Architectural Historians described the Washington Monument as "one of those structures created by process rather than by the talents of an individual designer," and the history of the monument more than bears him out. The first proposal for a monument to George Washington came in 1783, shortly after the end of the Revolutionary War, when the Continental Congress voted to honor Washington with an equestrian statue in which he would be "represented in Roman dress holding a truncheon in his right hand." The monument was supposed to be located where the current Washington Monument now sits, but from the start the statue raised questions about what historian Garry Wills in his study of Washington would call images of power in early America.

Federalists favored a larger-than-life Washington, whereas Republicans wanted a statue that showed a democratic Washington. In its Roman allusions the proposed statue of Washington spoke to the imperial example of the emperor Marcus Aurelius rather than the eighteenth-century American ideal of Cincinnatus, the farmer who abandoned his plow to direct the defense of Rome and then returned home. Indeed, the political issues that the equestrian statue raised were enough to cause even a hardened Federalist like John Jay, America's first chief justice of the Supreme Court, to suggest replacing the bas-reliefs of Washington's battle victories that were intended to go at the pedestal of the statue with a book inscribed "Life of General Washington—Stranger read it. Citizens imitate his example."[4]

Jay's compromise never got anywhere. Plans for an equestrian statue were dropped when no agreement could be reached on what the statue should finally look like, and it was not until Washington's death in 1799 that the movement to erect a monument to him was renewed. On December 24, 1799, Congress passed a unanimous resolution calling for a public tomb for Washington to be erected in the Capitol, despite Washinton's express wish for burial at Mount Vernon. However, this proposal fizzled, too, when the Federalists sought to turn the original plan for an indoor tomb into a much grander plan for an outdoor mausoleum, to be designed by future Capitol architect Benjamin Latrobe, in the form of a 100-foot-high pyramid. The Federalists' desire for a monument that would "impress a sublime awe in all" was counteracted by the Republicans' wish for a monument that would emphasize Washington's humanity, and shortly after Thomas Jefferson assumed the presidency in 1801, the second movement for a Washington Monument died out, just as the first had, with the architectural battle over how to symbolize Washington and America's national identity unresolved.[5]

It was not until 1832, the centenary of Washington's birth, that the movement to build a monument to him resumed. As Washington's birthday approached, Congress proposed that the bodies of both George and Martha Washington be moved to a mausoleum in the Capitol Rotunda, and in July 1832 Congress took a second step to honor the first president by authorizing payment of $5,000 for a marble statue of Washington that would also go in the Rotunda. The commission for the statue was won by Horatio Greenough, an American sculptor who had trained in Italy, but Greenough's statue, which was unveiled to the public in 1841, did anything but resolve the question of how best to honor Washington. The

12-foot-high, 20-ton sculpture, based on Phidias's *Olympian Zeus,* consisted of a bare-chested Washington sitting on a chair with drapery covering his legs and a sword in his left hand and immediately drew public disapproval. The statue was soon banished to the Capitol grounds, where the weather played havoc with its marble, and then in 1908, it found a permanent home at the Smithsonian Institution.[6]

In the meantime a very different attempt to honor Washington was developing in private circles. In 1833 the Washington National Monument Society was founded by a group of the capital's prominent citizens, led by former congressional librarian George Watterston. By 1836 the society, whose members thought Greenough's statue was a failure, had collected $28,000 and launched a public competition to find a designer for their Washington Monument. Nine years later, Robert Mills, the architect of Washington's Treasury Building and Patent Office, as well as a 220-foot-tall Washington Monument in Baltimore, was declared the winner.

The result was the start of the monument that would become the Washington Monument we know today, although Mills's design was very different from the unadorned obelisk that we now see on the Mall. In his Baltimore Washington Monument, Mills portrayed the first president in the humbling act of resigning his military command, but at the same time he placed Washington on a huge 220-foot column that was anything but humble in scale. Visitors to the monument were forced to look up at a Washington who towered over them. A similar penchant for grandeur was also characteristic of Mills's new design for the capital's Washington Monument. George Watterston had imagined the Washington Monument Society sponsoring the "most stupendous and magnificent monument ever erected to man," and Mills did his best to fulfill his client's wishes. With its juxtaposition of Greek, Roman, and Egyptian architecture, the most striking characteristic of the monument that Mills proposed building was its scale.[7]

Mills's monument, as he outlined it, consisted of a "grand, colonnaded building . . . one hundred feet high, from which springs an obelisk shaft . . . making a total elevation of six hundred feet." But what followed was a plan far more elaborate than Mills's description conveys. His was a monument designed to be the tallest in the world and to take the breath away of anyone who saw it. Mills's proposed colonnade building was 250 feet in diameter with thirty Doric columns, each 12 feet in diameter and 45 feet high. The coat of arms of each state was ornamented on the frieze above the columns, and within the colonnade thirty alcoves were reserved for statues that would form a pantheon of Revolutionary War heroes. On the outside of the monument, the awesome scale continued. Topping the colonnade off was a roof or "grand terrace" 700 feet in circumference, which featured a statue of George Washington, wearing a toga and driving a war chariot pulled by six horses, and then rising from the center of the grand terrace, just behind Mills's imperial Washington, was the obelisk itself. The obelisk was 50 feet square at its terrace base, tapering to 40 feet square at its summit, and it invited the viewer to gaze upward at its most prominent ornament, a star emblematic of the glory of Washington.[8]

In his July 4, 1848, speech at the laying of the cornerstone for the Washington Monument, Robert Winthrop, the Speaker of the House, confidently told a crowd of nearly 20,000 people, which included President James Polk, "Other structures may fitly testify our veneration for him; this alone can adequately illustrate his services to mankind." Winthrop was being overly optimistic. Although the Washington National Monument Society was able to get the states as well as foreign countries to contribute stone blocks for the monument's inner walls, it was not able to raise enough money to keep construction going. In 1854, after the monument had risen 152 feet, a marble slab from the Temple of Concord in Rome that Pope Pius IX had donated was stolen from the monument grounds, and immediately the monument was surrounded in religious and political controversy. A year later, members of the Know-Nothing Party, an anti-Catholic, anti-immigrant political group, who were, it would later be discovered, responsible for the theft of the Pope's gift, gained control of the Washington Monument Society in a rigged election that brought construction to a near standstill.[9]

Over the next three years, the Know Nothings were able to raise only $51.66, and by the time the original Washington Monument Society regained control of the monument, it was too late to do much building before the Civil War began and all work on the monument stopped. The "unfinished marble shaft" that so jarred Henry Adams when he came to Washington as a boy in the 1850s remained an ugly ruin until the 1870s.[10]

With the approach of the nation's centennial in 1876, the state of the Washington Monument once again became an issue. On July 5, 1876, Congress unanimously resolved to assume financial responsibility for the completion of the monument, and with that decision a new battle began over what the monument should look like. The first set of problems faced by the newly appointed Washington Monument Commission concerned engineering. The Army Corps of Engineers discovered that the monument's foundation could not support its proposed height, and from 1877 to 1880, the corps worked on stabilizing the monument while removing weakened sections of its original masonry. Only after this basic structural repair was completed was it possible to resume work on the shaft, and with the laying of a second cornerstone by President Rutherford B. Hayes in 1880, the monument entered its final and most controversial phase.[11]

This time the problems were all about design and taste. The idea of building a streamlined Washington Monument that consisted of an unadorned shaft was anathema to the Victorian architects of the 1870s. Mills had said that without its colonnade, his obelisk would look like "a stalk of asparagus," and in the 1880s architecture critic Henry van Brunt voiced similar sentiments in the *American Art Review,* arguing that the Washington Monument was in danger of becoming a "brute mass." Van Brunt was far from alone in feeling this way. In the wake of Congress's decision to assume the cost of building the monument, numerous proposals for beautifying its shaft poured in. The styles of the new proposals—from that of a Romanesque bell tower to that of an English gothic church—were wide-ranging, but what they had in common was the belief that the Washington Monument should avoid becoming what van Brunt called "an expression of bigness, but not of grandeur."[12]

Under the supervision of Colonel Thomas L. Casey of the Army Corps of Engineers, the monument steamed ahead to the quick finish Congress wanted. The American ambassador to Italy, George Marsh, had discovered in his research that a true obelisk should have a height ten times the width of its base, and so Casey, who was able to dominate a divided Washington Monument Commission, determined that with its base of 55 feet square, the completed Washington Monument should be 555 feet at its apex. Resisting the proposals of a sculptor to place a series of bas-reliefs at the base of the shaft, Casey opted instead for a smooth shaft with a barely visible marble door at its entrance and a pyramid-shaped top with an aluminum tip at its apex.[13]

The result was essentially the Washington Monument that we know today—a monument in which the president it honors is nowhere to be seen but the revolution that he led and the country that he helped found are exalted. What would not end with the setting of the Washington Monument capstone in 1884 were the quarrels over the monument's completeness. The *New York Times* reported in 1884 that the finished monument seemed "undesigned," but in 1885, following the dedication of the monument by President Rutherford B. Hayes, the *Times* quickly reversed course. It reported that the monument had now become an American symbol for "a new era of hope."[14]

A similarly intense controversy would surround the Lincoln Memorial, but fortunately for the country, it would not last as long as the controversy over the Washington Monument. In contrast to the eighty-six-year lapse between Washington's death and the dedication of the Washington Monument, the lapse between Lincoln's death in 1865 and the dedication of the Lincoln Memorial in 1922 was fifty-seven years. But with the Lincoln Memorial, as with the Washington Monument, the question of who and what were being memorialized was crucial. With Washington the tension had been between the man of republican virtue and the conquering, larger-than-life general turned president. With Lincoln the tension was between the humble man of the people, who freed the slaves, and the Christ-like martyr who preserved the Union. However, the issue of Lincoln's portrayal was laden with additional historic weight. In the decades following his death, Lincoln was constantly associated with George Washington. In the 1860s popular prints of Lincoln, rushed into circulation after his assassination, showed him being received into heaven as a second Washington, and at the start of the twentieth century the McMillan Commission made a parallel linkage when it called for a memorial on the Mall to "that one man in our history as a nation who is worthy to be named with George Washington."[15]

In Lincoln's case Congress did not wait long to begin the memorializing process. In 1867, the Fortieth Congress enacted a bill to create a private Lincoln Monument Association, and soon thereafter Representative Shelby Cullom, a Springfield, Illinois, lawyer who had been a protégé of Lincoln's, commissioned the design for a monument from Washington sculptor Clark Mills. Mills's monument was never built, but like the equestrian statue of George Washington that was supposed to go on the Mall, Mills's monument reflected the grandiose way in which people were thinking about the dead Lincoln. The Mills monument, which was intended for the northeast corner of the Capitol grounds, was both huge and complex. At its summit it showed Lincoln signing the Emancipation Proclamation. Just below the summit was a set of thirty-six statues of Union generals, cabinet officials, and prominent abolitionists, and just below that a third set of statues offered an allegorical representation of once brutalized slaves gaining their freedom.[16]

Whether a national monument on the scale of Mills's could ever have been successfully built in the 1860s is questionable, but with the end of Reconstruction and the Radical Republicans' loss of power, memorializing Lincoln as the Great Emancipator ceased to be an option. Thomas Ball's *Emancipation Monument*, which in 1876 was dedicated in Washington's Lincoln Park in a ceremony in which Frederick Douglass gave the principal speech while President Grant and his cabinet sat in attendance, marked the end of an era in which Lincoln and the freed slaves were paired in the same memorial. By the late 1880s, Augustus Saint-Gaudens's apolitical statue, *Abraham Lincoln*, unveiled in Chicago's Lincoln Park in 1887, represented the new norm. The statue portrayed a thoughtful Lincoln carefully weighing his words before speaking, and it mirrored an America in which the Civil War was now increasingly remembered as a glorious war that was to be celebrated for the bravery shown by both sides.[17]

The emergence of an unthreatening Lincoln, more concerned with union and reconciliation than with racial justice, had one distinct advantage when it came to the question of building a national memorial: It made support for a memorial easier to gather. When in 1896 the Republicans under William McKinley recaptured the presidency and began an extended period of political dominance, a second effort to erect a Lincoln Memorial in Washington was inevitable. The most dramatic plan came six years later from the McMillan Commission when it proposed for the new West Potomac Park extension of the Mall a memorial for Lincoln that would "possess the quality of universality" and have "a character essentially distinct from that of any monument either now existing in the District or hereafter to be erected." This proposed memorial, the work of commission member Charles McKim, consisted of "a great portico of Doric columns rising from an unbroken stylobate," or viewing platform, and was intended to be as dramatic as the Washington Monument. One entered the monument by climbing a flight of stairs and then passed through 40-foot columns that supported a structure 250 feet in length and 220 feet in width. But equally important, before one even entered the memorial, one felt its influence. At its eastern end, a canal 3,600 feet long set the memorial off, and at the head of the canal, facing the Washington Monument, a large outdoor statue of Lincoln dominated the prospect.[18]

Twenty more years—and a series of bitter architectural battles—would pass before the Lincoln Memorial became a reality. In 1902 a bill by Shelby Cullom, now a senator from Illinois, created a Lincoln Memorial Commission, but opposition to the location and the cost of the proposed memorial by House Speaker Joe Cannon put everything on hold. There was no way for supporters of the memorial to get around "Uncle Joe" Cannon, then at the height of his legislative powers.[19]

Matters would stay this way until 1909, the centennial of Lincoln's birth, when the delays in building a memorial for Lincoln became an embarrassment that could not be ignored. What remained, however, was an uphill fight. A move to honor Lincoln with a highway from Washington to Gettysburg had the support of the automobile manufacturers, and it also had the support of Progressives, who saw the highway as a chance to make needed internal improvements in the country. Similarly complex interests were reflected in a proposal to build a memorial to Lincoln in the area between the Capitol and the new Union Station. That proposal had the support of Washington real estate owners, but it also appealed to Progressives, who believed in the city beautification movement and saw the memorial as a way to initiate a slum-clearance project.[20]

Defeating both of these proposals was not easy, but between 1910 and 1911, the means for doing so became much easier. A revolution in the House stripped Joe Cannon of much of his power. A bill establishing a Commission of Fine Arts became law, and in 1911 Congress created a new Lincoln Memorial Commission, with none other than President William Howard Taft, a strong supporter of the McMillan Plan, as a member. When the Memorial Commission met in the White House on March 4, 1911, Taft was named its chair, and he quickly sponsored a resolution asking the new Commission of Fine Arts, which he had appointed, to give the Lincoln Memorial Commission advice on what action it should take next.[21]

The response of the Commission of Fine Arts on July 17, 1911, was all that Taft could have hoped for. The commission declared that the new western end of the Mall was the best site for the Lincoln Memorial because it would guarantee it "complete and undisputed domination over a large area, together with a certain dignified isolation from competing structures." And the commission also mirrored the provisions of the McMillan Plan in defining what the memorial should look like. "To avoid competition with the Capitol or the Washington Monument, the Lincoln Memorial should not include a dome and should not be characterized by great height, but by strong horizontal lines," the commission concluded. Nevertheless, the controversy over the Lincoln Memorial was only fueled by this report. With both House Speaker Joe Cannon and President Taft on the Lincoln Memorial Commission, the battles over the memorial continued to rage.[22]

In the wake of the report from the Commission of Fine Arts, two architects, Henry Bacon, a protégé of Charles McKim, and John Russell Pope, a young architect, who had studied at the American Academy in Rome and the École des Beaux-Arts in Paris, were asked to submit competing designs. Bacon was to focus on a Lincoln memorial for the Mall, and Pope was to develop a Lincoln memorial that would go on either the grounds of the Soldiers' Home at the head of North Capitol Street or on Meridian Hill in Washington. But when designs from both architects were submitted, the Memorial Commission refused to make a final choice. Instead, on January 22, 1912, the Memorial Commission concluded that the best site for the Lincoln memorial was the western end of the Mall and invited both architects to submit a second set of drawings for the competition.[23]

What followed were two very different proposals for a Lincoln memorial, each sufficiently compelling that the losing side was guaranteed plenty of ammunition to keep the controversy going. Pope's leading design of the three that he submitted was a variation on his Soldiers' Home proposal. It consisted, in his words, of an "open Doric colonnade," circular in form, that "guards but does not conceal" a quiet central area and a statue of Lincoln. Pope's colonnade was 320 feet in diameter and 60 feet high, a bold, eye-catching structure, but its round shape had the virtue of allowing it to harmonize, rather than contrast, with the traffic circle that enclosed the memorial site. By contrast, Bacon's most important design of the three that he submitted was a variation on the Greek temple he had always thought the memorial should be. Closed rather than open, rectangular rather than circular, Bacon's memorial sat on a stone terrace 256 feet long and 186 feet wide and welcomed the public into a colonnade supported by thirty-six Doric columns (the number of states reunited in 1865) 44 feet high and 7 feet, 5 inches in diameter.[24]

Finally, in December 1912 the Lincoln Memorial Commission made its decision. Bacon was declared the winner, and the long struggle to arrive at a design and a site for the Lincoln Memorial was officially over. Predictably, nobody, save those who favored Bacon's design, was satisfied with the outcome. Before Congress gave its approval in 1913 for the new Lincoln Memorial, the move for a highway memorial to Lincoln was revived, and complaints that the memorial was insufficiently American and too wedded to the past took on new life in the form of an attack that combined old-fashioned chauvinism with a call for architectural originality. The *Independent* of New York called the final design "a public confession of architectural insolvency." The Illinois chapter of the American Institute of Architects passed a resolution criticizing the new Lincoln Memorial as "purely Greek and entirely un-American," and Gutzon Borglum, who would later gain fame for carving the presidential heads on Mount Rushmore, complained, "Don't ask the American people to associate a Greek temple with the first great American." Indeed, until the memorial was dedicated, there would be no cessation of criticism, and even at the 1922 dedication ceremonies, in which blacks were segregated in a "colored section" far from the speakers' platform, there was much to complain about.[25]

For John Russell Pope, losing the Lincoln Memorial competition was a disappointment, but the attention that he had drawn while a young architect still in his thirties would boost his career. By the 1920s his command of the language of classical design prompted Charles Moore, the chairman of the Commission of Fine Arts, to insist that the best way to get the public buildings in the area between Pennsylvania Avenue and Constitution Avenue known as the Federal Triangle done correctly was to hire an architect "like John Russell Pope," and it was only natural that in 1935, when the Jefferson Memorial Commission decided that the Jefferson Memorial should be a domed Roman hall reflective of Jefferson's admiration for the Pantheon, the commission turned to Pope.[26]

Pope's selection as architect for the Jefferson Memorial would create as much trouble for him as losing the Lincoln Memorial competition. The idea of a memorial to Thomas Jefferson had been under consideration by the Commission of Fine Arts since 1914. At that time the commission thought the best place for a Jefferson memorial would be a site between Union Station and the Capitol or one near the proposed new State Department Building. But nothing came of these plans until January 1934, when President Franklin Roosevelt, a proponent of a memorial to Jefferson, wrote a letter to the Commission of Fine Arts asking the commission to consider locating a statue of Jefferson at the apex of the Federal Triangle, east of the National Archives Building. It was a suggestion that interested the commission, as did two other possible sites—the cross-axis of the Mall at Seventh Street and in front of the National Archives Building on Pennsylvania Avenue.[27]

Then in March 1934, a fourth and more prominent site, this one at the Tidal Basin on a southern axis with the Washington Monument and the White House, came under consideration. It was a site with a long history behind it. At the turn of the century the McMillan Commission thought the site might be a good place for a Pantheon to the illustrious men of the nation, and in the 1920s the site was the locale for a proposed Theodore Roosevelt Memorial competition, which Pope won in 1925. With all this discussion going on, the timing was right for the creation of a Jefferson Memorial Commission, and in March 1934, Congress passed the legislation that created the Jefferson Memorial Commission.[28]

In April 1935 the newly formed Jefferson Memorial Commission met for the first time, and led by its most architecturally sophisticated member, Fiske Kimball, a Jefferson scholar and the director of the Philadelphia Museum of Art, the commission began the process that would keep the Jefferson Memorial embroiled in controversy for the next eight years. Inherent in the controversy was the commission's decision to invite Pope and no other architect to its next meeting after coming to a general agreement that a Pantheon-style memorial located at the Tidal Basin would best suit Jefferson.[29]

At the Jefferson Memorial Commission's next meeting, Pope made the case that a monument to Jefferson should reflect Jefferson's reverence for classical architecture, and the next time that Pope appeared before the commission, he brought with him four site-specific designs that were classical in nature. The most important of the designs was of a gigantic, Pantheon-like building 220 feet in diameter and 144 feet high that would have its portico directly on the axis with the White House. It was this design that attracted the most interest when Pope's drawings were set up in the Red Room at the White House and viewed by the Jefferson Memorial Commission and President Roosevelt. The sticking point at this juncture was the projected $9 million cost of Pope's memorial. Roosevelt and the commission thought that in the midst of the Great Depression the $3 million Congress had appropriated was more than enough, and Pope was asked to scale back his Pantheon as well as come up with a second design, one resembling another building Jefferson admired, Palladio's Villa Rotunda, a square structure surmounted by a dome and faced on all four sides with identical porticos in the shape of temple fronts.[30]

By 1936 both design schemes were completed, and the Jefferson Memorial Commission went on to approve a smaller version of Pope's Pantheon-like memorial, which now rose to a height of 136 feet, identical to that of the Lincoln Memorial, and had an outside colonnade 165 feet in diameter. The Jefferson Memorial Commission had, it thought, completed its most important work. But the commission was in for a rude awakening. The final and most bitter phase of the battle over the Jefferson Memorial—one that would put the memorial itself in jeopardy—was just beginning.[31]

In February 1937 the Jefferson Memorial Commission went public and revealed its proposed design to the newspapers. Then on March 20, 1937, the commission submitted Pope's designs to the Commission of Fine Arts, which in conjunction with the National Capital Planning Commission, voiced serious reservations about the memorial, its estimated cost, and its potential effect on the Tidal Basin landscape with its Japanese cherry trees. It was a bad start for the Jefferson Memorial Commission, and it was made worse by the fact that more than a month had elapsed between the time the approving commissions had read about the memorial plans in the newspapers and when they actually got to see the plans for themselves.[32]

The minutes of the March meeting of the Commission of Fine Arts, which was attended by Pope, reveal how bitter the criticism of his memorial was. Commissioner William Lamb, whose firm had designed the Empire State Building, observed that "the reproduction of Imperial Rome in the shape of a pentagon" was a "purely academic" exercise that did not represent Jefferson. Charles Moore, the chairman of the Commission of Fine Arts, called for "something quieter and more in keeping with Monticello," and Fine Arts Commissioner Eugene Savage, himself a painter, concluded that the whole enterprise was "a dreary thing as it stands." Nor were critics outside the Commission of Fine Arts any kinder. The faculty of the School of Architecture at Columbia, from which Pope had graduated, condemned his memorial as a "lamentable misfit in time and place," and Frank Lloyd Wright in a letter to President Roosevelt was even more acerbic, describing the memorial as an "arrogant insult to the memory of Thomas Jefferson."[33]

In April, matters went from bad to worse for Pope. A flood of letters opposing his memorial, including ones from Alfred H. Barr, the director of the Museum of Modern Art, and painter Max Weber, were sent to the House Appropriations Committee, which was holding hearings on the Jefferson Memorial, and in May the American Federation of Arts joined the fray when at its Washington convention noted modern architect William Lescaze and Joseph Hudnut, dean of the graduate school of design at Harvard, heaped more scorn on Pope. Their criticism, published in the August 1937 *Architectural Record,* echoed Frank Lloyd Wright's earlier observations. "America has definitely outgrown the imitation of Greek or Italian architecture," Lescaze announced. Hudnut dismissed Pope's memorial by confidently insisting that if Jefferson were living today and practicing architecture, "he would be found in the ranks of the progressives."[34]

The toll of the attacks on Pope, who was battling stomach cancer, was enormous, and on August 27, 1937, four days after Congress halted appropriations for the Jefferson Memorial, Pope died. But the controversy kept going. On September 29, 1937, the Commission of Fine Arts met with Eggers and Higgins, the successor firm to Pope's.

The commission agreed to a new location for the Jefferson Memorial, 600 feet farther south, but rejected a Pantheon form for the memorial, calling attention instead to the open peristyle design Pope had done in the 1920s for the proposed Theodore Roosevelt Memorial. In February 1938 Eggers and Higgins again met with the Commission of Fine Arts and after presenting three alternative schemes, agreed, despite their misgivings, to develop the design that had been done for the Theodore Roosevelt Memorial. It was not a decision that the Jefferson Memorial Commission was happy with, and in an April 17, 1938, letter to the *New York Times* and in a still longer letter in May to the *Magazine of Art,* Fiske Kimball angrily observed, "There are many people who want to kill any memorial to Jefferson and will use any handle to do so."[35]

But it was Pope's widow, Sadie, heir to the rights on his work, who had the final say when she refused to bow to the Commission of Fine Arts and mounted a successful letter-writing campaign that won the approval of President Roosevelt, a distant relative by marriage. The result was a smaller Pantheon-like memorial than Pope had originally proposed, but it was a victory for Pope's classicism all the same. On June 15, 1938, Congress agreed to provide the funds for the memorial that it had earlier withdrawn. In February 1939 the Commission of Fine Arts, which had never been able to reach agreement with the Jefferson Memorial Commission, issued a report to the House and Senate giving its version of events, but by this time the Jefferson Memorial controversy was over. The construction of a memorial that President Roosevelt very much wanted (and even used a 1938 press conference to discuss) began with groundbreaking ceremonies in December 1938 and lasted until 1943, when on April 13, Jefferson's birthday, Roosevelt dedicated the memorial himself in a somber, wartime ceremony. Long before then, the last unresolved sore point, the destruction of Japanese cherry trees that needed to be removed to make room for the Jefferson Memorial, had become moot. In the wake of the bombing of Pearl Harbor, the cherry trees found themselves without their old defenders.[36]

There were, it would seem, lessons to be learned from the controversies surrounding the Mall's classic presidential memorials, all of which have enjoyed great popularity since they opened to the public. But since the 1980s there has been no letup in the battles over the most important additions to the Mall. Maya Lin's 1982 Vietnam Veterans Memorial has had two statues plus a flag added to it that Lin did not want. The designing of the Korean War Veterans Memorial was taken from the team of four architects from Pennsylvania State University who won the design competition and given to another firm to complete; similarly, the Franklin Delano Roosevelt Memorial, following a long controversy about whether Roosevelt should be shown in his wheelchair, had a new statue of FDR added to it against the wishes of its renowned landscape architect, Lawrence Halprin.

The Vietnam Veterans Memorial is the classic case of a memorial that generated controversy that quickly took on a life of its own. Indeed, the controversy over the Vietnam Veterans Memorial was so intense at the start that it was not until 1983, a year after the memorial was opened to the public, that President Ronald Reagan made his first visit to it. Approval for the memorial initially came very quickly. In 1979 Jan Scruggs, a Purple Heart Vietnam veteran trained in counseling psychology at American University in Washington, established the Vietnam Veterans Memorial Fund, and by July 1, 1980, Congress had authorized a site for the memorial on the west end of the Mall in Constitution Gardens. Three months later in October 1980, the Vietnam Veterans Memorial Fund opened the design competition for its memorial with two requirements: The memorial should be solemn, and it should contain the names of all the war's missing and dead. By March 31, 1981, when the competition came to a close, 1,421 entries had been submitted, and on May 6, the eight-member memorial jury, which Washington-based architect Paul Spreiregen, in his role as competition advisor had put together, was able to announce that it had chosen a winner. She was Maya Lin, a twenty-one-year-old Yale student, whose memorial scheme consisted of two black planes, bearing the names of those who died in the war, angled into the ground in a V shape.[37]

In just two years' time, Jan Scruggs's idea had gone from a wish to a reality. The *New York Times* hailed Lin's design for honoring the Vietnam veterans with "more poignancy" than "more conventional monuments," and on July 7, 1981, the Commission of Fine Arts, meeting for the first time to review Lin's preliminary design, approved it without dissent. The commission was impressed with the modesty of Lin's memorial and her characterization of it as a "rift in the earth" that would create a place for "personal reflection and private reckoning."[38]

By October 1981, when the Fine Arts Commission met to make its decision on the black granite sample to be used for the memorial, the situation had changed dramatically, however. The Cooper-Lecky Partnership, headed by architect Kent Cooper, had been chosen to implement the design of the memorial, but in the meantime, criticism of the memorial, especially by those who saw it as a covert anti-war statement, had mounted. The *National Review* concluded that Lin's way of listing deaths on the memorial made it seem that "they might as well have been traffic accidents," and the *New Republic* complained that the memorial treated those who died in the conflict as "nothing but victims." At the hearing the critics of the memorial were even more outspoken. James Webb, a highly decorated Vietnam veteran, the author of *Fields of Fire,* and a future secretary of the navy, submitted a letter to the commission that described the memorial as a "black hole" and a "cave," and in testimony that immediately made the news, Thomas Carhart, a West Point graduate and Purple Heart Vietnam veteran, attacked the memorial as a "black gash of shame and sorrow."[39]

The rift between the proponents and opponents of the memorial was as pronounced as it could be, and by the end of 1981, despite approval given by the Commission of Fine Arts for changes in the memorial that would lengthen its walls and alter the landscape around it, the Vietnam Veterans Memorial was in trouble. The controversy had become so bitter that Maya Lin herself was now under personal attack both for her youth and for her Chinese ancestry. "Designed by a Gook," one of Lin's critics was rumored to have said, ought to be the inscription on her memorial.[40]

What had most changed by the end of 1981 was the power that those opposed to Lin's memorial were now able to exert. In December, Ross Perot, the businessman and future presidential candidate who had contributed $160,000 toward funding of the memorial, now went public with his complaints and argued that a new competition should be held. Then in early January 1982, twenty-seven Republican congressmen, led by Representative Henry Hyde, circulated a letter declaring that Lin's design "makes a political statement of shame and dishonor rather than an expression of our national pride."[41]

For Ronald Reagan's Secretary of the Interior James Watt, the opposition by conservatives within his own party was enough for him to send a February 25, 1982, letter to the Commission of Fine Arts and National Capital Planning Commission stating that before he gave his approval for the groundbreaking of the memorial, he wanted to know how the two commissions felt about the addition of two new elements—a flagpole and a statue of servicemen. The proposal and the threat that went with it were not suggestions that had originated with Watt. They grew out of a closed-door meeting held in January 1982 by Senator John Warner with critics of Lin's memorial and with Jan Scruggs of the Vietnam Veterans Memorial Fund.[42]

For the Commission of Fine Arts in particular, it was showdown time. As its chairman, J. Carter Brown, who opposed altering Lin's design, later acknowledged, "If we refused to compromise, there was the risk that the whole design would be discarded, without knowledge of what would be proposed in its place." Brown's response was to persuade the members of the Commission of Fine Arts to agree that in principle the sculpture and flagpole would be incorporated in the memorial, and in March 1982 groundbreaking for the Vietnam Veterans Memorial went ahead on schedule. What had not been settled, however, were two crucial questions: Who would do the sculpture, and where would it go?[43]

The first question was resolved in July 1982 when a new memorial jury chose Frederick Hart, a Washington sculptor who had apprenticed under Felix de Weldon, the sculptor of the Marine Corps War Memorial. But what remained unsettled was where the two additions would go.

Those who favored them wanted the flag to be placed at the apex of the memorial and for the sculpture to go in front of the apex. The result, when the Commission of Fine Arts met in October 1982 to approve the changes, was a meeting that aroused so much interest it had to be held at the Cash Room of the Treasury Department rather than at the Commission of Fine Arts conference room. After four hours of testimony by those in favor of the additions and those opposed to them, the commission approved the flag and Hart's sculpture, but it put off deciding where the flag and statue would go until February 1983, three months after the memorial officially opened to the public on Veterans Day. But what the commission could not resolve with the decision it made in February 1983 to place the flag by two paths at the southwest entrance to the memorial and the statue, *Three Servicemen,* in a nearby glade were the bitter feelings over the memorial.[44]

Frederick Hart would later describe the commission's decision as "Solomon like," but even at a distance of some 300 feet, his realistic, 8-foot-tall statue of three heavily armed soldiers—one black, one white, one Hispanic—staring into space, would clash with Lin's abstract monument, honoring those who died but not the war they fought. At the October 1982 hearing of the Commission of Fine Arts, both sides in the dispute had used the occasion to air old grievances. The position of the anti-Lin side was summed up by Tom Wolfe in an angry article appearing on the morning of the hearing in the *Washington Post*. With its antiwar bias, Lin's memorial was, Wolfe wrote, an attempt to put the dead of Vietnam "in a pit, below ground, in funereal black" and might as well be titled "A tribute to Jane Fonda." The pro-Lin side was equally bitter. Michael Straight, the former deputy chairman of the National Endowment for the Arts, testified that Lin's design and Hart's sculpture "cannot be melded," and Robert Lawrence, president of the American Institute of Architects, went even further. "We should not allow a patched-up modified, compromised memorial to be built," he declared.[45]

As for Hart and Lin, they, too, would find themselves engaged in public combat, even after a "peace" meeting between them was arranged. Hart would insist that his statue *Three Servicemen* did not "intrude or obstruct" Lin's memorial, but he would later find her criticism of him disingenuous and annoying. "There is nothing more powerful than an ingénue," he argued. "The collision is all about the fact that Maya Lin's design is elitist and mine is populist." Most annoying to Hart was what he saw as Lin's arrogance. In a 1983 letter to *Art News,* he sardonically observed, "What a stunning day in the history of Art for Art's sake when a student, a mere student, can be indignant and outraged that a design intended solemnly to honor the bitter sacrifice and suffering of 2.7 million people is felt to be, in some ways inadequate." Lin, in her testimony before the Commission of Fine Arts, begged the commission to "protect the artistic integrity of my original design," declaring that Hart's additions would reduce her wall to "an architectural backdrop." When her pleas went unheeded, she grew furious. She claimed she had been treated by the Vietnam Veterans Memorial Fund "as female—as a child" and then went on to accuse Hart of "scabbing on other artists' work." "I can't see how anyone of integrity can go around drawing mustaches on other people's portraits," she declared. She was equally uncomplimentary about Hart's statue. "Three men standing there before the world—it's trite, it's a generalization, a simplification," she insisted.[46]

The war between Lin and Hart was not the final controversy surrounding the Vietnam Memorial. Long after their dispute stopped making headlines, it was replaced by the campaign of the Vietnam Women's Memorial Project to get a statue devoted to the women who served in the Vietnam War placed on the Vietnam Veterans Memorial grounds. Lin and Hart both opposed another statue, as did J. Carter Brown, who, in his role as chairman of the Commission of Fine Arts, voiced the fear that the additions to the Vietnam Memorial were endangering its integrity. "We shall never be able to satisfy everyone's special interest," Brown observed. "It will never end." Nevertheless, by the late 1980s, when the proposed sculpture became a feminist issue in Congress, the clamor to build it gained a momentum all its own, and in 1993, following a juried competition, a statue to the women who served in Vietnam by Santa Fe sculptor Glenna Greenacre was installed on a small, paved plaza 300 feet from Lin's wall. A decade after its dedication, the Vietnam Veterans Memorial had shown once again that neither its widespread popularity nor the many critics it had won over could insulate it from controversy or from being perceived as incomplete.[47]

An equally intense controversy between dueling visions would also occur with the Korean War Veterans Memorial. But unlike the Vietnam Veterans Memorial clash, the Korean War Veterans Memorial clash was not resolved by compromise. Instead, it was resolved in the courts with the architectural team originally chosen to build the Korean War Veterans Memorial losing a $500,000 lawsuit charging that a replacement design had been substituted for its winning design.[48]

The impetus for the Korean War Veterans Memorial came from Korean War vets, who in the wake of the Vietnam Veterans Memorial controversy decided that their service in a "forgotten war" should be remembered. On October 28, 1986, they were able to get Congress to pass legislation authorizing the American Battle Monuments Commission to establish the memorial and to create a Korean War Veterans Memorial Advisory Board, composed of twelve veterans appointed by the president, to oversee creation of the memorial. By September 1988, the American Battle Monuments Commission had won approval to build the memorial in Ash Woods, an area southeast of the Lincoln Memorial near the central axis of the Mall, and later in the year, the Memorial Advisory Board, using architect Paul Harbeson as their competition advisor, held a design competition.[49]

Relying on themselves as the final jury, the twelve veterans, aided by consulting architects, went through 540 entries before settling on one submitted by Veronica Burns Lucas, Don Alvaro Leon, John Paul Lucas, and Eliza Pennypacker Oberholtzer, a design team from the architecture faculty of Pennsylvania State University. To avoid a "Vietnam Veterans Memorial II," the Korean vets had stipulated that the winning design did not have to include any names but that it must incorporate an American flag. Their wishes could not have been clearer, and the four Pennsylvania State University architects followed those wishes to the letter in their winning 1989 design. Their memorial consisted of thirty-eight 8 to 10-foot-high granite soldiers, surrounded by barberry bushes to symbolize the rough terrain they faced, marching toward an American flag. The soldiers, impressionistically rather than realistically portrayed, move in a time line that reflected how the war went from retreat, to offense, to retreat, and finally to a stalemate that ended thirty-eight months later with a truce dividing North Korea and South Korea at the thirty-eighth parallel.[50]

It was an auspicious beginning, but in 1990, with the hiring of the highly experienced Washington architecture firm of Cooper-Lecky to implement the winning design, controversy began. By June the Pennsylvania State University architects, who under the terms of the award contract were assigned the role of "design consultants," found that as far as they were concerned, they were shut out of the design development process. When a revised Korean War Veterans Memorial design was submitted to the Commission of Fine Arts by Cooper-Lecky in December 1990, the winning architects saw a memorial that bore only a tangential relationship to their design. Their semi-abstract thirty-eight granite soldiers had become, through the work of newly commissioned sculptor Frank Gaylord, thirty-eight highly realistic soldiers made from aluminum or white bronze. The soldiers still moved toward a flagpole, but now, instead of moving from war to peace, the soldiers were fully engaged in a combat mission in a much softer landscape that included a black granite wall by Louis Nelson.[51]

The Commission of Fine Arts, with two designs on its hands rather than a single revised design, worried that what it was presented with by Cooper-Lecky had too many elements at work. The winning architects were less tempered in their judgment. Their memorial, they believed, invited "repose and reflection," and they felt that it had been transformed into "a G.I. Joe battle scene," as their lawyer put it. The response of the Pennsylvania State University architects was to initiate a lawsuit to regain control of the memorial. The suit, however, would only lead to more frustration for them; the court ruled that after receiving their $20,000 prize, their design work became the property of their clients to do with as they pleased.[52]

From here on in, the Pennsylvania State University architects would become secondary figures in the Korean War Veterans Memorial controversy, but the memorial battle would continue. Early in 1991, Cooper-Lecky submitted another revised scheme, and Commission of Fine Arts Chairman J. Carter Brown would praise them for acknowledging that their earlier scheme was "overstatement to the point of bombast." But Cooper-Lecky was doing anything but winning broad approval. Comparing the two competing schemes in February 1991, *Washington Post* architecture critic Benjamin Forgey praised the first design as "the more promising of the two" but condemned both for being "too big" for their surroundings. As 1991 wore on, the Commission of Fine Arts also kept up its criticism. Despite another Cooper-Lecky revision that reduced the number of soldiers in the memorial to nineteen and shortened the black granite wall from 214 feet to 180 feet, the Commission of Fine Arts withheld approval of the memorial design. As one commissioner observed in August, "This doesn't add up to a work of art."[53]

It was not until January 1992 that the Korean War Veterans Memorial gained the conceptual approval from the Commission of Fine Arts necessary for Cooper-Lecky to begin work on the design scheme that the public would finally see at the memorial's 1995 dedication. Cooper-Lecky had won a highly tainted victory, however. The view of the Korean War Veterans Memorial that has been voiced repeatedly over the years is the one expressed in 1991 by Joan Abrahamson of the Commission of Fine Arts, who refused to give the memorial conceptual approval, calling it a "jumble of elements" that reflects "endless tinkering with an unsuccessful approach."[54]

What the public saw in 1995 when the memorial was unveiled consisted of nineteen, 7-foot, stainless steel soldiers in ponchos marching toward a flag, backed by a black granite wall, serving as a mirror (which had the effect of doubling the number of soldiers to thirty-eight) and etched with the images of those who served as support troops in Korea. Although several years have passed since the dedication, critics have found it difficult to forget the Korean War Veterans Memorial controversy. That controversy and the maneuvering it reflected have made the final version of the memorial seem like a bad compromise, and the memorial, which in 1998—just three years after its dedication—required a $2 million appropriation in order to repair its waterlines, lighting, and landscaping, has been slow to shed its early history. Critics have labeled it "a soulless imitation of the Pennsylvania team's scheme," as well as a "knockoff" of Maya Lin's Vietnam wall, and have concluded that the memorial, with its "humanoid" soldiers, takes up too much space on an already crowded Mall.[55]

Like the Korean and Vietnam war memorials, the Franklin Delano Roosevelt Memorial, which was dedicated by President Clinton on May 2, 1997, was also dogged by controversy from the start. But what distinguishes the Roosevelt Memorial from its contemporary predecessors is the duration of the controversy surrounding it. The impetus to build a Roosevelt Memorial began in July 1946, fifteen months after FDR's death, when a congressional resolution was introduced creating the Franklin Delano Roosevelt Memorial Commission. But by the time the memorial opened to the public, more than a half century had elapsed, and two architectural teams had been dismissed before landscape architect Lawrence Halprin of San Francisco was able to complete his memorial.[56]

The extended controversy that the Roosevelt Memorial would generate was foreshadowed in the nine-year delay between 1946 and the actual formation of the Roosevelt Memorial Commission in 1955. Although no site or design yet existed, the potential cost of the memorial and the idea of honoring a president so soon after his death sparked intense controversy. By 1958, the newly created FDR Memorial Commission had, however, selected a site in West Potomac Park between the river and the Tidal Basin for the memorial and was ready to begin a two-stage juried competition. Interest in the memorial was high. Five hundred and seventy-four submissions poured in, and on December 30, 1960, when the jury settled on a design by William F. Pederson and Bradford S. Tilney of New York, it seemed as if the Roosevelt Memorial was on its way to being realized.[57]

What the jury—which consisted of some of the most distinguished modern architects of the time, including the dean of architecture at MIT and the head of the Harvard Graduate School of Design—had not anticipated, was that its tastes might not coincide with those of the public. The winning design consisted of eight gigantic concrete tablets, inscribed with quotations from Roosevelt speeches. Architect Philip Johnson praised the "powerful almost primitive tablets" as "a splendid expression of twentieth-century art." But the public saw a memorial that was out of scale and a challenge to the neoclassical memorials around it. When the distinguished planner and art critic Frederick Gutheim compared the new Roosevelt Memorial to "a set of bookends just out of the deep freeze" and labeled the winning design "instant Stonehenge," it was the beginning of the end for the Pederson-Tilney memorial. In response to the Commission of Fine Arts, which in 1962 withheld approval of the memorial on the grounds that it lacked "repose" and was not "harmonious" with the three presidential memorials around it, Pederson and Tilney came up with a revised design, which the Commission of Fine Arts approved. But in 1964, when Congressman James Roosevelt, FDR's oldest son, speaking on behalf of the Roosevelts, denounced the memorial on the floor of the House, saying, "We don't like it, and I'm sure father wouldn't either," the Pederson-Tilney Roosevelt Memorial was dead. With opposition from the Roosevelt family, any chance of congressional approval or successful fundraising was over. In April 1965, Pederson and Tilney resigned their commission.[58]

Worried that a second open competition might produce another unacceptable design, the Roosevelt Memorial Commission decided that its best alternative was to solicit proposals from fifty-five of America's leading architects, and in January 1966, the commission settled on Marcel Breuer, the designer of UNESCO's headquarters in Paris and the Whitney Museum in New York. With his impeccable architectural credentials, Breuer, then at the peak of his career, seemed like a perfect choice. The problem was that Breuer admired the design Pederson and Tilney had done, and what he submitted was perceived as a variation of their rejected design. The Breuer memorial consisted of a pinwheel scheme of seven gray granite triangles, 60 feet tall at their highest point, that rotated around a 32-foot cube of polished dark granite with an enlarged photographic portrait of Roosevelt recessed into the surface of the cube through a special sandblasting process. An electronic device in the center of the memorial was programmed to play recordings of Roosevelt's speeches for memorial visitors.[59]

"It's pure geometry," Breuer would say of his memorial, but critics had the same trouble with Breuer's design that they did with Pederson and Tilney's proposal. The comparative modesty of Breuer's memorial (it was 100 feet lower at its highest point than the Pederson-Tilney memorial, which peaked at 167 feet) did not spare it from being interpreted as a mix of pop art and dated Bauhaus modernism. In January 1967 the Commission of Fine Arts rejected Breuer's memorial, citing its lack of "artistic achievement and significance." In their discussion of the memorial design, the commission members were even more outspoken, as the minutes of the meeting reveal. What Breuer called pure geometry, commission members saw as "disrespectful and frivolous." "This might have been suitable for the Cabinet of Dr. Caligari," one joked, "but it doesn't have much to do with today." It was the end of Breuer's memorial. For two years senators sympathetic to the Roosevelt Memorial Commission sought to override the Commission of Fine Arts, but their resolutions never got out of committee, and in 1969 Breuer resigned his commission in disappointment.[60]

Although President Roosevelt once told his friend, Supreme Court Justice Felix Frankfurter, that he wanted a memorial "no larger than a desk," it seemed as if even a memorial of such minimal size was going to be impossible to build on the Mall. Two decades after his death, the only FDR memorial in Washington that people passed daily was a small block of stone, installed in 1965 outside the National Archives, bearing the inscription, "In Memory of Franklin Delano Roosevelt, 1882–1945." However, in 1971, the Commission of Fine Arts renewed its efforts to find an acceptable memorial design by approving a House resolution authorizing the secretary of the interior to help in the planning and design of a

Roosevelt Memorial. After the Interior Department held an open competition that drew ninety entries, it whittled the finalists down to seven in 1974, and the Roosevelt Memorial Commission settled on Lawrence Halprin, best known for such landscape projects as the Ira Keller Fountain in Portland, Oregon, and Freeway Park in Seattle, as its top choice.[61]

In contrast to his two predecessors Halprin, a World War II veteran with deep personal memories of Roosevelt, wanted a memorial that would reflect "the experience of living through the FDR presidency." The program for the competition that he won called for a landscape solution that would harmonize with its surroundings, and both Halprin's first design, a multilevel water garden that focused on a freestanding statue of Roosevelt, and his second design, four garden rooms that told the story of the Roosevelt presidency, fulfilled the Roosevelt Memorial Commission requirements. Halprin's conceptual design was approved by the Roosevelt Memorial Commission in 1975, and a scaleddown version of his design was approved in 1979 by the Commission of Fine Arts, which would continue to be involved with modifications of the FDR Memorial until 1990.[62]

But Halprin would not have clear sailing after 1979. A new version of the controversy that had derailed his predecessors would follow him for the next two decades and nearly stop his memorial from being completed. With an estimated price tag of $50 million, Halprin's memorial would be the costliest ever built on the Mall, and it immediately aroused concern. Syndicated columnist Jack Anderson accused the Roosevelt Memorial Commission of perpetuating one of the "nation's hoariest boondoggles," and Secretary of the Interior Cecil Andrus withdrew support for the memorial until Halprin, by eliminating 500 feet of wall, a costly theater, and an interpretative center, was able to reduce the estimated cost of his memorial to $24 million. Although the FDR Memorial won congressional approval in 1981, it would take another eight years and a dramatic last-minute appeal from Florida Congressman Claude Pepper, an old New Dealer, who in 1989 was dying of cancer at Walter Reed Army Hospital and left his hospital bed to deliver a passionate appeal to the House on behalf of honoring FDR, to get sufficient funding for the Roosevelt Memorial. A few days later, President George Bush visited Pepper in the hospital, and Pepper renewed his appeal again. This time Pepper was successful in getting the money the memorial needed, now estimated to cost $52.5 million. Groundbreaking for the Roosevelt Memorial began in 1991, and in 1994 construction on Halprin's third and final design got under way.[63]

As someone already known for his Taking Part Workshops, in which clients, designers, and users would gather to discuss a proposed building or park, Halprin was ideally suited for the challenges that lay ahead. But neither Halprin's natural diplomacy nor the accessibility of his Roosevelt Memorial, in which four massive outdoor rooms took the viewer in a straight line from the New Deal through World War II, could spare Halprin controversy. Even praise of his memorial seemed to come with qualifications. Benjamin Forgey, writing in the *Washington Post*, was typical, lauding Halprin for the "twelve-foot-high stone walls, magnificent trees, crashing waters" of his memorial, but complaining of "overstatement" that left him feeling "forcefully manipulated." Others were less restrained, whether speaking of the memorial's form or its content. In an op-ed revealingly titled, "The FDR Memorial Scam," columnist Charles Krauthammer argued that the memorial was an "embarrassment." "Grossly out of proportion," especially with regard to its monumental neighbors, it "goes on forever," Krauthammer complained. Architect Roger Lewis arrived at the same conclusion more than a year before the memorial officially opened, describing it as a "sprawling historically didactic ensemble" that was "excessive," and *Washington Post* writer Paul Richard made the same argument on a personal level, pointing out that the memorial pictured FDR "cloaked with weightiness, while Roosevelt the man was jauntiness itself."[64]

In 1997, the year the memorial opened to the public, it often seemed as if everything that Halprin did turned him into a target. The political left, which had clamored for a Roosevelt Memorial, refused to give Halprin a break. He was damned for modernizing FDR as well as for glorifying him. Mary McGrory, one of the *Washington Post*'s most consistently liberal writers, found the "aching political correctness" of the memorial stultifying, complaining that in deference to tobacco-haters

FDR's signature cigarette holder had been removed and that in deference to animal-rights activists Eleanor Roosevelt had been divested of
her trademark fox fur piece. Other liberal critics dug still deeper in their
analyses of the memorial. In the *Public Art Review* Harry Boyte and
Nancy Kari argued that the Roosevelt Memorial erred in the worst way
when it came to the question of political activism. The memorial, they
believed, reduced the people of the country to passive figures hanging
on FDR's every word but doing little for themselves. For Boyte and Kari
the memorial's political message was unmistakable and undemocratic:
Government in the person of FDR was the one true source of political
change in the 1930s.[65]

For Halprin, the controversy over the Roosevelt Memorial would not
end with its dedication in 1997. Like Maya Lin with her Vietnam Veterans Memorial, Halprin would be forced to deal with the demand for
an addition from a well-organized group dissatisfied with the original
memorial. In Halprin's case, the demand was for a fifth outdoor room
that showed FDR in his wheelchair. In his memorial Halprin had
included a biographical inscription, noting that after being stricken with
polio in 1921, Roosevelt "never again walked unaided." But Halprin
decided not to show Roosevelt in a wheelchair because, as he put it,
"FDR himself made every attempt to minimize his disability." In choos-
ing to stay "close to the historic record," Halprin was acting according
to Roosevelt's wishes. Among the 125,000 photographs in the Roosevelt
Library, only two show FDR in a wheelchair.[66]

But in the 1990s, there was no combating the power of the National
Organization on Disability, which in 1995, led by board member and
former Bush administration official, Michael Deland, began lobbying
for a statue of FDR in a wheelchair. A number of columnists—the *New
York Times*'s Russell Baker and the *Washington Post*'s Marc Fisher—
protested the introduction of historical revisionism into a memorial
dealing with the thirties and forties, but far more influential was a column of *Time*'s Hugh Sidey, which began with a headline that asked,
"Where's His Wheelchair?" The disability lobby soon had Presidents
Ford, Carter, and Bush, as well as the Roosevelt grandchildren, on their

side, and on July 24, 1997, at the urging of President Clinton, Congress passed a joint resolution requiring the Roosevelt Memorial to build a new outdoor room featuring a statue of FDR in a wheelchair. For Halprin, the option that remained, as he later acknowledged, was a Hobson's choice. "I could take on the assignment or allow someone else to do it." He chose to keep final control of his memorial and have sculptor Robert Graham, who had done a bas relief in the first room of the memorial, work on a wheelchair depiction of Roosevelt, and in January 2001, the new statue of FDR was unveiled in a dedication ceremony presided over by President Clinton.[67]

Six months later Halprin, who had tried to be so considerate of everyone's feelings with his Take Part Workshops, expressed his feelings in a letter to *Landscape Architecture.* "A process needs to be evolved that can help us avoid such painful afterthoughts," he observed. "At both the Vietnam and FDR memorials, special interest groups were able to override thoughtful processes and established procedures. The results dilute the art and send equivocal messages to the future." It was a message of frustration that other memorial builders, not just Maya Lin, would understand all too well, and the kinds of conflict it reflected would prove equally relevant to the battle over the National World War II Memorial.[68]

# 4

## SITE SEEKING

When General P. X. Kelley, the former commandant of the Marine Corps, opened his *Washington Post* on the morning of March 23, 1994, he knew that his stint as chairman of the American Battle Monuments Commission was over. "I'm history," he told his wife. What caught Kelley's eye was a headline that warned, "Clinton Could Face Enemy at Omaha Beach." The enemy consisted of conservative Republican appointees to the ABMC, who, according to the article, were going to be accompanying Clinton to Normandy for the fiftieth anniversary of D-Day unless he replaced them with commissioners of his own choosing.[1]

General Kelley, a much decorated retired general and former member of the Joint Chiefs of Staff, who did campaign ads for President George Bush in 1992 and who had offered to resign from the American Battle Monuments Commission when Bill Clinton was elected, did not feel bitter about the story. Founded in 1923 to deal with establishing and maintaining burial grounds in Europe for American soldiers killed during World War I, the American Battle Monuments Commission, which oversees twenty-four military cemeteries around the world, is an eleven-member agency to which presidents regularly appoint veterans and political allies. The ABMC's first chairman, World War I hero General

John J. Pershing, served from 1923 to 1948, and General George Marshall, the chief of the armed forces in World War II, served from 1949 to 1959, but in recent years, as Kelley knew, the ABMC chairmen had served shorter terms, changing along with the administrations that appointed them. Indeed, in 2001, following the election of George W. Bush, Kelley would resume his chairmanship of the Battle Monuments Commission, succeeding the chairman who had succeeded him.[2]

In the case of the Clinton administration, which in April and May of 1994 appointed eleven new members to the American Battle Monuments Commission and replaced Chairman Kelley with Fred Woerner, a Clinton-friendly, retired four-star army general forced into early retirement by President Bush for opposing the 1989 Panama invasion, the timing of the new ABMC appointments was also revealing. Worried about the opposition it faced on issues ranging from gays in the military to health care reform, the Clinton administration had not made the ABMC a high priority when it came into office.[3]

As a result a great deal of time was lost before the Clinton-appointed American Battle Monuments Commission, which by law had the responsibility to do the planning and fund-raising for the National World War II Memorial, was in a position to get down to serious work on the memorial. As the summer of 1994 began, the best that the new ABMC could do was fulfill the ceremonial demands on it. On May 30 the new commission held its first meeting, and the next morning the commissioners were off to Europe for ceremonies that would culminate at the American cemetery at Normandy on the fiftieth anniversary of D-Day. It was not until the fall that the new commission actually began the task of making the National World War II Memorial a reality. At their second meeting on September 29, the new commissioners received an extensive briefing on the status of the memorial and were told of the problems they faced. They also learned that a second group, a twelve-member World War II Memorial Advisory Board, would be appointed shortly by President Clinton and would be expected to advise and assist the commission. "I was impressed with the magnitude of the task ahead and the lost time," General Woerner would later say. The lost time was particularly worrisome to the general, and in October made a key decision. To streamline the operations of ABMC and get decisions on building the National World War II Memorial made on a much quicker basis, General Woerner appointed a three-member World War II Memorial Committee composed of ex-New York governor and World War II army veteran Hugh Carey, former ambassador and World War II navy veteran Haydn Williams, and retired army Brigadier General Evelyn "Pat" Foote. The committee was expected to report to General Woerner on all key decisions, but it would also have wide leeway to act on its own. In December the Memorial Advisory Board took a similar step to streamline its operations, forming a Site Advice Committee and a Design Advice Committee that would report to its chairman, retired Georgia Army National Guard Brigadier General Pete Wheeler, the commissioner of veterans affairs for the state of Georgia for more than fifty years.[4]

The American Battle Monuments Commission was now ready to begin making day-to-day decisions on the National World War II Memorial. Years later Fred Woerner would look back on this period and remember how concerned he was about getting the money to pay for the National World War II Memorial. But he also knew that he could not let that problem distract him and the ABMC from what in 1995 was the first order of business, finding a site for the National World War II Memorial.[5]

As a result of the October 1994 passage of House and Senate Joint Resolution 227, the ABMC had the legal authority to establish a national World War II memorial within the monumental core area of Washington, and on January 20, 1995, the ABMC's World War II Memorial Committee and the Memorial Advisory Board's Site Advice Committee held their first joint site-selection session, meeting in Washington with representatives from the Commission of Fine Arts, the National Capital Planning Commission, the National Capital Memorial Commission, and the National Park Service. At that meeting the American Battle Monuments Commission learned the full range of its choices from John

Parsons, the National Park Service's associate director of land, resources, and planning for the National Capital Region.

The members of both the World War II Memorial Committee and the Memorial Advisory Board Site Advice Committee visited the sites on Parsons's list on January 20. The sites included the Capitol Reflecting Pool, the Tidal Basin, West Potomac Park, Constitution Gardens, the Washington Monument grounds, and Freedom Plaza. A seventh site, the Marine Corps's Henderson Hall, adjacent to Arlington National Cemetery, was dropped from consideration because of its unavailability at the time. With these possibilities before it, the American Battle Monuments Commission's next move came later in January, when it retained the firm of Washington architect Davis Buckley, which had broad experience in designing memorials, to conduct an evaluation of the six sites John Parsons had put forward.[6]

"I wanted to be as balanced as I could," Buckley would say of the *Site Selection Report* he prepared for the American Battle Monuments Commission, and when the World War II Memorial Committee met again on March 2, 1995, in Washington, it was clear that Buckley had been true to his word. He had prepared a detailed report for the World War II Memorial Committee on the accessibility, historical associations, and proximity to other monuments of the six sites under consideration.[7]

The first site, "Capitol Reflecting Pool, Western Sector," had the advantage of a conspicuous location within Washington's monumental core. It was bounded by Pennsylvania Avenue to the north, Maryland Avenue to the south, First Street and the Reflecting Pool to the east, and Third Street to the west. Visually linked to the Capitol, which was just to its east, the Capitol Reflecting Pool, Western Sector, also had good pedestrian access, and because of the nearby Grant Memorial, it was a site that was frequently visited.

The second site, "Tidal Basin," was located in the triangle formed by Independence Avenue, the Tidal Basin, and Fifteenth Street and had the virtue of being relatively flat and easy to build on. It would not compete with other memorials, and although it was not an easily accessible site, it was, as a result of the Tidal Basin's Japanese cherry trees, a beautiful locale enhanced by strong visual links with the Jefferson Memorial to its south and the Washington Monument to its north.

The third site, "West Potomac Park," was defined by the triangle formed by Independence Avenue, Ohio Drive, and the Tidal Basin and had the benefit of being in a large, open field. It could accommodate a good-sized memorial; it had a good visual linkage to the Lincoln Memorial, and it was close to the Franklin Delano Roosevelt Memorial with its ties to World War II. With the Tidal Basin to its east, and the Potomac shoreline to its west, West Potomac Park also had the advantage of being a particularly scenic locale.

The fourth site, "Constitution Gardens," consisted of three-quarters of an acre located between the Rainbow Pool and Constitution Avenue and bounded on the east by Seventeenth Street and on the west by a small lake. It came with an enormous advantage because of its location just off the central axis of the Mall. It was near public transportation and easily accessible by pedestrians, and because it was so central to Washington's monumental core, the Constitution Gardens site could be sure of a steady stream of visitors. The Washington Monument and Lincoln Memorial were within easy walking distance of it.

The fifth site, "Washington Monument Grounds," consisted of an area west of the Museum of American History, south of the Department of Commerce, bordered by Constitution Avenue and Fourteenth Street. The American Battle Monuments Commission found this site unappealing from the start because of its crowded location, but the site had the virtue of being highly accessible. Visitors could get to it on foot or by public transportation with no difficulty, and since it was linked to the nearby Washington Monument, the site was sure to draw a steady stream of visitors.

The sixth and final site, "Freedom Plaza," was at the western end of Pennsylvania Avenue between Thirteenth and Fourteenth streets and came with the disadvantage of being off the Mall. But Freedom Plaza also had a number of advantages. Immediately to its west was the American Expeditionary Forces Memorial, which commemorates America's role in World War I and the hero of that war, General John J. Pershing, the commander-in-chief of the American Expeditionary Force. In addition there were important military associations with this site; it was central to Washington's most important parades. Inaugural parades and the victory parades for World War I and World War II went by it, and so a World War II memorial that was built at Freedom Plaza would in a very real sense be occupying familiar territory.[8]

Haydn Williams would later look back on these site options and the long drawn-out site selection process and observe, "In my opinion the site decision was the single most important one made in the history of the National World War II Memorial." What Williams had in mind was the degree to which the site chosen for the National World War II Memorial would shape its design, be crucial to its public acceptance, and affect fund-raising. It was a view shared within the American Battle Monuments Commission, and when it came time to choose a site, the World War II Memorial Committee and Site Advice Committee were, after a certain amount of debate at their March 2, 1995, meeting, able to reach a unanimous decision on how to rank the choices before them. Heading the list of potential sites was Constitution Gardens, and in second place was the Capitol Reflecting Pool. In making these sites its two top choices, the World War II Memorial Committee was acting on the basis of what it thought its viable options were. After early 1995, the American Battle Monuments Commission considered the Rainbow Pool to be a superior site for the National World War II Memorial, and Haydn Williams would recall how in informal conversations the ABMC had tried, without success, to see if the National Park Service could be persuaded to include the Rainbow Pool as part of the Constitution Gardens site. In order to give the National Park Service incentive to change its mind, the World War II Memorial Committee had even spoken of the ABMC's willingness to make the long overdue repairs that the crumbling Rainbow Pool needed. But John Parsons was unpersuaded by this argument, and at this stage in the site search the World War II Memorial Committee thought it unwise to push him on the matter.[9]

For the remainder of March and all of April 1995, the World War II Memorial Committee worked on preparing for its appearance at a May 9 public hearing with the National Capital Memorial Commission, an advisory agency created by Congress in 1986 to help the Department of the Interior and General Services Administration implement the Commemorative Works Act. For the ABMC, getting the National Capital Memorial Commission to approve its site choice was a crucial first hurdle in the memorial process, and the World War II Memorial Committee viewed its meeting with the Memorial Commission as a test of the road ahead.

It would turn out to be a bumpy road. In his presentation to the National Capital Memorial Commission, Haydn Williams stated that of all the sites available, the ABMC's unanimous preference was Constitution Gardens and that its alternative choice was the Capitol Reflecting Pool. Williams also spoke of the ABMC's willingness to provide for "a restoration of the Rainbow Pool lying immediately to the south of the proposed site," but his offer was not taken up. With Charles Atherton, who also served as secretary of the Commission of Fine Arts, leading the way, a third site, Freedom Plaza, was also introduced into the discussion as a possible memorial locale. In the debate that followed, the Memorial Commission then tried to narrow its choices, but the best the commissioners could do was agree to eliminate recommending the Freedom Plaza site. Unable to choose between the Constitution Gardens and Capitol Reflecting Pool sites, they ended the meeting by voting to give "equal weight" to both and to ask the American Battle Monuments Commission to study each site further before returning to the next Memorial Commission meeting on June 20. That there might also be trouble ahead was foreshadowed by Charles Atherton, who near the end of the meeting warned that from the perspective of the Commission of Fine Arts, "It just may be that these two sites you mentioned would not meet the approval of the Commission."[10]

Three days later on May 12, at its regular biannual meeting, the full American Battle Monuments Commission visited the Capitol Reflecting Pool and Constitution Gardens sites, and after being briefed on what had happened at the National Capital Memorial Commission meeting by Haydn Williams, the commissioners in a unanimous vote reaffirmed their preference for the Constitution Gardens site. The ABMC commissioners nonetheless remained hopeful about the Rainbow Pool as a potential site for the memorial.

When the American Battle Monuments Commission met with the National Capital Memorial Commission on June 20, the ABMC did manage to make the Rainbow Pool a topic of discussion. In his opening statement to the commission, Haydn Williams reaffirmed the ABMC's preference for the Constitution Gardens site over its second choice, the Capitol Reflecting Pool, but then Williams went on to discuss defining the Constitution Gardens site so as to allow for "a major exploration of the Rainbow Pool." John Parsons, however, countered Williams by saying that in his judgment the Constitution Gardens site should be limited to three-quarters of an acre and not extended farther south, and with this assertion the Rainbow Pool as a potential site for the National World War II Memorial seemed off the table. The June 20 meeting ended with the National Capital Memorial Commission recommending, without stating a preference, both the Capitol Reflecting Pool and the Constitution Garden sites. The Rainbow Pool was a consideration at this point for rehabilitation but not as a site for the National World War II Memorial, despite the observation by Charles Atherton, "If I had my own personal preference, I would stick the memorial out in the Rainbow Pool."[11]

After the June 20 meeting there was still hope within the American Battle Monuments Commission that the Rainbow Pool might become the site for the National World War II Memorial, but as the ABMC prepared for its next big challenge, same-day meetings on July 27, 1995, with the Commission of Fine Arts and the National Capital Planning Commission, the ABMC knew its hope rested on shaky ground. For the ABMC the July 27 meetings were crucial. Under the terms of the 1986 Commemorative Works Act, the ABMC needed to get approval for the National World War II Memorial from three sources: the Secretary of the Interior, whose immediate representative was the National Park Service; the Commission of Fine Arts; and the National Capital Planning Commission. A rejection from any one of these three agencies on either the site or the design of the memorial was in essence a veto.

The meetings on July 27 began early in the morning when Chairman J. Carter Brown of the Commission of Fine Arts led a tour of three possible National World War II Memorial sites—the Capitol Reflecting Pool, Freedom Plaza, and Constitution Gardens—for members of both the Commission of Fine Arts and the National Capital Planning Commission. Then at midmorning, at the official meeting between the ABMC and the Commission of Fine Arts, Haydn Williams began his testimony by stating why the ABMC thought that in view of the options before it, the Constitution Gardens site was superior to the Capitol Reflecting Pool site. Williams's stance had taken into consideration a memo, formally titled "World War II Memorial Suggested Program Elements," that the American Battle Monuments Commission had received on July 19, 1995, from John Parsons and the National Park Service. Parsons's memo was unequivocal when it came to its section on "suggested design guidelines" for Constitution Gardens: "The Rainbow Pool will not be a part of the memorial," the memo declared.

When Williams was done with his remarks on potential National World War II Memorial sites, a discussion did not, however, immediately follow on the options he had proposed. Instead Chairman J. Carter Brown of the Commission of Fine Arts read into the record three letters that he had received. The first letter, from Sarah McClendon, a member of the World War II Memorial Advisory Board, expressed dissatisfaction with the Constitution Gardens site. The second letter, from David Childs, the Skidmore, Owings, and Merrill partner who was the principal designer of Constitution Gardens, argued that a large memorial in Constitution Gardens would spoil the park atmosphere it was intended to have. The third letter, from Frederick Hart, best known for his controversial *Three Servicemen* sculpture near the Vietnam Veterans Memorial, suggested that the best solution for the World War II Memorial was a gateway memorial, such as a tri-

umphal arch, that would be located at the Columbia Island traffic circle on the drive between the Lincoln Memorial and Arlington Cemetery. The reading of the letters was a significant indication of what was
to come. Collectively, the letters reflected the unwillingness of the
Commission of Fine Arts to settle on Constitution Gardens as a site for
the National World War II Memorial.[12]

For the American Battle Monuments Commission, the reading of
the letters was a surprise but, as it turned out, a welcome surprise. The
letters and the discussion that followed on the importance of placing
the memorial on a prominent axis allowed Haydn Williams to work
into the meeting, and the conversations after it, his and the ABMC's
belief that the Rainbow Pool site south of Constitution Gardens was
the right place for the National World War II Memorial and that such
a site would put the Korean War Veterans Memorial and Vietnam Veterans Memorial in proper historical perspective. It was a view that J.
Carter Brown found congenial. By contrast, Brown referred to the
Constitution Gardens site as safe but a "cop-out," and years later in an
interview, he would be still more critical, describing the Constitution
Gardens choice as the equivalent of "burying the World War II Memorial into this little ghetto of its own as a kind of postage stamp footnote
to the Vietnam Memorial."[13]

For the American Battle Monuments Commission, Brown's disdain
for the Constitution Gardens site was welcome, and the concluding
pages of the July 27 Commission of Fine Arts minutes show Haydn
Williams speaking in a way that he had not publicly done before of the
Rainbow Pool as the right place for the World War II Memorial and
Carter Brown in turn reacting to Williams's remarks by observing, "A
site at the Rainbow Pool might be one the Commission could support."
But the meeting would not end with the Commission of Fine Arts
endorsing the Rainbow Pool site and putting to rest the American Battle Monuments Commission's problems. The meeting would instead
conclude on a more open-ended note with the commission suggesting
that in addition to the Rainbow Pool site, further consideration should

be given to Frederic Hart's Columbia Island proposal as well as the Capitol Reflecting Pool and Freedom Plaza sites.[14]

In view of the morning's action in which the Commission of Fine Arts had said no to the Constitution Gardens site, Haydn Williams, who was representing the ABMC, was reluctant to go ahead as he had planned and meet later in the day with the National Capital Planning Commission. But the chairman of the National Capital Planning Commission, Harvey Gantt, an architect best known to the public as the victim of Jesse Helms's infamous "white hands" commercial during the 1990 North Carolina Senate race, was anxious for his commission to evaluate on its own the proposed National World War II Memorial sites and to reach a decision independently of the Commission of Fine Arts. Gantt specifically asked Haydn Williams to make the same case to the National Capital Planning Commission that he had to the Commission of Fine Arts. The results were very different from earlier in the day. After hearing Haydn Williams make the case for building a National World War II Memorial in Constitution Gardens, the National Capital Planning Commission voted to approve the Constitution Gardens site, despite their awareness of the earlier negative reaction by the Commission of Fine Arts to the same proposal.[15]

The next day's *Washington Post,* in an article written by its architecture critic Benjamin Forgey, focused on what had happened with a headline that declared, "No Accord on WWII Memorial; Two Agencies Send Mixed Signals About Location." What the *Post* headline did not pick up on in emphasizing the differences between the two commissions were signs of an important shift in perspective going on at the National Park Service. After the meeting of the Commission of Fine Arts, John Parsons (who, in addition to being the associate director for lands, resources, and planning at the National Park Service's Capital Region, served on the National Capital Planning Commission) voiced a position on the Rainbow Pool closer to the one J. Carter Brown had adopted when he said the Commission of Fine Arts might support the Rainbow Pool site for the memorial. In the afternoon, Parsons, despite voting for

the Constitution Gardens site, observed in discussion that in his judgment the Rainbow Pool could be treated "as an element in this memorial or, indeed, the memorial itself." It might even be regarded as an
"extension" of the Constitution Gardens site.[16]

As the American Battle Monuments Commission pondered what to
do next, it found itself in a very different position from the one it faced
going into the two July 27 meetings. On the one hand, the ABMC had
been given new site options that it did not particularly want. On the
other hand, the Rainbow Pool was now a genuine possibility as a site for
the National World War II Memorial. The ABMC still, however, faced
the problem of bridging the differences between the two approving
commissions, one of which had said no and the other yes to Constitution Gardens.

On August 3, the ABMC took the first step toward solving its problem by sending a letter seeking a resolution of these differences to the
three commissioners—J. Carter Brown, Harvey Gantt, and John Parsons—on whose judgment it was dependent. Three days later on August
6, 1995, the three commissioners and Haydn Williams held a crucial
conference call that Williams would later look back on as a site-selection
turning point because the call put the Rainbow Pool in full contention
for the first time as a National World War II Memorial site. After the
call, the Rainbow Pool, Columbia Island, and sites along Arlington
Memorial Drive took over as the leading contenders for a National
World War II Memorial site, while two other sites that had once been
thought of as good alternative possibilities, Freedom Plaza and the Capitol Reflecting Pool, were dropped from contention.[17]

Then on September 15, after the ABMC's reports on the new sites were
completed and the staffs from the approving commissions went over the
reports, another breakthrough occurred. The National Park Service clarified its new position when it sent J. Carter Brown a letter in which it formally stated, as it had not done before, that it believed the Rainbow Pool
might be an appropriate site for the National World War II Memorial and
that it thought placing a memorial at Columbia Island or along Arlington

Memorial Drive brought with it problems of varying degrees. The Rainbow Pool site, Park Service Field Director for the National Capital Area Robert Stanton, wrote "could possibly also service the important contemplative needs of the memorial." By contrast, the "automobile, pedestrian, and bicycle traffic" of Columbia Island, Stanton argued, created a "visual distraction" that worked against any memorial there, and placing a memorial along Arlington Memorial Drive, while possible, would require that two established memorials, the *Seabees Memorial* and a Spanish-American War memorial known as *The Hiker,* "be relocated."[18]

A similar set of observations was at the center of the evaluations of the new sites that Davis Buckley, who had done the first site evaluations for the ABMC, was asked to do. In his analysis, Buckley was, as he had been earlier in the year, highly professional in his assessment of what it would take to build on the areas he was asked to consider, but as he explored the virtues of the Rainbow Pool site, there was no mistaking the advantages he saw in it or the degree to which his views of the site reinforced those of the American Battle Monuments Commission. The Rainbow Pool site is of "great historical importance" and "carries great symbolic importance," he wrote, before going on to add that the significance of World War II for America supports the idea that a World War II memorial is worthy of "center stage position."[19]

For the American Battle Monuments Commission, the consequence of these shared summer deliberations and discussions with Brown, Gantt, Parsons, and their staffs was that the ABMC began its fall meetings with the Commission of Fine Arts and the National Capital Planning Commission with, as Haydn Williams put it, a "better and more sharply focused vision of the site we are recommending." In making the case for the American Battle Monuments Commission, Williams and the World War II Memorial Committee felt increasingly confident that the ABMC would be authorized to build the memorial at the Rainbow Pool, and after he had a September 15 meeting in Washington with J. Carter Brown, Williams finally felt sure of the liklihood of ABMC getting the Rainbow Pool site.[20]

Four days later at the September 19 meeting of the Commission of Fine Arts, Williams began making the American Battle Monuments Commission's case for the Rainbow Pool site by recalling the positive impact the past months of discussion had had. "We now have a site recommendation that is far better for having been reshaped and honed by questions, suggestions, and criticisms" from both approving commissions, Williams observed. He then went on to point out that the Rainbow Pool site answered the criticisms that the Commission of Fine Arts had voiced over the limited visibility and importance of the Constitution Gardens site. Building the National World War II Memorial at the Rainbow Pool would, Williams concluded, guarantee the memorial a locale "commensurate with the importance and impact of World War II on the life of America and the world." Williams's presentation, which took up thirteen pages of transcript, was long and detailed, but in contrast to July, the response from the Commission of Fine Arts was overwhelmingly positive. The vice chairman of the commission, Harry Robinson, wanted the ABMC to be sure to consult with the Commission of Fine Arts on architectural guidelines so that any future National World War II memorial would not infringe on the landscape around it, and J. Carter Brown expressed similar concerns, pointing out that a memorial at the Rainbow Pool could not go deep into the ground without causing problems and could not extend far north or south without infringing on the Mall's elms. Both Robinson's and Brown's caveats were, however, purely cautionary. They were not raised as objections to the proposed memorial site, and after a comparatively short discussion, the Commission of Fine Arts voted unanimously to approve the Rainbow Pool as the site for the National World War II Memorial.[21]

Two weeks later on October 5, Haydn Williams made an appeal to the National Capital Planning Commission that was very similar to the one he had made earlier to the Commission of Fine Arts. "The clock is ticking, and there is a growing sense of urgency," Williams declared, as he argued that of all the sites the American Battle Monuments Commission had before it, the Rainbow Pool site was the one that would best allow the National World War II Memorial to establish itself in its own right and occupy the center line of the Mall. If the Rainbow Pool had been among the original six sites the American Battle Monuments Commission was given to consider, it would, indeed, have been the "first choice from the beginning," Williams went on to say. As at the Commission of Fine Arts meeting, the response to the ABMC was extremely positive, and after discussing the site question, the National Capital Planning Commission gave its approval to the Rainbow Pool site by a nine-to-three margin. What was significant, however—and would become more so with the passage of time—was the dissent voiced by Pat Elwood, of the National Capital Planning Commission. Elwood found it difficult to imagine building anything of significance at the Rainbow Pool site. "I have reservations about the ability of any design to not impact this spacious grandeur," she declared. For Elwood, there was not enough evidence at this stage of the memorial process to cast a yes vote for the Rainbow Pool site, but what worried her most was that in giving the ABMC the green light to build at the Rainbow Pool, the Commission of Fine Arts and the National Capital Planning Commission had put themselves in a box. "Once committed to the site, it is really hard to draw back," she warned before casting her no vote.[22]

What had just been accomplished with the National Capital Planning Commission's approval of the Rainbow Pool site was summed up the next day in the headlines of Benjamin Forgey's October 6 *Washington Post* story: "WWII Memorial Gets Choice Mall Site; 2nd Panel Approves Location, Clearing Way for Design Phase." A month later, on Veterans Day 1995, everything still seemed to be going smoothly for the American Battle Monuments Commission. No protests followed the official approval of the Rainbow Pool site, and on the afternoon of a drizzly November 11, 1995, in front of a Veterans Day crowd of more than 5,000 people, President Clinton marked the fiftieth anniversary of the end of World War II by dedicating the National World War II Memorial site with a bronze plaque that read, "At this site will be erected the World War II Memorial—A Monument to the spirit and sacrifice of the American people and a reminder of the high moral purposes and idealism that motivated the nation's call to arms as it sought victory in concert with its allies over the forces of totalitarianism." "From this day forward this place belongs to the World War II generation and their families," the president declared in a speech that he concluded by reminding his audience, "America must never forget the debt we owe the World War II generation. It is a small down payment on that debt to build this monument as magnificently as we can." The soil from four-teen World War II cemeteries was then used to sanctify the ground around the plaque, which was placed directly on the Mall's center line at the eastern edge of the Rainbow Pool, and with this final gesture the dedication ceremony was over.[23]

A major hurdle had been cleared for the American Battle Monuments Commission, and in the fall of 1995, the ABMC would also take the time to streamline its organizational structure. In September, ABMC chairman Fred Woerner authorized the formation of a World War II Memorial Site and Design Committee, which would have primary responsibility for dealing with work on the National World War II Memorial. The new committee, with Haydn Williams as its chairman and Hugh Carey as an ex-officio member, would initially include retired brigadier generals Douglas Kinnard and Pat Foote plus Memo-rial Advisory Board member Helen Fagin, a Holocaust survivor and former director of Judaic studies at the University of Miami, and in the coming years, it would lead the ABMC's effort to get the National World War II Memorial approved and built, staying on the job until new ABMC commissioners were appointed by President George Bush in September 2001. For the opponents of the National World War II Memorial, 1995 was by contrast a very different turning point. Five years later, they would look back on 1995 and insist that they were, in the words of Neil Feldman of the National Coalition to Save Our Mall, "in the dark—shut out of the process" when it came to choos-ing where the National World War II Memorial would be located. In a June 11, 2000, *Washington Post* op-ed reply to Bob Dole's sardonic observation that the critics of the National World War II Memorial site were a "little late," Feldman pointed to the problems that preservationists and critics like himself had in getting basic information during 1995.[24]

Feldman's op-ed addressed a key problem that opponents of the National World War II Memorial faced: mobilizing public opinion before the memorial had a design. "When I look back and ask what could have been done differently, I do wish we had paid more attention when the site was being chosen, that we had weighed in earlier in the process," Sally Berk, the president of the D.C. Preservation League from 1995 to 1998, would later observe. The National Park Service's John Parsons, no friend of the National World War II Memorial opponents, would concede that preservationists like Berk were in a bind. "It's very difficult to get people interested in the siting of memorials," he would observe. "The interest doesn't grow until people see the design." But Feldman's op-ed also ducked dealing with the fact that in 1995 it was more than possible to know that a site for the National World War II Memorial was being chosen and that the Rainbow Pool was a leading contender. For anyone interested, there had been ample opportunity to speak out. Nothing was secret about any of the approving commission meetings in which the site was discussed.

The minutes of the Commission of Fine Arts regularly contained notice of the commission's next meeting, and in 1995 the National Capital Planning Commission sent out mailings of its agenda to more than a thousand individuals, media outlets, and organizations. Furthermore, there had been steady newspaper coverage of the National World War II Memorial site deliberations. Between July 1 and October 6, 1995, *Washington Post* architectural critic Benjamin Forgey wrote four feature articles on the National World War II Memorial site-selection process. Two of his first three articles explicitly discussed the Rainbow Pool as a possible National World War II Memorial site option, as did the July 27 Commission of Fine Arts and National Capital Planning Commission meetings, both of which occurred months before the Rainbow Pool received final approval.[25]

Although those opposed to locating the National World War II Memorial at the Rainbow Pool had missed an opportunity in 1995 to challenge the site decision, they did not stop trying to have the site changed, even after the debate on the memorial had moved on to the question of its design. The site opponents were undeterred by J. Carter Brown's assertion in a July 30, 1997, letter to Fred Woerner, the chairman of the ABMC, that as far as the Commission of Fine Arts was concerned, "The design was the only issue before it; the site had been approved previously in 1995, and the members have vigorously and unanimously reaffirmed that approval." Beginning in 1996 and continuing until 2001, the opponents to the National World War II Memorial mounted an attack on the Rainbow Pool site, arguing that it was a bad choice on four key grounds: (1) It interfered with the Mall's vista; (2) it was anti-preservationist; (3) it constituted an environmental danger; and (4) it violated space historically reserved for civil rights demonstrations.[26]

Would such an attack have succeeded if it had been mounted in 1995 before the Commission of Fine Arts and the National Capital Planning Commission approved the Rainbow Pool site? We will never know. The site arguments themselves—their rise and fall, or more accurately, their rise and failure to carry the day—are, however, an important part of the National World War II Memorial story. They speak to the question that is always asked about every important Mall memorial, How might it have been different?

Of all the arguments made in opposition to the Rainbow Pool site, the vista argument was the one with the widest appeal. Even people who had never been to the nation's capital had usually seen postcards of the Mall showing the vast green space between the Lincoln Memorial and the Washington Monument. They had no trouble grasping the idea that the Mall might be adversely altered if this open space was filled with an obscuring monument.

Senator Bob Kerrey of Nebraska, who in 1997 became an outspoken critic of the Rainbow Pool site and whose Senate office became an early meeting place for National World War II Memorial critics, made the vista argument a powerful oppositional tool. In interviews Kerrey could be both caustic and funny about the new National World War II Memorial site. "This is a permanent haircut," he told a *New York Times* reporter in a March 1997 interview. "Once it is done, this will not grow back." Kerrey was, however, dead serious in his opposition to the Rainbow Pool site, and over the course of 1997 and into 1998, the case he made was a deeply impassioned one.[27]

In May, Kerrey wrote Chairman Harvey Gantt of the National Capital Planning Commission, "I am currently working with a group of concerned architects, historians, citizens, members of Congress, and the Guild of Professional Tour Guides of Washington, D.C., on a presentation regarding the many difficulties associated with this site and, upon completion, hope to present it to the commission at the earliest possible date." But in Kerrey's mind it was already clear that building anything new at the Rainbow Pool was a mistake. "This quiet, uninterrupted space between the Washington Monument and Lincoln Memorial is one of the most sacred spaces in our Capital," he told Gantt. "Constructing a large and popular destination at this site will permanently and irrevocably change the entire nature of this space."[28]

A month later on the floor of the Senate, Kerrey repeated these objections in even more forceful language. "I am deeply opposed to this selection of this expansive, reflective space at the key axis of the National Mall between the Lincoln Memorial and the Washington Monument as the site of a Memorial," he observed. "The memorial proposed for the Rainbow Pool would forever alter the openness and grandeur that is America's front lawn." To augment his own view, Kerrey read into the June 25, 1997, *Congressional Record* a letter from architectural historian Richard Longstreth that declared, "It is the site that is inappropriate, so much so that I believe this ranks among the very worst proposals ever made for the monumental core. Nothing—from John Russell Pope to Maya Lin—would be suitable at the proposed location."[29]

At the end of July, when Kerrey appeared in person before the National Capital Planning Commission, he was even more outspoken. He put on record a six-page white paper that asserted, "The World War II Memorial proposed for this site interrupts the symbolic and special continuity between Washington and Lincoln," and then added to the white paper his own testimony. "This site is already today a hallowed, quiet place," he stated. "If what is being proposed is built, we must consider that what we are doing is destroying what is already there."

Kerrey's campaign against the Rainbow Pool did not end with his testimony before the Senate and the planning commission. In February 1998, Senator Kerrey took his final and politically boldest step. Aligning himself with arch conservative Republican Strom Thurmond, a World War II veteran, Kerrey sent a letter to President Clinton in which he and Thurmond pleaded with the president to become involved in the World War II Memorial controversy. "We respectfully ask you to support a relocation of the World War II Memorial to a less controversial, more accommodating, location—off the main axis of the Mall," Kerrey and Thurmond wrote in a letter they knew would make headlines across the country.[30]

In contending that the Mall's most important vista was in danger of being obscured, Kerrey had not only made a broad appeal that was easily understood but also put himself in a position in which he was at odds with the majority of World War II veterans. In addition, as long as it could not be shown that the National World War II Memorial did in fact block the sight lines between the Lincoln Memorial and the Washington Monument, Kerrey's argument lacked credibility. When in the spring of 1998 the American Battle Monuments Commission submitted revised plans for a smaller memorial that would clearly not block the north-south or east-west sight lines, Kerrey's vista argument was in trouble.[31]

After seeing plans for the new memorial and meeting on May 13, 1998, with Haydn Williams of the American Battle Monuments Commission, Kerrey issued a statement in which he endorsed the Rainbow Pool site and the memorial design. "My original concerns about the use of the Rainbow Pool site were based primarily on my fears that this site would be used in an inappropriate manner that would jeopardize the integrity of the National Mall both aesthetically and environmentally. These concerns appear to have been heard and answered," Kerrey declared. With reporters Kerrey was still more upbeat. "The vista will be as it was," he told the *Omaha World-Herald*. "I'm not abandoning the fight but claiming victory." Four years later Kerrey would concede, "I yielded in the end and supported the National World War II Memorial because of Bob Dole and the entire World War II generation. I felt that having reduced the size of it, it was the best I was going to get." Others—from Deborah Dietsch, the editor of *Architecture,* to Roger Lewis, a columnist for the *Washington Post*—would continue the battle against the Rainbow Pool site, but without Kerrey, who had been instrumental in organizing the early opposition to the site, the vista argument lost its steam, and in the House and Senate, petitions favoring "the timely construction of the World War II Memorial on the National Mall" took center stage.[32]

The second major argument against building at the Rainbow Pool site—namely, that placing a memorial there was an anti-preservationist act—had less popular appeal, except in the architectural community, but it had the advantage of being an argument with a clear basis in law. The Site and Design Approval section of the 1986 Commemorative Works Act is very explicit in stating, "A commemorative work shall be so located as to prevent interference with, or encroachment upon, any existing commemorative work and to protect, to the maximum extent practicable, open space and existing public use."

Judy Feldman, a Washington-based art historian, and her husband, Neil Feldman, the outspoken critics who in 2000 formed the National Coalition to Save Our Mall, were quick to seize the preservationist argument and link it to the idea that building the National World War II Memorial at the Rainbow Pool was an intrusion on the Lincoln Memorial itself. The evidence they found most telling was in the National Park Service's own publications, particularly its *Cultural Landscape Report: West Potomac Park, Lincoln Memorial Grounds* and its *Revised National Register of Historic Places,* which spoke of the Reflecting Pool and Rainbow Pool as "related features" of the Lincoln Memorial grounds. As far as the Feldmans were concerned, the National Park Service not only had been deceptive in ignoring its own findings on the close relationship of the Lincoln Memorial grounds to the Lincoln Memorial but had been aided in this deception by J. Carter Brown, chairman of the Commission of Fine Arts. According to the Feldmans, Brown and John Parsons of the National Park Service were guilty of trying "to deceive the public" and "disseminating false, misleading, and even damaging information."[33]

A similar argument, although couched in more diplomatic terms, was advanced by the Advisory Council on Historic Preservation, which under the terms of the National Historic Preservation Act of 1966 was authorized to comment on projects such as the National World War II Memorial. In a September 5, 2000, letter to Secretary of the Interior Bruce Babbitt, the chairwoman of the Advisory Council, Cathryn Slater, joined the Feldmans in attacking the National Park Service. The National Park Service, she argued, had delayed releasing its *Cultural Landscape Report: West Potomac Park, Lincoln Memorial Grounds* until July 2000, knowing that the report provided insight into the "historic properties and possible effects of the National World War II Memorial proposal." Slater did not call for the resignations of Brown and Parsons, but despite her calm tone, there was no mistaking her disgust with the National Park Service or her belief that building the currently proposed version of the National World War II Memorial at the Rainbow Pool site was a terrible mistake. The Advisory Council on Historic Preservation, Slater went on to say, "has accepted that it is possible to design a World War II Memorial on this site that would harmonize with its historic surroundings," but this memorial does not meet that challenge. The proposed National World War II Memorial would, she concluded, have "serious and unresolved adverse effects on the preeminent historic character of the National Mall." Indeed, so dire was the situation that in Slater's judgment only "reconsideration" of the National World War II Memorial project could stop these "unacceptable impacts" from happening.[34]

Unlike Senator Kerrey, neither the Feldmans nor the Advisory Council on Historic Preservation would back off their argument that building the National World War II Memorial at the Rainbow Pool was an anti-preservationist act. But in linking their arguments so closely to interpretations of National Park Service documents, the Feldmans and Advisory Council also found themselves entangled in textual battles more appropriate to a college seminar than a public discussion on how best to memorialize World War II veterans.

The counterresponse to the Feldmans' argument, which depended on the National Park Service's view of the Lincoln Memorial corresponding to the historical record and to the intentions of both the turn-of-the-century McMillan Commission and the Lincoln Memorial Commission, was an August 27, 2000, op-ed by art historian Michael Richman, an authority on Daniel Chester French, the sculptor of the Lincoln statue that dominates the interior of the Lincoln Memorial. The idea that the Rainbow Pool—or for that matter, the Reflecting Pool—was part of the Lincoln Memorial was historically wrong, Richman argued. To get at the truth, one had to do some historical digging, and to prove his point, Richman cited the minutes of the January 28, 1922, meeting of the Lincoln Memorial Commission, which offered a very different view of the Rainbow Pool than the one the Feldmans were advancing as the historical truth. There the chairman of the Lincoln Memorial Commission, Supreme Court Chief Justice and former President William Howard Taft, referring to the pools east of the memorial, is quoted as saying "while the Lagoon was part of the plan for beautifying the park surrounding the Memorial, it was not a part of the Memorial, and the Lincoln Memorial Commission had no connection with its construction."[35]

A similar textual battle also occurred between the National Park Service and the Advisory Council on Historic Preservation. Insisting that in favoring placement of the National World War II Memorial at the Rainbow Pool, it had indeed paid attention to its own *Cultural Landscape Report,* the National Park Service answered Cathryn Slater's September 5 letter by quoting back the *Landscape Report*'s published guidelines, which said, "Future commemorative features should be located in the Lincoln Memorial study area only if they will have minimal impact on the historic setting." The design of the National World War II Memorial was, the Park Service insisted, "respectful of the integrity" of the Lincoln Memorial landscape and consistent with Park Service guidelines.[36]

The result was the kind of argument that neither side could ever really win and that to those outside the preservationist community often seemed like hairsplitting. Asked to comment on the battle between the Feldmans and Michael Richman, Christopher Thomas, the author of *The Lincoln Memorial and American Life,* the definitive book on the Lincoln Memorial, avoided taking sides and observed that the kinds of arguments he was hearing reminded him of "the battles fourth-century Christians fought over the canon of Scripture." But more to the point, what was lost when textual warfare took over the preservationist debate was the reality that Professor Richard Longstreth, the editor of the monumental study *The Mall in Washington, 1791–1991,* addressed when he observed, "The Mall is going to continue to evolve. Preservation doesn't freeze dry something. It is about managing change."[37]

By contrast, the third major argument against placing the National World War II Memorial at the Rainbow Pool site—the environmental argument—was anything but abstract in its implications. It raised issues ranging from the impact that additional tour buses would have on the area to how construction of the memorial might damage the Mall's elms. The environmental argument that drew the most attention related to the fact that the Rainbow Pool was located in a flood plain. Critics charged that building a memorial on such a site could increase the amount of pollutants being pumped into the nearby Tidal Basin as well as undermine the foundations of the Washington Monument, just a few hundred yards away on the other side of Seventeenth Street.[38]

The leading advocate on these issues was Lisa Jorgenson, who opened her 1997 testimony before the National Capital Planning Commission by pointing out that she was "an international water specialist." Jorgenson, whose clients included the World Bank and Global Environment Facility, had not in fact been educated primarily as a scientist. Her undergraduate degree was in economic geography, and she held a master's degree in city and regional planning from Harvard University. The usual work she did for her clients was, as she put it, "to review international development sites and look at how they are going to be financed." But in her testimony before the National Capital Planning Commission in 1997 and 1998 and in her June 4, 1998, report, *Hydrology Concerns About the Proposed World War II Memorial Site,* Jorgenson argued that there was a strong scientific basis for regarding the future National World War II Memorial as an environmental threat. In dramatic fashion Jorgenson warned the National Capital Planning Commission that during rain storms the National World War II Memorial would in all likelihood be adding "water that has to be treated just like sewage" to the Washington sewer system. The constant pumping required to maintain the National World War II Memorial posed an even greater danger, Jorgenson declared. It had the potential to create a "cone of depression" that threatened the "structural integrity" of the Washington Monument. To prove her point, Jorgenson supplied the National Capital Planning Commission with drawings of the Washington Monument's nineteenth-century foundations and a geological survey showing how often flooding conditions occurred in the area around the Reflecting Pool and the Rainbow Pool. There was no mistaking Jorgenson's pessimism about the problems she believed that the memorial would cause, and in the concluding paragraph of her *Hydrology Concerns* report, the last piece of advice she had for anyone foolish enough to construct a memorial at the Rainbow Pool site was "have financial insurance against damage to the Washington Monument."[39]

It was explosive testimony, and in combination with a subsequent survey by Gavin and Associates, a Virginia-based geotechnical engineering firm hired by the National Coalition to Save Our Mall, it served as the basis for a press release by the coalition that in huge capital letters warned, "IF THE WWII MEMORIAL IS BUILT ACROSS THE MALL, THE WASHINGTON MONUMENT MAY FALL OVER." What were the odds of such a catastrophe really happening? No engineering firm would say, of course. But in the period before construction of the National World War II Memorial began, the American Battle Monuments Commission was in a tight spot. All it could do was insist that it had the tools for dealing with any environmental challenge the National World War II Memorial posed. In May 1998 the National Park Service released its own report, *Environmental Assessment: The National World War II Memorial,* which declared that the noise, flooding, and contaminated soil problems associated with the National World War II Memorial were all manageable, but like the reports critical of the memorial's future impact on the environment, the National Park Service's *Environmental Assessment* was based solely on projections.[40]

It was not until after August 27, 2001, when construction on the National World War II Memorial officially got under way, that the American Battle Monuments Commission was in a position to say that it was not damaging the environment by pointing to tests done on the water and soil at the Rainbow Pool that confirmed its claims. With the passage of time and with test results from the Environmental Protection Agency and independent laboratories in hand, the American Battle Monuments Commission has increasingly found itself daring critics to challenge its environmental record. At the National World War II Memorial site, workers replaced the Rainbow Pool's old fractured storm pipes with new ones, and around the periphery of the new memorial, they put in a 2-foot thick concrete slurry wall that extends into the bedrock below and creates a bathtub effect that prevents water from leaking in or out of the Rainbow Pool site. As for the Washington Monument, to few people's surprise, it is still standing. In January 2002, the trade paper *Civil Engineering* carried a story with the headline, "Washington Monument's Foundations Not Threatened by Memorial," but it was not a story that got much notice or that had the legs to continue. It was as if nobody had really believed the Washington Monument was in danger in the first place.[41]

The fourth major argument against placing the National World War II Memorial at the Rainbow Pool site—the civil rights argument— would, on the other hand, leave everyone feeling uneasy, even after it ceased to be a factor in the campaign to get the National World War II Memorial moved. The charge that building the memorial at the Rainbow Pool amounted to disrespect of the civil rights movement and its historic marches was an argument that carried weight in Washington.

In her December 14, 2000, testimony before the National Capital Planning Commission, Judy Feldman of the National Coalition to Save Our Mall used the civil rights argument as grounds for opposing the National World War II Memorial, and that same year, in its presentation to the National Capital Planning Commission, a Virginia law firm went even farther, arguing that building the memorial at the Rainbow

Pool interfered with the "Right of Assembly found under the First Amendment of the Constitution."[42]

What made the civil rights argument truly formidable, however, was the decision of Washington congressional delegate Eleanor Holmes Norton to take it up. As a black woman who grew up in Washington and who had roots in the civil rights movement dating back to the 1960s, Norton was in a position to make the civil rights case. She had public credibility, and she started out with a genuine hatred for the National World War II Memorial. It was in her eyes "a gargantuan obstruction" with "Germanesque features." The memorial honored an event that Norton did not believe was "the equivalent of the birth of our country, the equivalent of keeping our country together," and it was going to sit on land that she thought was sacred. "The Mall is the urban equivalent of the Grand Canyon. There should never be anything in the middle of the Grand Canyon," Norton insisted.[43]

Before the National Capital Planning Commission, Norton voiced all of her doubts about the National World War II Memorial, but what made her testimony especially powerful was the racial argument she chose to emphasize. "The African-American civil rights community strongly objects to the proposal before you, because it trespasses both physically and thematically on the Lincoln Memorial," she declared. "Marian Anderson sang on the steps of the Lincoln Memorial when she could not sing at Constitutional Hall because of her race. Martin Luther King Jr. and 250,000 Americans made equality a living and national aspiration for the first time at the Lincoln Memorial." To place "a large, multifaceted memorial in the virtual lap of Lincoln crowds and overwhelms the universality of the American ideals associated with the Lincoln Memorial," she insisted, before going on to conclude, "As a black American who reveres the site for the African-American history, in particular, that was made there, I would especially regret the insensitivity of commissions that allowed one great message to step on another."[44]

At the September 21, 2000, National Capital Planning Commission hearings, Luther Smith, one of the last surviving Tuskegee Airmen, implicitly challenged Norton's testimony with the pro–National World War II Memorial testimony he gave, and National Capital Planning Commission Chairman Harvey Gantt, the former black mayor of Charlotte, North Carolina, did the same by casting a yes vote for the memorial. But what finally neutralized the civil rights argument were not direct challenges to Norton, which few were willing to risk, but the fact that the distance from the steps of the Lincoln Memorial to the eastern edge of the Reflecting Pool—765 yards, or more than seven football fields placed end to end—was so great that it was too much of a stretch of the imagination for most people to believe that the memorial would intrude on the area where Anderson sang and King spoke and the bulk of the crowds listening to them stood. At the new National World War II Memorial site, as well as at the old Rainbow Pool site, one could sit comfortably on the hillside east of the Rainbow Pool and look back at the Lincoln Memorial in the distance. As before, the only real problem for marchers and demonstrators was that they might get wet from the Rainbow Pool and its fountains.[45]

For the opponents of the National World War II Memorial, losing the location battle was a major defeat that was hard to accept. Five years after the site issue was officially settled, Jonathan Yardley, the *Washington Post* book columnist, still continued to hope for a last-minute compromise that might save the day. On September 11, 2000, in an article titled "Tunnel Vision: A Compromise for the Mall," a desperate Yardley proposed a total reworking of the area between the Rainbow Pool and the Washington Monument. His plan was to run Seventeenth Street underground and construct the National World War II Memorial on the new Mall space that would be created above Seventeenth Street. Then in order to speed up and simplify the memorial process, Yardley wanted the Marine Corps statue of the flag being raised on Mt. Suribachi during the bloody battle for Iwo Jima moved from its location in Arlington to the new Seventeenth Street space. Everyone, Yardley concluded, could claim victory. The American Battle Monuments Commission would have its memorial, and pedestrians would be free to walk from memorial to memorial across an expanse of grass and water that was now uninterrupted by traffic.[46]

What the opponents of the National World War II Memorial had lost sight of by this time, however, was the impact of historic events over which they had no control. If the decision to erect a National World War II Memorial had been made at the end of the 1940s or in the years before the Vietnam Veterans Memorial and the Korean War Veterans Memorial were erected, then there would have been a wide range of site options for a National World War II Memorial in Washington. But once the memorials for the Vietnam War veterans and Korean War veterans had been built on the north and south sides of the Lincoln Memorial Reflecting Pool, the site options for the National World War II Memorial narrowed dramatically. The magnitude of World War II and the ideals for which it was fought necessitated a memorial site that was more prominent than the sites for the Vietnam Veterans Memorial and the Korean War Veterans Memorial. The logic of the Mall—with the Grant Memorial at its east end, the Washington Monument in the middle, and the Lincoln Memorial at the west end—carried with it a clear link between geography and historical significance. By the 1990s the only question was whether that logic would be applied to the National World War II Memorial.

Beginning in 1995, in hearing after hearing, Haydn Williams of the American Battle Monuments Commission based the case for siting the National World War II Memorial on the main axis of the Mall on American history. Williams insisted that what the Revolutionary War was to the founding of America in the eighteenth century and the Civil War was to the preservation of America in the nineteenth century, World War II was to the continuation of America's ideals in the twentieth century. It was a powerful argument, made even more formidable by the fact that with the Vietnam Veterans Memorial and the Korean War Veterans Memorial lying so near the center line of the Mall, a decision that sited the National World War II Memorial off the center line had been all but eliminated.[47]

# 5

# THE COMPETITION

With the site for the National World War II Memorial finally approved, the American Battle Monuments Commission quickly moved in the fall of 1995 to set up the guidelines for what it knew could be another controversial process—the design competition. It was a process that the new, Clinton-appointed American Battle Monuments Commissioners had not been through, but many of the staffers at the ABMC had learned about competitions the hard way. At the start of the decade the competition to design the Korean War Veterans Memorial had proved to be a public relations nightmare for the ABMC when the winning design team from Pennsylvania State University filed a suit against the American Battle Monuments Commission, the Army Corps of Engineers, the Korean War Veterans Memorial Board, and the Washington architecture firm of Cooper-Lecky, accusing them of breach of contract for the changes they made in the winning design.[1]

It was a suit that the American Battle Monuments Commission finally won when a federal court ruled that having paid for the winning design, the ABMC could do with it as it chose. But six years later the ABMC did not want another litigation-plagued controversy. In addition to getting the highest quality design, the ABMC wanted to be sure it ran a smooth competition that did not cause problems down the road. As Commissioner Haydn Williams told the *Washington Post*, "We looked very carefully at the experiences of the Vietnam Veterans Memorial and the Korean War Veterans Memorial."[2]

This time the American Battle Monuments Commission took an approach to its design competition that it believed would be as fair and as free from controversy as possible. At the beginning of March 1996, after two months of intensive consultations with the National Park Service, the Commission of Fine Arts, and the National Capital Planning Commission, the American Battle Monuments Commission officially put responsibility for running its design competition into the hands of the General Services Administration, which, under the guidance of its chief architect, Ed Feiner, administered a highly respected Design Excellence Program that selected the architects and engineers for federal government building projects throughout the country.

It was a decision that seemed to make sense. It reflected not only the high regard in which Ed Feiner was held but the reputation of the General Services Administration commissioner of public buildings, Robert Peck, a former member of the Commission of Fine Arts. Since its inception in 1994 the Design Excellence Program, which operates through the Public Buildings Service of the General Services Administration, has cut costs and streamlined the way architects and engineers are hired for the multibillion-dollar building programs of the federal government. The key to the success of the Design Excellence Program has been a two-stage competition in which, as Ed Feiner noted, "We make sure that not only will the design be superb but that the team that is selected to do the design is able to execute it." In stage one, interested firms are asked to submit to a review panel portfolios of their accomplishments that reflect their history and capabilities. In stage two, a short list of three to six firms is then chosen to discuss design philosophy, meet with the review panel, and submit design concepts. The winner is then selected on the basis of the ranking and written recommendations of the review panel.[3]

*Roger Durbin, shortly before shipping overseas in 1944.*

(Durbin family)

*Roger Durbin, Representative Marcy Kaptur, Marian Durbin, and Senator Bob Dole at a 1997 luncheon for veterans services organizations.*

(American Battle Monuments Commission/ Carl Cox)

*The Mall with canal in foreground and
uncompleted Capitol dome in background, 1860.*

(National Archives)

*Lincoln Memorial and Reflecting Pool with temporary government buildings, 1930s.*

(National Archives)

*Roger Durbin and President Bill Clinton at*
*National World War II Memorial site dedication, November 11, 1995.*

(© 1995, *The Washington Post*. Photo by James A. Parcell. Reprinted with permission.)

*Groundbreaking, Memorial Day, 2000.*

(American Battle Monuments Commission/ Richard A. Latoff)

*Brian and Katherine Ambroziak,*
*National World War II Memorial, Perspective. Finalist submission.*

(Brian and Katherine Ambroziak)

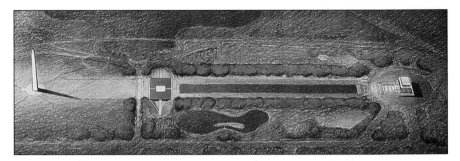

*Diana Balmori, National World War II Memorial, Day View.*
*Finalist submission. Designed by Diana Balmori. Perspective John Picard.*

(Balmori Associates, Inc.)

*Rafael Viñoly, National World War II Memorial. Finalist submission.*

(Photo Roy Wright/ Rafael Viñoly Architects, PC.)

*Marion Weiss and Michael A. Manfredi,*
*National World War II Memorial, Semi-aerial view. Finalist submission.*

(Photo Jock Pottle/ Marion Weiss/ Michael A. Manfredi, Architects)

*Bernard J. Wulff and William C. Jackson,*
*National World War II Memorial, Bell Garden. Finalist submission.*

(Model photo: David Whitcomb/ Bernard J. Wulff and William C. Jackson)

*Friedrich St. Florian, National World War II Memorial.*
*Winning competition submission, 1997.*

(Illustration: Advanced Media Design)

*Friedrich St.Florian, 1998 design of National World War II Memorial.*
*Memorial Arch: View from Plaza.*

(Friedrich St.Florian Studio)

*Friedrich St.Florian, 1999 design of National World War II Memorial.*
*View of Sacred Precinct.*

(Friedrich St.Florian Studio)

*Friedrich St.Florian, National World War II Memorial.*
*View from across Seventeenth Street. Final architectural submission, 2000.*

(Friedrich St.Florian Studio)

*Friedrich St.Florian Studio. Left to right: Justin Minda, Dan Grady,*
*Maggy Madarentz, Nicola DePace, Friedrich St.Florian,*
*Pablo Ortiz-Peña, Joowan Lee.*

(Friedrich St.Florian Studio)

*Kaskey Studio Inc. Left to right:*
*Perry Carsley, Joanna Blake, Aaron Sykes, Ray Kaskey.*

(Kaskey Studio, Inc.)

*Model of relief for "Tanks in Action."*

(Kaskey Studio, Inc.)

*World War II Re-enactors at Ray Kaskey Studio.*

(Kaskey Studio, Inc.)

It's the right time. It's the right place.

Please help build the National
World War II Memorial, here on
the Mall in Washington, D.C.

Because, incredibly, there is still no
national memorial to honor the
achievements of this great generation.

It's time to say thank you.

*Tom Hanks*

NATIONAL
**WWII**
MEMORIAL

1-800-639-4WW2
WWIImemorial.com

Ad
Council

AMERICAN BATTLE
MONUMENTS COMMISSION

*National World War II Memorial public service ad with Tom Hanks.*

(Printed courtesy of the American Battle Monuments Commission and the Advertising Council.
Creative credit: Marsteller Advertising, part of Burson-Marsteller.)

*Herblock cartoon of National World War II Memorial controversy.*

(Copyright 2000 by Herblock in *The Washington Post*)

*Conrad cartoon of National World War II Memorial controversy.*

(Copyright 2003, Tribune Media Services, Inc. All rights reserved. Reprinted with permission.)

*Stonecarver Nick Benson at work.*

(American Battle Monuments Commission/ Richard A. Latoff)

*National World War II Memorial arch under construction.*

(American Battle Monuments Commission/Richard A. Latoff)

*Pipe installation for National World War II Memorial vaults.*

(American Battle Monuments Commission/ Richard A. Latoff)

*Pile driving at National World War II Memorial.*
*Washington Monument in background.*

(American Battle Monuments Commission/ Richard A. Latoff)

*Pennsylvania, Georgia, and Massachusetts pillars after a snowstorm,
with the Lincoln Memorial in the background.*

(American Battle Monuments Commission/ Richard A. Latoff)

*Pacific arch and baldacchino.*

(American Battle Monuments Commission/
Richard A. Latoff)

*National World War II Memorial baldacchino. View from floor of arch.*

(American Battle Monuments Commission/ Richard A. Latoff)

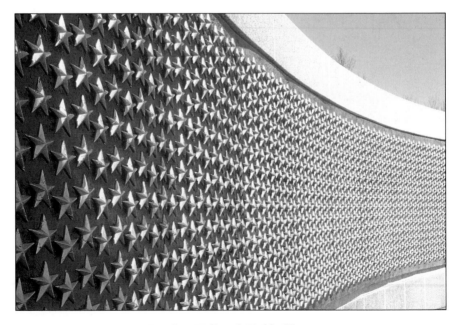

*Freedom Wall with Field of Stars.*

(American Battle Monuments Commission/ Richard A. Latoff)

The problem for the American Battle Monuments Commission was that applying the Design Excellence Program to a high-profile project like the National World War II Memorial was very different from applying it to the federal courthouses and office buildings that the General Services Administration normally dealt with. Ever since Maya Lin, while still a twenty-one-year-old Yale architecture student, won the competition to build the Vietnam Veterans Memorial, open competitions—ones that invite proposals from all comers—have been the preferred method for choosing a design for a public memorial.

The rules that were initially set up for the National World War II Memorial design competition were intended to combine the virtues of the General Services Administration's traditional competitions and an open competition. As Haydn Williams told the ABMC commissioners, the decision was to take somewhat of a middle course between a one-stage competition open to all and a closed competition open only to an invited few. The rules, as posted in the April 19, 1996, *Commerce Business Daily,* the journal where announcements of General Services Administration architecture competitions are posted, reflected this attempt at compromise. To move from the first stage to the second stage of the competition, an architect needed both a strong submission and a strong past record to go along with that design submission. The weighting for the criteria told the story: (1) Past Performance on Design (40 percent); (2) Lead Designer's Vision (30 percent); (3) Philosophy and Design Intent (20 percent); (4) Lead Designer's Resumé (10 percent).

The problem with these requirements was that as a practical matter, they worked against young, unknown architects. Past performance and the lead designer's resumé—two categories no beginner could hope to compete in—added up to 50 percent of the total score, and in addition, the amount of paperwork and drawings required by the June 17, 1996, due date the General Services Administration set for submissions was sure to burden the resources of any small firm, let alone an independent architect.[4]

It did not take long for criticism of the National World War II Memorial design competition to emerge, and on May 5, an angry op-ed by architect Paul Spreiregen, who had served as the professional advisor for the Vietnam Veterans Memorial competition, appeared in the *Washington Post*. "The American Battle Monuments Commission," Spreiregen charged, "is planning to select a design through an exclusionary, cumbersome, restrictive, arbitrary and—worst of all for the subject at hand—undemocratic process." The ABMC, in using the General Services Administration's invited-competition format rather than an open competition, was trying to avoid controversy, but there was no reason to do so, Spreiregen argued. A design competition as important as the National World War II Memorial competition should invite controversy. Moreover, it was possible, Spreiregen believed, for the ABMC to have a two-stage competition without being exclusionary. In the first stage, architects would simply be asked to submit their basic concepts in modest, yet graphic, formats. In the second stage, the finalists would then be asked to refine their plans based on comments from a design jury, and from this field a winner would be chosen.[5]

It was the kind of op-ed that called for a reply, and twelve days later, on May 17, the American Battle Monuments Commission and General Services Administration announced a change in the criteria that were issued on April 19 and set a new due date of July 15 for all submissions. The change in criteria reflected the views of many within the ABMC who wanted a more open design competition and confirmed that the criticism by Spreiregen and other architects had been heard. But the change itself was very modest. Past design performance was now reduced to 30 percent, and the lead designer's vision was increased to 40 percent, but everything else remained the same, and so in essence did the National World War II Memorial design competition. Creativity, the lead designer's vision plus design philosophy and intent, now added up to 60 percent—a small improvement but a sign that the American Battle Monuments Commission and the General Services Administration had responded to the criticism. Nonetheless, it was still clear that large firms and experienced architects would start with a significant advantage before their submissions were ever seen.[6]

The 10 percent shift in the competition criteria did little to satisfy critics, and on May 20, at a competition pre-submission meeting held at the auditorium of the General Services Administration Building, what was supposed to be a routine information session quickly turned into an angry confrontation between the General Services Administration and a group of students and architects led by Jaan Holt, the director of graduate studies at Virginia Tech's Washington-Alexandria Architecture Consortium. With a petition in hand signed by the deans of architecture schools from fourteen states, Holt challenged the American Battle Monuments Commission to change its first-stage requirements and to make the National World War II Memorial competition truly democratic. As Holt later observed, "We and a lot of our other colleagues thought there should be an open competition like the Vietnam Memorial."[7]

It was not the kind of pre-submission meeting Ed Feiner was expecting. The staged protest dominated the coverage of the meeting, and very little attention was paid to Feiner's assertion, "We want to keep the competition open for that diamond-in-the-rough." The next day's *Washington Post* article focused on the anger of architecture students waving red-lettered banners that accused the National World War II Memorial design competition of being "undemocratic" and "elitist" rather than on Feiner's assertion that "the diamond-in-the-rough will be in competition with Pritzker Prize winners." The students and their banners embodied the view expressed in the May 16 Petition of Protest from the Washington Area Architecture Group, which accused ABMC of running a competition that "neatly eliminates students, sole practitioners, intern architects, architect/educators unless they are fortunate enough to hitch themselves to one of the dozen established firms whose client references will ensure their bureaucratic acceptability."[8]

For the American Battle Monuments Commission, the choices were clear: It could continue down the path the General Services Administration had established and face more protest, or it could change direction and make the National World War II Memorial design competition an open competition in which experienced and inexperienced architects were on the same footing. Behind the scenes, many in the ABMC had been pushing for a more open competition long before May 20, and reversing course became easier with the one piece of good news that emerged from the May 20 pre-submission meeting: the announcement that Bill Lacy, president of the State College of New York at Purchase, had accepted an invitation to become the professional advisor to the National World War II Memorial design competition. As someone who had served as the executive director of the prestigious Pritzker Architecture Prize and had spent seven years in Washington as director of the architecture and design program of the National Endowment for the Arts, Lacy brought to the National World War II Memorial competition not only a calming presence but a record of professional accomplishment that gave him enormous standing among architects.[9]

Lacy was delighted to be chosen as the professional advisor for the National World War II Memorial design competition. "It was an opportunity that doesn't come along very often in your whole career," he would later say. "I had done some major projects, but never anything that had this kind of national significance. I immediately said yes." However, when Lacy signed his contract with the General Services Administration on May 17, he was not fully aware of the degree to which the General Services Administration had "gotten off on the left foot" and backed itself and the American Battle Monuments Commission into a corner.[10]

Nonetheless, Lacy did not feel trapped by the position in which the General Services Administration and the ABMC now found themselves. In his own mind, he was very clear about what was wrong with the competition. "I thought it was deficient and heading in the wrong direction," he would recall. "It was neither an open nor a closed competition." Lacy's response was to work to change the competition rules once again. When he arrived in Washington on May 28, he brought with him a draft for new competition rules, and by June 7, after consultations with the American Battle Monuments Commission Site and Design Committee, the draft was approved. On June 11, a new announcement in the *Commerce Business Daily*, reflected a May 28 memo that Lacy had written to the American Battle Monuments Commission and the General Services Administration in which he declared that the World War II Memorial design competition "must be an open competition in every sense of the word," one that "neither excludes the Maya Lins of the country nor the I. M. Peis."

The new rules were a sharp break with the previously announced rules. In essence they conceded that the protesting critics and architects had been right and that the General Services Administration had not gone far enough in opening up the National World War II Memorial design competition. In the first stage of the new competition, neither the record nor the identity of an entrant would be revealed. All design proposals would be submitted anonymously. As Lacy told the *Washington Post*, "The rating in the first stage is now based 100 percent on design."[11]

The official first-stage competition rules reflected this new emphasis. All previous information on the National World War II Memorial design competition was "cancelled in its entirety" and replaced with a streamlined submission process that now had a due date of August 12, 1996. The only material designers were expected to submit at this point in the competition was a sketch or graphic of their preliminary design vision, either in black and white or color, mounted on a quarter-inch foam core board measuring 20 inches by 20 inches. The rest of the requirements were equally clear. In addition to their illustration, designers were asked to integrate three elements within the borders of their board: (1) a narrative describing their intentions and philosophy as they related to the memorial; (2) the location of the memorial on the site; and (3) the scale of the principal elements of their design.[12]

The new competition rules did not completely satisfy everyone. Jaan Holt, who had led the criticism against the early competition requirements, was concerned that a two-month submission period, coming in the middle of the summer, would limit entries. But there was no comparing the new competition rules with the old. They put "the project back on a positive track," as Lacy observed, and they quieted a controversy that Haydn Williams and others on the American Battle Monuments Commission worried might affect "the success of the memorial's fund-raising campaign." In the end, even Jaan Holt would conclude, "We felt we had helped the project in a positive direction."

Nevertheless, the new rules, while leveling the playing field and reversing the previously overwhelming advantage given to large firms, still imposed significant challenges. In stage one of the design competition, the names of those doing the judging, the Architect-Engineer Evaluation Board, were not disclosed, and so entrants could not shape their designs to meet the tastes of someone whose architectural history they knew. In addition, the competition's preliminary program for the National World War II Memorial design established a set of complex demands. Not only did it require that the new memorial capture in architectural form what it called a unique moment in American history, but it placed significant constraints on the memorial design, requiring entrants to submit specific solutions for dealing with the fact that the memorial would be built on a flood plain that was only 2.6 meters above river level. In addition, the design of the National World War II Memorial had to fulfill a number of other objectives: It could not "detract from the Mall's east-west vista formed by the rows of elms bordering the Reflecting Pool between the Lincoln Memorial and Washington Monument"; it had to contain enough below-grade interior space for a hall of honor, interactive education facilities, and an auditorium; it had to provide enough above-ground space for commemorative services and ceremonies; and it had to rehabilitate the Rainbow Pool so that it became an important part of the memorial's total design.[13]

It was not an easy challenge, but by August 12, the deadline for entries, the American Battle Monuments Commission had received 407 submissions. Bill Lacy's faith that a large number of architects and designers would be drawn to the National World War II Memorial design competition had been justified, as had his belief that on short notice a first-rate Architect-Engineer Evaluation Board and Design Jury could be assembled. The Evaluation Board for the first-stage competition was made up of an impressive cross section of architects and veterans. Headed by architect Hugh Hardy of the New York firm of Hardy Holzman Pfeiffer Associates, it included architect Max Bond of Davis, Brodie and Associates of New York; *Boston Globe* architecture critic Robert Campbell; the General Services Administration's chief architect, Ed Feiner; retired colonel Mary Hallaren, the former commander of the Women's Army Corps; landscape architect Mary Margaret Jones of Hargreaves Associates of San Francisco; curator Diane Hauserman Pilgrim from the Cooper-Hewitt Museum in New York; engineer and former Tuskegee Airman Luther Smith; architect Cynthia Weese, dean of the school of architecture at Washington University in St. Louis; military historian Russell F. Weigley of Temple University; Haydn Williams of the American Battle Monuments Commission; and retired Marine Corps Commandant General Louis H. Wilson.[14]

Equally encouraging, as far as Lacy was concerned, were the six finalists selected by the Architect-Engineer Evaluation Board. They were chosen on August 15 and 16 in a two-day selection process in which the ground floor of the National Building Museum in Washington was closed to the public and all 407 submission boards were hung on portable panels for the Architect-Engineer Evaluation Board to view and comment on through the use of numbered tally sheets. After three rounds of judging on the first day, the Evaluation Board had whittled down the number of submissions they wanted to consider to twenty-five, and on the second day, after a morning of intense debate, they had arrived at a consensus on six finalists.

The six finalists were a diverse lot. They ranged from graduate students still in their twenties to world-famous architects, and they reaffirmed the notion that in anonymous architecture competitions, unknowns could get noticed. The six finalists included Brian and Katherine Ambroziak, 1992 University of Virginia graduates, who in 1996 were in architecture school at Princeton; Diana Balmori, a professor at Yale and head of Balmori Associates, an architect celebrated for both her writing on gardens and projects like the World Financial Center Winter Garden in New York; Friedrich St.Florian, the former dean of architecture at the Rhode

Island School of Design in Providence, best known in 1996 for his theoretical work and domestic architecture; Rafael Viñoly, much-honored head of Rafael Viñoly Architects, an international firm that has designed buildings ranging from the Tokyo International Forum in Japan to the Philadelphia Regional Performing Arts Center in America; Marion Weiss and Michael A. Manfredi, partners in Weiss/Manfredi Architects, a firm with such diverse projects to its credit as the Women's Memorial and Education Center at Arlington National Cemetery and the Olympia Fields Park and Community Center in Illinois; and Bernard J. Wulff and William C. Jackson, architects at the Washington office of RTKL Associates, the fourth largest design firm in the world, who had worked on buildings ranging from the Little Rock Courthouse to the Grand Hyatt in the Cayman Islands.[15]

In the second stage of the design competition, the challenges remained as complex as before. As Haydn Williams told the six finalists at the August 29 orientation session held for them, "What you will be designing will symbolize and memorialize a moment in time which, in profound ways, changed forever the face of American life and the direction of world history." The catch was that at the same time the memorial needed to have what Williams called "its own unique identity," it needed to be humble and "respectful of its surroundings." It had to keep open the vista between the Washington Monument and the Lincoln Memorial, which meant that while the memorial could extend underground or horizontally, it could never at its center have a significant vertical element. The highest points on the National World War II Memorial would have to be at its northern and southern ends.[16]

The official program for the second stage of the National World War II Memorial design competition, as well as the announcement that appeared in the August 23, 1996, *Commerce Business Daily*, reiterated this requirement for a unique memorial that blended in with its surroundings and the fact that in the second stage of the competition, there would be new priorities. In the second-stage judging, the design concept would count for 60 percent of the total score rather than 100 percent, as it had in the first stage of the competition; the remaining 40 percent would depend on the quality and experience of the team that the finalists chose to be part of their projects.

Precisely how the new standards would apply to the finalists was spelled out in a list of the five evaluation criteria that appeared in the *Commerce Business Daily.* The finalists would be judged according to the following weighted criteria: 60 percent for a design concept that was expected to be an amalgamation of art, landscaping, and architecture that took advantage of the National World War II Memorial's location; 15 percent for the past performance of the project team in managing comparable undertakings; 10 percent for the suitability of the team for the type of work required by the National World War II Memorial; 10 percent for the professional qualifications of the project team and individuals on it; and 5 percent for the ability of the team to accomplish the work required on the National World War II Memorial in timely fashion.[17]

It was a formidable task, made still more formidable by the desire of the American Battle Monuments Commission to have the memorial contain an estimated 7,400 square meters of interior space, which would allow it to hold exhibitions and patriotic ceremonies. With a two-month due date that required all of their materials to be in by October 25, 1996, the finalists did not have a lot of time to refine their original submissions, nor with the $75,000 fee they were given, did they have a lot of money to hire support staff. They also were not in a position to evaluate the strengths and weaknesses of one another's submissions. Their six designs were not put on display, because, as Bill Lacy put it, "At this early stage I think it would be wrong for each of the entrants to view what the others have done."[18]

The only meeting the finalists had with each other after August 29 came at an April 26, 1997, symposium at the Rhode Island School of Design, and the only chance to see all of the competition entries came the following summer in an exhibition at the Mellon Auditorium in Washington from June 17 to June 22, 1997. The one break the finalists did get was that for the second stage of the design competition they knew in advance who was sitting on the Design Jury that would evaluate their submissions. Although the makeup of the Design Jury changed slightly between the time it was first announced in August 1996 and when it met in October, its core remained consistent. Chairman of the Design Jury was architect David Childs, a senior partner at Skidmore, Owings, and Merrill and the principal designer of Constitution Gardens, and assisting him were architect Hugh Hardy of Hardy Holzman Pfeiffer Associates, who had also served on the Architect-Engineer Evaluation Board, Pulitzer Prize winner and former *New York Times* architecture critic Ada Louise Huxtable, Houston architect John Chase, landscape architect Laurie Olin, San Francisco architect Cathy Simon, Earl A. Powel III, the director of the National Gallery of Art, Pepsico CEO Donald Kendall, retired Admiral Robert Long, and retired General John W. Vessey, the former chairman of the Joint Chiefs of Staff.[19]

For the finalists, the next two months were ones of intense work in which they not only sought to develop their designs but made plans to gather around them a team of architects and engineers who would impress the Architect-Engineer Evaluation Board. The National World War II Memorial would not, however, remain out of the news, even though only a very small group of people, linked either to the American Battle Monuments Commission or the General Services Administration, knew what the drawings of the six finalists actually looked like.

Between July and September 1996 the yet-unseen National World War II Memorial designs came under attack in a series of articles by architecture critics who were concerned that the amount of interior space the memorial was expected to contain would make it impossible to build successfully at the Rainbow Pool site. The attack was launched in the July 1996 issue of *Architecture* by its editor, Deborah Dietsch, who in an article titled "Memorial Madness" declared that only "an unmonumental monument—low, limited, and landscaped," could begin to meet the requirements of the American Battle Monuments Commission but that by definition "such deference" would be at odds with a memorial built to remind Americans of one of the world's most colossal conflicts.

A month later, Roger Lewis, a professor of architecture at the University of Maryland, in an August 17 *Washington Post* article that began by quoting Deborah Dietsch, carried the argument further. After insisting that the Rainbow Pool site was a bad choice, Lewis honed in on the dilemma of interior space. The National World War II Memorial's space requirement created too many contradictions, he argued. It was "bizarre to build what amounts to a museum at a site such as this, to create a huge subterranean structure with little or no visual and architectural presence on the Mall." A month later, in the September 7 *Washington Post,* architecture critic Benjamin Forgey took up the same theme. Asserting that the requirement that the National World War II Memorial have so much interior space blurred the distinction between a museum and a memorial and would surely undermine the memorial's integrity, Forgey argued that there was only one alternative—elimination of the interior space proposed for the National World War II Memorial. The precedent that the FDR Memorial set when it blurred the distinction between a memorial and a museum should not be extended to the central axis of the Mall, Forgey concluded.[20]

For the American Battle Monuments Commission, the criticism, especially from a respected critic like Benjamin Forgey, was a serious concern, and in a September 29, 1996, *Washington Post* op-ed, Haydn Williams tried to dampen the controversy. While the American Battle Monuments Commission did want its National World War II Memorial to contain interior space, the ABMC did not plan anything approaching a conventional museum that would have historical material or memorabilia, Williams wrote. It was, Williams went on to say, "a misunderstanding of our intention" to assume that the ABMC would build anything on the scale of a museum or anything that would require a staff and curator. The fact that Williams was put in a position in which he had to explain the American Battle Monuments Commission's design intentions even before there was a National World War II Memorial design for the public or for the media to see revealed, however, just how much tension the prospect of the memorial was already creating.[21]

In the drawings they submitted for the second stage of the National World War II Memorial design competition, the finalists showed that they, too, understood the controversy and issues swirling around the memorial. There is enormous variety in their designs, but what unites them is the finalists' shared belief that in order to meet the American Battle Monuments Commission's requirement for interior space, they must find a way to keep the memorial's interior space below grade. This sense is especially true of the five finalists who were runners-up and whose submissions offer us a view of what might have been the winning design.

In the case of Brian and Katherine Ambroziak, the youngest finalists, the focus on building underground and eliminating large above-ground elements was directly tied to their belief that the best form for the National World War II Memorial was that of the bunker. They saw in the modern bunker both a military architecture that was unique to World War II (America built bunkers on its east and west coasts) and a monolithic structure that, although not classical, nonetheless fit in with the two other monolithic structures, the Washington Monument obelisk and the Lincoln Memorial Greek temple, that dominate the central axis of the Mall. As Brian Ambroziak explained it, "The goal of our memorial was to create a language or create architectural elements that carry secondary meaning, that were not necessarily classical but fit within the context of the classical system that already exists on the Mall."

For the Ambroziaks, the bunker brought to mind the idea of a structure designed for survival, and in their eyes the "two distinct bunker forms" that they used in their design blended the image of war with the image of individual citizens and soldiers struggling to survive the war's violence. For Brian, whose grandfather, a World War II fighter pilot, led the first squadron of P-38s in the North African campaign, it was particularly important to take into account the home front and the war front, and in the memorial that the Ambroziaks proposed, with its main hall 180 meters long, they provided more than enough space to deal with both phases of the war.

Visitors would enter the main underground hall of the Ambroziaks' memorial through a low, angled bunker north of the Rainbow Pool and exit from a larger circular bunker south of the Rainbow Pool. Except for four emergency exits, visitors would see nothing of the memorial when they looked from the base of the Washington Monument to the Lincoln Memorial. Indeed, what was unique about the Ambroziaks' memorial was that the vista its two bunkers called attention to was on a cross-axis with the central spine of the Mall and took the viewer's eye south to the Jefferson Memorial and north to the White House.

The underground hall of the Ambroziaks' memorial, which would be illuminated with the kind of light found in the bunker war rooms that the allies used in London throughout the 1940s, took the visitor chronologically through World War II. The idea, as the Ambroziaks put it, was to layer the information about the war and its sacrifices. The north entrance of their memorial was marked with inscriptions about America's early involvement in the war with the Lend-Lease Act, the Atlantic Charter, and the Declaration of War on December 8, 1941. Then in the main hall of their memorial the time line continued. As visitors walked down the hall, they would encounter four small rooms—each devoted to a single year of the war—that continually showed newsreels. They could enter these rooms directly or view them from benches positioned in eight niches on the west wall of the main hall, but in both cases, thanks to the newsreels, visitors could see the same scenes from the war that Americans were being shown in the 1940s.

The visitor could not, however, simply move from room to room doing nothing but watching newsreels. After the first two rooms and before the last two, the hall was interrupted with a critical, central map room located just beneath the Rainbow Pool. Etched into the floor of this fifth room was a map showing battle sites around the globe, and at the east end of the room was an eternal flame with an oculus above it that let light in from the outside. A plinth that the Ambroziaks would install in the Rainbow Pool just above the water line kept its waters from flowing down into the oculus, but the oculus was not shielded from the outdoor elements. It was deliberately left open to allow in snow and rain.

Visitors stopping in the map room were now halfway through the memorial, but their departure from the memorial was not intended to be a repeat of the experience of their entrance. Like the floor on many World War II factory assembly lines, the floor on the Ambroziaks' memorial deliberately sloped downward, taking the visitor deeper into the memorial with every step. On the west wall of the main hall, across from the map room, the Ambroziaks planned sculptural representations of Norman Rockwell's 1943 series of paintings, *The Four Freedoms,* and as visitors exited the memorial by the circular ramp at its southern bunker, they came across the most gripping part of the memorial. Enclosed in an internal bunker room, which visitors could look into but not enter as they ascended the bunker by its circular ramp, was a statue of a grieving mother, looking down on the memorial floor at a gold star representing the death of her son. For visitors, the mother with the gold star was the last image of the memorial that they would take with them before they exited, and as they returned to the Mall, the mother, who initially could only be seen through slits in the interior bunker room surrounding her, became increasingly visible, a symbol of the ultimate cost of the war.[22]

For Diana Balmori building below grade was also the key to keeping the vista between the Washington Monument and Lincoln Memorial uncluttered. "If you wanted to be respectful of that axis, it meant putting it all underground," she said of her memorial design. For Balmori this decision meant taking advantage of the Rainbow Pool site and creating a memorial that did not revolve around a literal narrative but reflected the change that Maya Lin's Vietnam Veterans Memorial made in what could be built on the Mall. As Balmori put it, "The thing that was foremost in my mind was to create a place or a space more than an object."

The outside of Balmori's memorial was thus very minimal in appearance. It consisted of an alabaster cube, 35 meters on a side, located at the center of a black granite Rainbow Pool that had been reconfigured into a rectangle. When the pool was drained, the cube turned into a stone stage. Otherwise, it appeared as an alabaster island in a black sea. Balmori's memorial was anything but an inert geometric construct, however. Incised into the center of her cube was a glass star, exactly like the kind of star families hung on a banner in the window during World War II to indicate they had someone in the service. The star let light in and out of the memorial and was, in Balmori's words, "sensitive to what was happening in the atmosphere." At night the star became part of a memorial that glowed and thereby created a space for itself between the Washington Monument and Lincoln Memorial.

The richness of Balmori's memorial deepened on entry. Her underground space served multiple functions. The floor of the alabaster island that visitors would see from the Mall was also the ceiling of a below-ground room, that constituted a central hall of honor, and surrounding the hall of honor was a 425-seat auditorium, an exhibition area, two visitors centers, rest rooms, and a book and gift shop. Balmori's floor plan made it easy to move from one room to another, but her rooms never isolated visitors. Visitors would always be able to get to the central hall of honor from wherever they were, and once in the central hall of honor during the day, they had only to stand on the bronze star set in the floor and look up to see the light pouring in from the glass star directly above them. The memorial's symmetry connected its exterior with its interior.

Equally important, in Balmori's plan the crisscrossed axes that would take people to and from the center of her memorial not only moved them from place to place but also engaged them in the process of understanding World War II. Along her north-south axis, where she deliberately put her main entrance-exit area so that it would not compete with the east-west axis leading from the Washington Monument to the Lincoln Memorial, Balmori created what she called an axis of space. On the north section of this axis, which ended with the hall of honor, Balmori placed an interactive hall of monitors, to which visitors could go to look up on computers anyone who served during World War II, and on the south side of this axis, which began on the other side of the hall of honor, she placed a hall of exhibits that was intended to contain the letters and memorabilia of individual servicemen.

On her east-west axis, the axis of time, as she called it, Balmori provided a time line that reflected what America was doing during World War II. Starting with the Lend-Lease Act and moving chronologically through the war in the Atlantic and the Pacific, Balmori's axis would take the visitor through the important battles and domestic events in the years from 1941 to 1945. In her time line the war front and the home front blended, and the memorial visitor who had just come from her north-south axis and looked up a serviceman on the computers there would now be in a position to see how that serviceman's life intersected with what was happening to the nation as a whole.[23]

For Rafael Viñoly, too, the starting point for a successful memorial was the assurance that nothing would interfere with the vista between the Washington Monument and the Lincoln Memorial. "The initial idea," he observed, "was based on precisely one of the restrictions that was so clear and also so right in the brief for the competition, which was not to obstruct the main axial perspectives." For Viñoly the answer to the vista problem meant not only putting the interior space of his memorial below grade but also creating an above-ground memorial in which two natural, nonarchitectural elements—water and fire—were crucial.

Viñoly's design placed a circle of fire, which was fueled by methane gas, around the periphery of the Rainbow Pool and then relied on the interaction of the fire and the water to create a peaceful cloud of mist. This encounter was designed to reflect both the destructiveness of World War II and the final victory of America and the allies over totalitarianism. This central image of Viñoly's memorial did not end here, however. It was embraced by two semicircular colonnades of glass prisms placed around the edge of the memorial in a way that let them highlight, but not intrude upon, the Mall's central axis. The 8-meter high prisms, one for each state and territory in America at the time of World War II, were designed to refract light during the day and night and then, in the rainbows they created, to duplicate the rainbow stripes on the ribbon of the Victory Medal that all American servicemen were given at the conclusion of the war.

Viñoly's design would also expand the Rainbow Pool site. To the Rainbow Pool he added two more pools designed to represent the war that took place in the Atlantic and Pacific. It was here that Viñoly would place his glass prisms and also modify the edge of his two new pools. Around each would be educational time lines that reflected the chronology of events in each theater of war. Visitors following the chronologies were in a position to follow the war's progress, but they were also directed by the time lines to the main stairway at the Seventeenth Street side of the memorial. From the elliptical stairway, with steps that were designed to double as seats for an outdoor theater, visitors were then led below grade to the hall of remembrance, the circular room that Viñoly thought of as "the heart of the memorial."

Here, too, the memorial was surprising. Even after visitors were completely inside the hall of remembrance in the lower level of Viñoly's memorial, they were still connected to the circle of fire and water that first drew their attention to the memorial. The floor of Viñoly's new Rainbow Pool was made of glass, designed to act as a skylight for the hall of remembrance below it. The hall with its white marble walls and continuous relief of men and women returning from the war was thus always affected by what was going on above. In the day, visitors could see the light from the sun and the ring of fire as it filtered through the waters of the Rainbow Pool; at night, depending on the weather conditions, there was the light of the moon in addition to the ring of fire.

For Viñoly this connection between what was above and below grade was in many ways a political statement. He did not want visitors to his World War II Memorial to lose track of the complexity of World War II. He wanted, as he put it, to be "non–politically correct." But also shaping Viñoly's design was his desire to make sure that his memorial was both practical and respectful of the real estate on which it stood. The fuel for the methane gas that allowed Viñoly's ring of fire to burn twenty-four hours a day was to be generated from clippings and leaves collected from the Mall. Viñoly had commissioned a study that found that there was enough organic material to sustain the ring of fire year-round. In creating a memorial that by the neoclassical standards of the Mall was unquestionably theatrical, Viñoly wanted to make sure that anyone looking into how his memorial worked would find an ecologically sound piece of architecture.[24]

For architects Marion Weiss and Michael A. Manfredi, building below grade was also fundamental to the design of their National World War II Memorial. But in contrast to the other finalists, Weiss and Manfredi were willing to go against the notion that it was taboo to place anything vertical on the Mall's central axis in the area between the Washington Monument and the Lincoln Memorial. The most visible part of their memorial was a grid of fifty crystalline glass columns, each 39 feet high, that filled the Rainbow Pool. The columns, five deep and ten across, rested on the floor of a Rainbow Pool, from which Weiss and Manfredi deliberately removed the old fountains, but which otherwise remained the same, in order to show, as Weiss put it, that the Mall's "honorific landscape as it had been established was not really going to change."

The grid of columns, Weiss and Manfredi wrote four years later in their book *Site Specific,* "represents the collective efforts of United States citizens" during World War II. But that was as far as they would go in assigning meaning to their columns. As Marion Weiss would say, "Our feeling was that we wanted to be as abstract as we could be with the symbolism, because issues of representation start to become very finite because of who, what, and where they include." Nonetheless, the glass columns in the Weiss-Manfredi memorial would perform a very clear function in linking their memorial to its Mall surroundings and connecting what was visible to what lay below ground.

As visitors approached the Weiss-Manfredi memorial from Seventeenth Street, they would see a low colonnade in the foreground and the Lincoln Memorial in the background. At night, when the columns were lit, the view would be more striking, with the illuminated Weiss-Manfredi memorial providing a visual continuum with the Washington

Monument and the Lincoln Memorial. The most important function of the glass columns, however, was the way they shed light into the memorial's hall of honor 25 feet below the surface of the Mall. During the day the light pouring in from the columns would naturally fall downward onto the inscriptions on the floor of the hall of honor, which recorded on a state-by-state basis the number of those who served in World War II, the number killed, and the number taken prisoner. At night shafts of light from the internally lit columns would perform the same function. For visitors to the memorial, the war front and the home front, like the nation's victory and sacrifices, would thus be always presented in tandem.

The hall of honor below the glass columns, which in the hot Washington summers would naturally provide visitors with a measure of relief, was designed so that it would be filled with changing shadows and light, but the area below the surface, which Weiss and Manfredi often referred to as a crypt, would also contain a great deal of practical space. In addition to the hall of honor, there was a theater, an archive, exhibition space, and a library. Visitors could easily get to them, but they could also simply stay in the hall of honor and follow its great map of the war from beginning to end. The Weiss-Manfredi memorial was, above all else, a commemorative space. The slow descent into the memorial was designed to mark the war before America entered it; the deepest part of the memorial, to address America's participation in the fighting from 1941 to 1945; and the steep ascent out of the memorial, to observe the end of war and the return to peace.[25]

Like Marion Weiss and Michael A. Manfredi, Bernard J. Wulff and William C. Jackson of RTKL Associates also took an unexpected approach to the vista problem created by the location of the National World War II Memorial. Their strategy, however, was to avoid the problem altogether by making the most significant element of their memorial a bell colonnade, which they set among the double rows of elms on the north and south sides of the Rainbow Pool. Although the bell colonnade they created was not small, it was not immediately noticeable. More than 30 feet high and covering 300 total feet, with each of its four segments stretching approximately 75 feet, the bell colonnade, hidden by the trees around it, did not visually dominate the Rainbow Pool site so much as permeate it with sound. The 192 bells in the colonnade were grouped in clusters of 48 bells, with each cluster tuned to play four twelve-note octaves that would ring quietly at different hours during the day as if driven by the wind. Visitors, unless they were actually walking under the elms, would hear the bells before they saw them. As they approached the Rainbow Pool or looked down the vista between the Washington Monument and the Lincoln Memorial, the rows of bells, separated on the north and south from each other by 442 feet, the length of a World War II Liberty Ship, were out of their line of sight.

The inspiration for the bells, as Wulff and Jackson freely acknowledged, was Ronchamp, France, where bells in the woods near the Chapel of Nôtre Dame du Haut, designed by Le Corbusier and built in the early 1950s, create a sound that visitors to the chapel hear without knowing exactly where it is coming from. For Wulff and Jackson, whose aim, as they wrote, was to "join the elements of sound, landscape, and water to create a restrained and reverent place," the sound from their bells was intended to provide background for the experience of being at the National World War II Memorial and to remind visitors that the end of World War II was celebrated in America and Europe with the ringing of church bells. On one day each year, Wulff and Jackson expected that their bells would be played in concert, along with the music of various groups, to mark the end of World War II and the victory of freedom over tyranny.

The impact of Wulff's and Jackson's bell garden on their National World War II Memorial was more than auditory, however. In addition to maintaining the open vista between the Washington Monument and the Lincoln Memorial, the bell garden avoided encroachment upon the outline of the Rainbow Pool, and there was no need to undertake major alterations at the site.

Wulff and Jackson were then free to concentrate their energies on establishing a meaningful link between the above-ground elements in their memorial and the below-ground elements required by the American Battle Monuments Commission program. They began by rebuilding the floor of the Rainbow Pool (renamed the Pool of Peace by the designers) out of a honed black granite that they set slightly above the surrounding plaza. In the center of this pool, Wulff and Jackson inserted an oculus, which would allow a shaft of light to descend down into the memorial below and thereby visually connect the two levels of their memorial.

A white-granite ceremonial plaza, similar in size to that of the central space of the East Plaza of the Capitol, was then placed by Wulff and Jackson at the east side of the Pool of Peace and linked to ramped walkways that traced a semicircular path along the north and south sides of the pool and embraced the bell colonnades and elm trees to the west. For the visitors who followed these paths the result was a guided tour that led them directly into the lower level of the memorial.

There they would find a hall of honor, a gallery, a three-hundred-seat auditorium, and a memorial chamber. On the outer wall of the hall of honor Wulff and Jackson placed two time lines, one for the war in Europe, the other for the war in the Pacific, and within the hall they created room for exhibitions. But it was the memorial chamber, an underground room directly beneath the pool and linked to the hall of honor by four narrow passageways, on which Wulff and Jackson lavished the most attention. On the chamber's curved stone walls, they placed inscriptions of the Four Freedoms that Franklin Roosevelt first articulated to the nation in 1941, and in the center of the chamber, they made sure that the outside world became an integral part of the memorial's interior. They allowed the sunlight coming through the oculus in the floor of the Pool of Peace to create a "hallowed space" on the floor of the memorial chamber below during the day, and at night they took advantage of the darkness and reversed the process. They projected the light from within the memorial chamber upward through the oculus, so that when visitors came to the memorial in the evening they would see reflections of the bell garden within the trees as well as a glow that added a point of light to the vista linking the Washington Monument and Lincoln Memorial.[26]

The problem that beset the other finalists—creating interior space without encroaching on the Mall vista—was also a matter of concern for Friedrich St.Florian. The challenge, as he put it, was to create "a space with autonomy without disturbing the open vista." Where St.Florian differed from the other five finalists was in his solution to this problem. As Benjamin Forgey shrewdly noted in his *Washington Post* review of the April 26, 1997, Rhode Island School of Design symposium on the World War II Memorial competition, "Only St.Florian figured out a way for the memorial's visitors to enter its exhibition halls without feeling as if they were going underground. He did this by lowering the entire plaza, including its centerpiece, the existing Rainbow Pool, by about fifteen feet." With St.Florian's memorial, everything was thus below grade, but nothing was subterranean.[27]

Visitors entering the memorial from either Seventeenth Street on its east side or from the Lincoln Memorial on its west side had only to walk down a series of descending stairs to get to the Rainbow Pool. Then, whether they turned north or south, they would face architecturally identical halves of the memorial. Immediately before them would be a semicircular colonnade of fifty 40-foot-high columns, twenty-five on the north, twenty-five on the south. The fluted columns, truncated at the top with their capitals cut off to signify the deaths of the soldiers who had died in battle, were the most symbolic element in St.Florian's memorial. The columns, equal to the current number of states in America, were designed to reflect the enormous toll World War II took on the United States and to employ an architectural language in which the classical style that is part of the Mall's oldest presidential memorials was combined with the modern.

Just behind the columns and rising 10 feet above them, two earthen berms, each 68 feet wide and 360 feet long, encompassed the memorial's educational and exhibition space. Visitors would enter this covered space, which included a 400-seat auditorium and a series of smaller rooms, as if they were entering a giant shell. But from outside the memorial, the berms were very different in appearance. They were designed to look as if they were part of the Mall's landscape rather than part of a structure that had been engineered. All the visitor would see from most vantage points on the Mall were two large embankments planted with white Bonica roses, which in the Washington climate were expected to bloom much of the year. By virtue of the shape of the semi-circular colonnade at its edge, St.Florian's memorial kept open the Mall's central axis and a view of the Lincoln Memorial and the Washington Monument.

St.Florian was very happy with the way he had worked around these vista–interior space tensions. "I thought the winning design had the right balance between the classical elements and modern elements," he would later say. But there was a price to pay for St.Florian's particular solution to the National World War II Memorial's vista–interior space problem. Because of its length, his memorial would require some of the Mall's oldest elms to be cut down, and although his memorial would leave the Mall's east-west vista open, it would block its north-south vista. A visitor standing just beyond the north edge of St.Florian's World War II Memorial would not be able to look south and see the Tidal Basin or the Jefferson Memorial. The berms on his memorial were striking, but they were also too large for anyone to see over or around.[28]

It would be months before the winner of the design competition was chosen. Who lost and who won would in the end be determined by three days of reviews and interviews that took place in Washington from October 29 to October 31, 1996. On October 29 the Design Jury for the National World War II Memorial competition, headed by David Childs, met for the first time at breakfast and, after a trip to the Rainbow Pool, gathered at Blair House to begin its deliberations. The ten-member Design Jury then spent the rest of the day reviewing the seven boards each finalist had been asked to submit. It was a long and arduous process. The boards were placed on easels in front of the jury, and the jury took the morning to review three of the finalists' boards, then came back in the afternoon to review the remaining three before it reached a decision on whom it would recommend to the World War II Memorial Competition Architect-Engineer Evaluation Board.

The Architect-Engineer Evaluation Board, which started its deliberations the next day, October 30, at the offices of the General Services
Administration, without knowing the decision of the Design Jury,
would take two days to reach its decision. After learning from a techni-
cal team headed by Ed Feiner that the finalists' architecture teams had
all met the General Services Administration's stage-two requirements,
the Architect-Engineer Evaluation Board then began the process that
would take up most of its time—personally meeting with each architectural team in sessions lasting an hour or more in which the design architect of each team made an oral presentation and then the team went
through a question-and-answer period.[29]

At the end of the three days, Friedrich St.Florian's design emerged as
the first choice of both the Design Jury and the Architect-Engineer Evaluation Board. It was a decision that J. Carter Brown of the Commission
of Fine Arts would later applaud by observing, "I've seen the design concept, and I like it. It has a certain inevitability that I think is quite inspiring." But there was nothing inevitable about St.Florian's victory. Hugh
Hardy, who would do double duty in Washington, serving as chairman
of the Architect-Engineer Evaluation Board and as a member of the
Design Jury, would say of St.Florian's design, "The big gestures were so
clear and evocative that they won the day." But Hardy would also admit
that members of the Design Jury were divided in their loyalties to classical and contemporary design. In order to make St.Florian their first
choice, they had to overcome the strong admiration a group of jurors,
headed by landscape architect Laurie Olin, had for Diana Balmori's
entry, and in addition they had to decide that St.Florian, who, despite a
highly successful academic career, did not in 1996 have a worldwide reputation, could in the end design a better memorial than an international
architecture superstar such as Rafael Viñoly.[30]

Friedrich St.Florian was in Providence getting a haircut when Bill Lacy
called and left a message with Livia St.Florian that her husband should
ring him back as soon as he got in. It was Saturday morning, an unlikely
time for any but a congratulatory call, and after his wife reached him at

the barbershop, St.Florian felt relief for the first time since he had entered the World War II Memorial competition. "At that moment I knew," he would recall thinking. "They don't call people who don't win. They write them."[31]

For the American Battle Monuments Commission, which had spent 1995 trying to get a site for the memorial and 1996 trying to get a design, there was also a sense of relief. The ABMC still had a long way to go before actual construction of the National World War II Memorial could begin. But at least one crisis was over. As Design Jury chairman David Childs observed of the pressure he and others felt to pick a winner and not delay the memorial process by insisting on further design refinements, "The timing was critical. There was a lot of controversy about the site. There was an eagerness to move things forward." On November 6, the ABMC's World War II Memorial Site and Design Committee affirmed the recommendation to declare Friedrich St.Florian the winner of the National World War II Memorial design competition and forwarded the recommendation to American Battle Monuments Commission Chairman Fred Woerner. On November 18, the ABMC's Memorial Advisory Board gave its affirmation, and on November 20, the full American Battle Monuments Commission followed suit.[32]

Two months later at the January 17, 1997, unveiling of St.Florian's design at the White House, there was even more reason for optimism. The coverage of the event was upbeat, and there was widespread approval of the choices that St.Florian, as a design finalist, had made during the second stage of the competition to assemble a project team. The team had the international firm, Leo A Daly, in a lead role with responsibility for architect-engineer design services for the World War II Memorial Project and featured a group prominent in architecture and the arts. In his front-page *Washington Post* account of the White House ceremony, Benjamin Forgey singled out for special mention the presence on the project team of George Hartman of Hartman-Cox Architects as associate architect, landscape architect James van Sweden of the landscape architecture firm of Oehme, van Sweden & Associates, and sculptor Ray Kaskey and then went on to report that the American Battle Monuments Commission had also decided to scale down its requirements for interior space at the new memorial.[33]

At the White House unveiling, President Clinton, who in 1995 had spoken at the site dedication for the National World War II Memorial, gave the building of the memorial still more publicity when he used the occasion to award his 1996 presidential opponent, Bob Dole, the nation's highest civilian honor, the Medal of Freedom. At seventy-three, Dole, who was wounded during the fighting in Italy's Po Valley, was the embodiment of the World War II veteran who sacrificed for his country and then returned home to make still more contributions. The president's decision to honor Dole so quickly after a bitter election made news throughout the country. "With Ballots Still Warm, Clinton Pays Homage to Dole," the *New York Times* next-day headline ran. "Two Political Opponents Score a Mutual Victory at Emotional Award Ceremony," the *Washington Post* headline announced.[34]

In his speech President Clinton went out of his way to give his personal support to the construction of the National World War II Memorial. "I have reviewed it, and it is very impressive," he said of St. Florian's design, before going on to add, "Fittingly, it will be flanked by the Washington Monument and the Lincoln Memorial. For if the Revolutionary War marks the birth of our republic, and the Civil War its greatest trial, then surely America's triumph in World War II will forever signal our coming of age." Dole, after joking that he hoped the gift from the president was going to be the front door key to the White House, was equally eloquent. "No one can claim to be equal to this honor," he declared, "but I will cherish it as long as I live, because this occasion allows me to honor some others who are more entitled."[35]

For the American Battle Monuments Commission, the design-selection process and the unveiling ceremony would continue to reap benefits long after January 17. When the Design Jury finished its work on October 29, several of its members at the Blair House reception expressed their concerns about the future of the National World War II Memorial to Haydn Williams. It was a conversation that led Williams, after conferring with Ed Feiner, to ask those who had been members of the Architect-Engineer Evaluation Board and the Design Jury to participate in a series of informal review sessions to discuss the design of the National World War II Memorial as it was being developed for approval by the Commission of Fine Arts and the National Capital Planning Commission. The General Services Administration agreed to pay for transportation to these sessions, and over the next four years the group became the core of an unofficial advisory process, meeting nine times between April 1997 and April 2000 with Friedrich St.Florian as he went through the lengthy design-approval process.

After the memorial unveiling ceremony at the White House, Senator Dole in turn became intrigued with the idea of getting the National World War II Memorial built without further delays so that as many aging World War II veterans as possible would be able to see it, and on March 19, 1997, Dole agreed to become national chairman of the National World War II Memorial Campaign, presiding over a fund-raising effort that would spare the National World War II Memorial the money problems that, beginning in the nineteenth century with the Washington Monument, had beset so many Mall memorials.[36]

# 6

# St.Florian at Work

In August 2001, just before construction on the National World War II Memorial began, Friedrich St.Florian looked back on the long struggle to get his design approved and observed, "I did not realize when we won the competition that it would be so difficult." St.Florian, who was sixty-four in 1997, the year his winning design was unveiled at the White House, was not being disingenuous. He was speaking as an architect whose private clients and academic career at the Rhode Island School of Design had allowed him to remain free during most of his working life from the kind of controversy that comes with high-profile commissions.[1]

In an era when we think of architects as master builders with enormous egos, St.Florian is the opposite—a quietly confident man who does not seek out the limelight and who speaks admiringly of the architects, classical and contemporary, who have influenced him. Typical of St.Florian was his reaction to being told that he had won the National World War II Memorial design competition but that he must keep the news secret until the American Battle Monuments Commission made an official announcement. While happy himself, St.Florian was anguished that he could not share his good fortune with those who had worked with him at his studio in Providence or with members of the winning design team in Washington.[2]

St.Florian was born Friedrich Florian Gartler in 1932 in Graz, Austria, a middle-size city of 226,000 people, closer to Slovenia and Hungary than to the Austrian capital of Vienna, a two-hour train ride away. During the World War II years St.Florian's father, who worked as an engineer in hydroelectric power plants, was exempted from military service, and Kaprun, the alpine village in which the Gartlers lived, was spared from allied bombing by virtue of its remoteness. St.Florian can recall watching bombers flying overhead, but his most vivid memory of the war came in 1945 when he was twelve and an American soldier suddenly appeared at the door of his classroom and told the teacher to send the students home. For St.Florian, the friendly G.I. and the American troops who later came through his village were an impressive sight, whose presence marked the return of peacetime for the Gartlers and their neighbors.[3]

After Catholic boarding school, St.Florian returned to Graz, where in 1958 he received his architect's degree from the Technische Universitaet, and soon thereafter, with his friend and fellow student Raimund Abraham, best known in America for designing the new Austrian Cultural Forum on East 52nd Street in New York, St.Florian surprised everyone by winning third prize in the competition to design the Pan Arabian University in Riyadh, Saudi Arabia. For St.Florian, it was a wonderful career start, and it prompted him to undertake what he would look back on as a "youthful utopian gesture." With the example of the great Swiss architect Le Corbusier (Charles-Edouard Jeanneret) in mind, St.Florian formally petitioned the Austrian government to allow him to adopt an artist's name. The Florian half of the artist's name that he chose for himself came from his mother's side of the family, where there was a beloved Uncle Florian as well as a martyred Roman officer with the same name. The St. part of his artist's name came from the Italian futurist, Antonio Sant'Elia, who, while a young man with a promising career ahead of him, was killed in 1916 during the fighting of World War I.[4]

"If I had discussed it with others, I probably would not have done it," St.Florian would later say of his name change, but as the fifties drew to an end, he was in no mood to settle down. After graduation from university, St.Florian and Abraham moved to Vienna, where, as architectural partners, they were able to get commissions designing a photographer's studio house and later an apartment house on Maxingstrasse. Even more important, the two continued to thrive in architectural competitions. In 1959 they won first prize in an international competition to design a Belgian Cultural Center (it was never built) for Leopoldville in the Congo, and in 1960 they won both third prize for their design for a Catholic church in Linz and fourth prize for their design for a vocational school in Vienna. This early recognition was not, however, enough to make St.Florian feel that he was ready to begin an architecture practice. By comparison with America, where the work of Paul Rudolph in particular caught his eye, Austria seemed out of date to St.Florian, and in 1961, supported with a Fulbright Fellowship, he enrolled in the master's program at Columbia University School of Architecture.[5]

At Columbia, where St.Florian received his master's degree in 1962, the quality of his work immediately brought him notice. He was offered an instructorship at Columbia in 1962. Then the following year Albert Bush-Brown, the new president of the Rhode Island School of Design (RISD), hired St.Florian as an assistant professor in the school's architecture program. It was the start of an association with RISD that would span four decades and initially send St.Florian back to Europe. Required by the conditions of his study visa to leave America after 1963, St.Florian spent the next two and a half years teaching in RISD's program in Rome.

The years in Rome were invaluable for St.Florian. It was in Rome that he met his future wife, Livia Campanella, a painter, then working in a film animation studio, and it was in Rome that he began to do what he had not done in his twenties either in Austria or the United States—study classical architecture. The modernist impulse that had shaped St.Florian's early design work in Austria did not, however, disappear as he began to study the classical architecture around him. In Rome, St.Florian initiated what he describes as his theoretical period by designing a vertical city, and after returning to America in 1967, the year he and Livia Campanella married, St.Florian continued to experiment still more. Influenced now by the work of Buckminster Fuller and the possibilities opened up by the space program that America had begun during the Kennedy administration, St.Florian began what he would later call "my first utopian work."[6]

"I began in earnest to create the things that Buckminster Fuller was talking about," St.Florian would say. The result was an "imaginary architecture" in which St.Florian, taking at face value Fuller's notion that air travel would soon make highways unnecessary, began to create imaginary spaces in the sky that were based on the holding patterns of airplanes over the New York City airports. It was an approach to architecture that was enthusiastically received at RISD, where by the late 1960s Bush-Brown had assembled an avant-garde faculty that in addition to St.Florian included his friend Raimund Abraham, Adolfo Natalini of Italy, and Michael Webb of London's Archigram, a movement that combined architecture and pop art. For St.Florian the high point of this period was a 1969 installation at the Moderna Museet in Stockholm, where, using laser beams and mirrors, he created an "Imaginary Room."[7]

The Stockholm installation got St.Florian still more notice in America, and in 1970 Gyorgy Kepes, the director of the Center for Advanced Visual Studies at the Massachusetts Institute of Technology, invited St.Florian to become a fellow there. The result was a series of imaginative works—including the "Statue of Liberty on Loan over South Africa" and an "Imaginary Bridge" over Boston's Charles River—that culminated with a 1973 show at MIT's Hayden Gallery and three years later with a retrospective at the University of Texas Art Museum in Austin. During this period St.Florian came close to getting the commission of a lifetime when in 1972 he, Raimund Abraham, and John Thornley, another young RISD professor, finished second in the competition to build the Georges Pompidou Center for the Visual Arts in Paris. But it was the Texas retrospective that turned out to be a turning point. It drove home to him the limits of his theoretical projects, and when in 1977 St.Florian, who four years earlier had become an American citizen, was offered the chairmanship of the architecture department at the Rhode Island School of Design, he had no hesitation about throwing himself back into the academic world. "I had hit a point where I could go no further in my theorizing," he would remember thinking.[8]

For the next eleven years, including three as provost of the Rhode Island School of Design, St.Florian threw himself into university life in a way that he had not done before as either an assistant professor from 1963 to 1970 or as an associate professor from 1974 to 1977. The eleven years from 1977 to 1988 that St.Florian spent as chairman and then dean of architecture at the Rhode Island School of Design were among the happiest in his life, but as the years wore on, St.Florian also found himself neglecting his own creative work. "I felt ten years behind some of my colleagues," he would recall.

A Rome Prize Fellowship at the American Academy in Rome settled the question of what he should do next. Although from 1991 to 1993, St.Florian served as the chief critic for RISD's European Honors Program in Rome, after 1988 he was finished with the kind of intense academic work that he had done for over a decade. He was now free to devote himself to the small architectural practice that he had been running since 1978. In St.Florian's case, the new work that, beginning in 1993, his sixtieth year, would emerge from his reborn practice was not confined to the domestic architecture that he had specialized in during the 1980s. The new work included proposals for the National Opera House in Norway, the New England BioLabs in Ipswich, Massachusetts, and most significant of all, a 1994 commission (now completed) to design the Pedestrian Skybridge and Winter Garden for Providence Place, the $450 million new shopping and entertainment center in the historic district of downtown Providence.[9]

It was a history that, in terms of what he had accomplished, made Friedrich St.Florian a relative unknown by comparison with many of the famous architects whose submissions were eliminated in the first stage of the National World War II Memorial design competition. Even J. Carter Brown, the longtime head of the National Gallery and the Commission of Fine Arts, who seemed to have connections that reached everywhere in the American art world, would admit that before St.Florian won the National World War II Memorial design competition, he did not know who he was. But as a man in his sixties who had just returned to a full-time architecture practice after years of teaching, St.Florian brought with him a sensibility that made him very different from both an unknown architect at the start of a career or a veteran architect trying to land one more commission.[10]

What St.Florian brought to the National World War II Memorial design competition was a sense of freshness plus an inner confidence that made him believe he was at a point in his life where he was ready to do his best work. In the case of the National World War II Memorial, the significance of this sensibility was that even before he began his preliminary drawings, St.Florian was sure he needed to build a memorial in which the classical and the modern were made to exist side by side. As he later explained, "I wanted to work within the classical spectrum of architectural language, but I also wanted to bring an element of modernity to it."

The starting point for St.Florian, as for the American Battle Monuments Commission in its program for the second stage of the design competition, was the historic significance of World War II. "It changed forever the face of American life," St.Florian believed. America's renewed focus on World War II more than a half century later was, he felt, a product of the nation finally arriving at a true perspective on the preceding one hundred years. "The interest in World War II could not be dismissed as a nostalgia episode," he was convinced. In St.Florian's eyes the National World War II Memorial was not to be thought of like the Vietnam Veterans Memorial, as a healing memorial designed to bind up the nation's wounds. The analogy for the World War II Memorial was a much larger one. "The World War II Memorial is not about healing," he insisted. "The World War II Memorial, like the Lincoln Memorial, like the Washington Monument, is a statement about an absolutely significant moment in our history. This time on a global level, not on a national level or on a continental level, the ideals of democracy were challenged. We had dictatorships threatening to take control of the world."

From this historical perspective, St.Florian then reached the conclusion that in designing a National World War II Memorial he had to work within "the classical language and classical principles of architecture" despite the fact that all his life he had been "fundamentally a modern architect." His reasoning, which dovetailed with the American Battle Monuments Commission's call for a memorial that was contextually respectful of the memorials around it, was very straightforward and reflected his years in Rome. The classical language of architecture, he insisted, brought with it "the greatest sense of timelessness" and showed how classicism could be renewed again and again. For St.Florian the challenge of combining the modern and the classical was one that he viewed himself well suited for, and he believed such architecture had an important precedent in America in two of the architects whom he most admired: Louis Kahn, whose work between the late fifties and early seventies included the Richards Medical Research Building at the University of Pennsylvania and the Kimbell Museum in Fort Worth, Texas; and Paul Cret, Kahn's professor as well as employer, best known for the stripped classicism that in the 1930s he brought to Washington in the Folger Shakespeare Library and Federal Reserve Board Building, but also admired for the classicism that he adapted to the funerary architecture he did for the American Battle Monuments Commission after World War I, when he designed the Flanders Field Cemetery Chapel in Belgium and the Aisne-Marne Memorial at Château-Thierry, France. St.Florian was not worried, especially with these precedents in mind, that by combining modernism and classicism in his National World War II Memorial, he was creating a memorial that would prove unappealing for Mall visitors. "Architecture is not like an open book. It does not have to be understood right away," he told himself as he got further and further into the design process.[11]

The next four years would test that belief time and again, and by 2001 St.Florian would make no secret of the toll that gaining design approval had taken on him. "We went through twenty-two public hearings," he wearily told the *Boston Globe* shortly before construction on the National World War II Memorial began. "My heart suffered, both literally and emotionally." The "we" in St.Florian's statement to the *Globe* included not only himself but the memorial project team as well as the American Battle Monuments Commission and its World War II Memorial Site and Design Committee. In the end, however, the ultimate burden for designing the National World War II Memorial was always felt most deeply by St.Florian. Moreover, even had the process that the American Battle Monuments Commission, St.Florian, and the memorial project team were required to follow to gain design approval from the Commission of Fine Arts, the National Capital Planning Commission, and the Secretary of the Interior gone smoothly, it would have been an ordeal. After winning the competition to design the National World War II Memorial, St.Florian, on behalf of the ABMC, was in effect required to win three more official approvals: (1) for his design concept; (2) for his preliminary design; (3) for his final design.[12]

St.Florian's first big test came in the summer of 1997, when on July 24, he appeared before the Commission of Fine Arts and on July 31, before the National Capital Planning Commission to present his design concept. At this time the concept that St.Florian presented to the two commissions was a modified version of his original design. It reflected the American Battle Monuments Commission's decision in January 1997 to remove a requirement for a 400-seat auditorium that the ABMC had originally wanted. As Haydn Williams told the *Washington Post* in a January interview, "Our own thinking has been changed, and we're scaling down the amount of enclosed space considerably." For St.Florian the ABMC's reconsideration meant that instead of lowering the memorial 15 feet below grade, he could now lower it just 6 feet and still have all the interior room he needed.[13]

Nonetheless, the design that St.Florian submitted to the approving commissions in July 1997 was still basically his initial design. The core of his original memorial—the sunken plaza, the fifty columns with their capitals cut off, and the earthen berms to the north and south—remained, and when St.Florian addressed the Commission of Fine Arts and the National Capital Planning Commission in July 1997, he offered the same explanation of his design that he had put forward when he had won the competition in 1996. At the heart of his memorial, St.Florian pointed out, was an "urban design strategy" that was intended to take advantage of the space the National World War II Memorial would occupy. By gently depressing the new Rainbow Pool, the memorial would maintain the unbroken plane between the Washington Monument and the Lincoln Memorial, St.Florian argued, and then by surrounding that plane with berms, the new memorial would "orchestrate" the vista between the Washington Monument and the Lincoln Memorial. A waterfall placed at the western end of the memorial would complete matters by optically linking the new Rainbow Pool and the nearby Reflecting Pool.

The deepest symbolism of the new memorial would in turn be borne by the colonnade of fifty columns, twenty-five to a side, that were arranged in semicircles in front of the berms. In St.Florian's scheme these 35-foot-high columns represented the individual states and the unity that resulted when Americans joined together to fight a common enemy. But with their capitals cut off, the columns also carried a second meaning: They harkened back to their Greek and Roman roots and symbolized young soldiers who had gone to war and had their lives cut short in battle. Like the white roses planned for the slopes of the berms, the columns, St.Florian contended, would give the National World War II Memorial its tragic ethos.[14]

At the meetings of the Commission of Fine Arts and the National Capital Planning Commission, testimony favoring St.Florian's design concept came from the American Battle Monuments Commission, veterans groups, and some of the critics and architects who had served as jurors for the National World War II Memorial competition. It was not, however, the memorial's supporters who in the end dominated the news. As a disappointed Haydn Williams of the American Battle Monuments Commission observed in a letter to architect David Childs, it was the memorial's opponents who got the headlines while the ABMC's gains were ignored. The memorial opponents' attacks ranged far and wide. Some wanted to reopen the question of where to locate the National World War II Memorial. Others were concerned with what Deborah Dietsch, the editor of *Architecture* magazine, called a stripped-down classicism "painfully reminiscent of designs by Nazi architect Albert Speer." But the attack that resonated most deeply was one that charged the National World War II Memorial with being unclear in its symbolism and unclear about whether it was a museum or a memorial. At the July 24 meeting of the Commission of Fine Arts, University of Maryland architecture professor Roger Lewis summed up this problem when he cited the official memorial competition call for roughly 7,400 square meters of interior space, and then observed, "I hate to see us get into semantics. We may or may not choose to call it a museum, but I think everyone has to agree that it has the scope of such a building." Lewis's concern, which architect Paul Spreiregen addressed in his testimony at the July 31 meeting of the National Capital Planning Commission when he spoke about the "architectural heft of the memorial," was one for which there was no good answer, and what followed was that after their July meetings both the Commission of Fine Arts and the National Capital Planning Commission refused to give their full approval to the National World War II Memorial design concept.[15]

The *Washington Post* carried the story of what had happened with the front-page headline, "WWII Memorial Goes Back to Drawing Board." The real story was a good deal more complicated, as Chairman J. Carter Brown of the Commission of Fine Arts made clear in public interviews and letters. The decision to ask St.Florian to modify his design concept, as Brown told the *Providence Journal-Bulletin,* was "not unusual in a project of this size and significance," and what lay behind the decision was a mixed view of St.Florian's design. As Brown observed five days later in a July 30, 1997, letter he wrote to American Battle Monuments Commission Chairman Fred Woerner, there was, on the one hand, "much about the present design concept that the commission approved." The commission liked the "lowering of the Rainbow Pool and its surrounding plaza," the fact that there was no "architectural obstruction to the central vista" of the Mall, and the memorial's "water features." On the other hand, there was, Brown believed, a need for a "simplified program" for the National World War II Memorial, an issue that *Washington Post* architecture critic Benjamin Forgey had addressed with great insight a year earlier in a lengthy article, "Tactical Error; World War II Monument Site Is No Place for a Museum."[16]

There were, J. Carter Brown would later recall, three major problems about the National World War II Memorial's design concept that particularly worried him. With its interior spaces, the St. Florian design confused the requirements of a museum with those of a memorial. With its truncated columns, which were supposed to make the visitor feel good about the unity of the country but sad about those who died fighting for it, the memorial offered, he believed, a contradictory symbolism, and with the amount of space it took up, the memorial required more elms to be cut down than the public would tolerate.[17]

In both the minutes of the Commission of Fine Arts meeting and in his testimony at the conclusion of the meeting, Brown spelled out these objections in terms that were unmistakable and that anticipated the objections the National Capital Planning Commission would voice a week later when it, too, refused to give its full approval to St. Florian's design concept. The key for the future, Brown tartly observed, was "to see how less can be more for a World War II commemorative space." In its present form the memorial simply tried to do too much, he believed. Entering the interior spaces of the memorial was, he opined, "going to seem like going into caves." The memorial's columns attempted to be "tragic and celebratory" at the same time. Its berms were too intrusive, and as for the openness the memorial created by having such a large footprint, it came at too high a price. "If openness and vistas were the only criterion of the success of the Mall, we would be out there with chain saws taking care of all the elms," Brown sardonically noted.[18]

It was tough criticism, coming as it did from someone who believed the Rainbow Pool site made sense and who thought that St. Florian's idea of lowering the National World War II Memorial's plaza was a brilliant stroke. It was, moreover, criticism that increased in importance when one added to it a series of July 1997 newspaper editorials—"Hallowed Ground in Jeopardy," the *New York Times* wrote; "Not This Design," the *Washington Post* declared—that attacked the National World War II Memorial without acknowledging the obstacles St.Florian had been forced to overcome just to meet the requirements of the memorial design competition.[19]

For Friedrich St.Florian, the 1997 calls of the Commission of Fine Arts and the National Capital Planning Commission for reworking his design concept were a disappointment as well as a relief. "I was very proud of it," he would say of his winning design. "It was very difficult to recapture the strength the original design had." The white roses on the slopes of the berms were, in St.Florian's judgment, very moving, and the two commissions' criticisms of the truncated columns were mistaken, he believed. "They took away the columns, which I was sad about. They were a strong statement," he would recall thinking at the time.

On the other hand, St.Florian had no qualms about eliminating the National World War II Memorial interior space that the two commissions had criticized and that J. Carter Brown described as "cavernous and uncompromising." "Initially we did it much too much because it was conditioned by the competition requirement," St.Florian would say of the interior space he had created. *Washington Post* architecture critic Benjamin Forgey's objections to the memorial's large interior and the distinction that Forgey drew in his articles on the difference between a museum and a memorial were embraced by St.Florian from the moment he read them. "The man who had tremendous influence on me was Benjamin Forgey," St.Florian would later say. "He said a memorial is not a school. It is a shrine. A memorial is not to teach. It is to inspire."[20]

As he started in on his revised design concept, St.Florian's new work reflected his sensitivity to these criticisms and to new design guidance from the ABMC that eliminated the need for enclosed space. It also reflected the influence of a July 1997 trip that he and his wife took to

Europe, where, at the invitation of the American Battle Monuments Commission, they toured military cemeteries supervised by the ABMC. In addition, St.Florian was now meeting periodically with a group of the architects and critics who had served on the panels judging the National World War II Memorial competition and who had volunteered to serve as unpaid consultants as the memorial moved through the approval process. The group, which in addition to the ABMC's Haydn Williams, included Laurie Olin, Bill Lacy, David Childs, Hugh Hardy, Robert Campbell, Max Bond, Ed Feiner, and Ada Louise Huxtable, met at the request of the American Battle Monuments Commission nine times between April 21, 1997, and April 20, 2000, at gatherings in New York and Washington and provided St.Florian with a sounding board on which he could try out his ideas and receive both theoretical and practical advice.[21]

In 1998 when he met on May 21 with the Commission of Fine Arts and on July 9 with the National Capital Planning Commission, St.Florian was in a much better situation than he had been the year before, and so was the American Battle Monuments Commission, which, after its 1997 difficulties, began doing much more advance work with the Commission of Fine Arts and the National Capital Planning Commission before going into formal public meetings with them. The ABMC still believed in what Haydn Williams in a September 18, 1997, letter to Senator Bob Kerrey, the most politically important memorial critic, called the "musts" of the National World War II Memorial: (1) It must be "commensurate" with the importance of World War II; (2) it must have "memorable landmark qualities"; (3) it must have "great architectural and aesthetic merit"; and (4) it must be "respectful" of its historical surroundings. Notwithstanding these four musts, St.Florian now had fewer design requirements to worry about than a year earlier, especially since the interior space requirements had been dropped. The principal elements of his original design—the lowered plaza, the semicircular colonnade framing the Mall's central spine, and the waterfalls at the western end—all remained, but in 1998 St.Florian was in a position to employ these elements in a much more compact design.

In place of the berms, which with the removal of the interior space requirements were no longer needed, the new design concept featured a Rainbow Pool that was 15 percent smaller than the original Rainbow Pool and a plaza that was 130 yards across. The elms, which in the first design concept had to be removed, were now preserved and used as a canopy for the memorial at its north and south ends. Gone, too, were the fifty truncated columns that had seemed so contradictory to both commissions. In their place were what St.Florian described as fifty-six "shield-like architectural structures" of stone and metal that represented the states and territories of the country during World War II and that together appeared as "embracing arms," reflective of the bonding of the nation during the war. Each shield had the seal of a state or territory on it, but because the grillwork on the shields was transparent, the north-south axis of the new memorial now remained open, in contrast to the initial design, in which the earthen berms that housed the memorial's interior space blocked sight lines.

In the revised design concept, what now distinguished the north and south ends of the National World War II Memorial were two arches— one for the Atlantic-European theater of war, the other for the Pacific-Asian theater of war—that were open at the top and that rose 36 feet from ground level. Each of these arches would have a small fountain and pool at its base, but in addition to the Rainbow Pool, there would also be, as there had been in the original design, water elements at the western end of the memorial on its Lincoln Memorial side. There cascading waterfalls would provide a transition between the Reflecting Pool and the Rainbow Pool as well as bracket a curvilinear commemorative wall designed to be the location for a Light of Freedom symbolizing the sacrifice and heroism of World War II. The curvilinear wall would have a niche in its center framing the view of the Lincoln Memorial, but at this western end of the National World War II Memorial, in contrast to the other three ends, there would not be a way out. On this subject St.Florian was adamant. "A memorial is not a traffic circle," he told the National Capital Planning Commission members, who had requested that he add a western entrance for the convenience of visitors. It was essential, St.Florian reminded the commissioners, to orchestrate the National World War II Memorial experience so that it had a sequence to it and visitors did not shortcut the transition they made from the Mall's pathways to the memorial's sacred ground.[22]

This time the reception to the memorial design concept from the two commissions was very different from what it had been in 1997. By the time the National Capital Planning Commission met, there were even petitions to its chairman, Harvey Gantt, from the House and Senate calling for "timely construction of the World War II Memorial" and asking for "favorable consideration of the modified design concept." The difference in tone between the 1997 and 1998 meetings was apparent even before the Commission of Fine Arts met on May 21. A week earlier Senator Bob Kerrey signaled his approval of the memorial by telling the press, "It's not obtrusive; it doesn't require any loss of trees or any loss at all of the vista. I'm not abandoning the fight but claiming victory." At the same time John Parsons of the National Park Service gave his agency's approval, observing of the new design concept, "It mitigates all the concerns we expressed," and Charles Atherton, the secretary of the Commission of Fine Arts, announced that he, too, saw "no major stumbling blocks" to the memorial's approval. "It should defuse some of the critics of the first design," he declared.[23]

At the May 21 meeting of the Commission of Fine Arts the same approving tone was present early on. Architect David Childs, a senior partner at Skidmore, Owings, and Merrill, who had chaired the National World War II Memorial Design Jury, testified that the new memorial had kept its "original concept" but become "gardenesque" as a result of the improvements to it, and landscape architect Laurie Olin, who also had served on the Design Jury, praised the memorial for providing a "landscape solution" that made use of "classic and timeless forms" to harmonize with its Mall setting. The result was that by the end of the meeting the chairman of the Commission of Fine Arts, J. Carter Brown, was able to announce that the commission "unanimously and enthusiastically endorses" the National World War II Memorial design concept, and in early July, by an eight-to-two vote, the National Capital Planning Commission gave its approval to the same design concept and issued a report declaring, "Staff is very pleased with the evolution of the design of the National World War II Memorial when compared to the original design concept."[24]

The laudatory language that the Commission of Fine Arts and the National Capital Planning Commission used in announcing their 1998 approval of St.Florian's second design concept did not, however, tell the whole story. Both commissions had a number of qualms that would affect the next stage in the memorial approval process, the development of a preliminary design, and each commission provided St.Florian with a wish list that specified the concerns it had. In a May 26, 1998, letter to the American Battle Monuments Commission, J. Carter Brown noted that although his Fine Arts Commission felt that many of the comments of those who spoke in opposition to the National World War II Memorial were "off the mark," the commission was worried that the memorial did not yet have "an artistic unity" that "adds up to more than the sum of its parts." Brown then went on to list fourteen items that the Fine Arts Commission believed needed more work. Only two of the items on Brown's list—the memorial's arches and its metal screens—were major, but the tone of Brown's letter to the American Battle Monuments Commission, while upbeat, remained serious. The members of the Fine Arts Commission, Brown went on to say, wanted him to remind the ABMC, "There is still a lot to be done." The National Capital Planning Commission in its July 9 report was equally specific and serious in categorizing its worries. "There is no central focusing element that effectively solidifies the total memorial experience," the commission announced, and then went on to say that the Light of Freedom needed to "be more clearly defined," the screens on the memorial stone walls made less "fussy," and the memorial plaza itself given a more "textured landscape."[25]

For Friedrich St.Florian, the criticism that the Commission of Fine Arts and the National Capital Planning Commission voiced while giving their approval to his design concept corresponded to many of his own worries, as back in Providence he set to work on his preliminary design for the National World War II Memorial. In making the memorial smaller, greener, and more transparent, St.Florian believed that his revisions had cost him some of the unity, particularly the tragic sense of war, that his original design had with its decapitated columns and hillside of white roses. "The problem was that the memorial lost its punch. It had become so gentle and so garden-like," St.Florian would later say. It was a concern that the American Battle Monuments Commission's Site and Design Committee also had as it made clear to St.Florian in a 1998 letter. The observation that went to the heart of what St.Florian was feeling at this time came, however, from an aging veteran who told him, "World War II was not a walk in the park." Without telling him what to do architecturally, the vet had described what St.Florian now saw as absent from his World War II Memorial. "There was no connection to the horror of war in it."[26]

As he prepared for meetings on May 20, 1999, before the Commission of Fine Arts and on June 3 before the National Capital Planning Commission, St.Florian saw the challenge that lay ahead as twofold: He must retain the transparency he had achieved with his revised design concept and at the same time find a way to ensure that the sacrifices World War II required of Americans at home and abroad were made palpable for those visiting his memorial, even if they did not know much about the history of the 1940s. It was, as St.Florian made clear in his 1999 testimony before the two commissions, an architectural balancing act.

To enhance the spaciousness of his design, which featured an open unblocked memorial plaza, St.Florian widened the approach to the plaza from the eastern side of West Potomac Park, where he placed his ceremonial entrance. That entrance was now 170 feet across, 25 feet wider than in the 1998 design concept. In addition, the ramp system, which carried visitors around the plaza, was pushed farther to the side, so that the center of the plaza was more spacious. The ramps were also made easier to use for anyone in a wheelchair or on foot; they were widened from 10 to 11 feet, and their slope was made gentler, which meant that they no longer required handrails.

The biggest changes in the memorial's preliminary design came, however, in the development of what now had become its dominant symbolic elements—its arches, its pillars, and its Sacred Precinct. The arches, which were criticized earlier by the Commission of Fine Arts for their heaviness, were now made less compact and more airy, going from 21 by 21 feet to 24 by 24 feet at their base and increasing in height from 36 feet to 41 feet from grade. The most significant change in the arches, however, was the result of a suggestion by Ray Kaskey, the sculptor on the memorial design team. Kaskey, who in the fall of 1998 had become much more involved in the memorial design process, came up with the idea of placing a baldacchino in each arch. Unlike a baldacchino in a church, which is traditionally a freestanding covered structure that is placed over an altar and is topped by a cross, Kaskey's baldacchino was totally secular and uncovered. It had the effect of transforming St.Florian's original arch into a structure in which the interior meaning was now as important as the exterior meaning. Kaskey's baldacchino featured four eagles, perched on four narrow bronze columns, holding in their beaks stainless steel ribbons with a bronze cladding from which a laurel wreath, the historical symbol for triumph in battle, was suspended. For anyone standing on the floor of the arch and looking through its oculus to the sky above, the result was a sight very different from that produced by a traditional, closed victory arch. The baldacchino within each arch now made the point that for America winning World War II was a matter of transcendent importance, not simply a question of defeating the enemy.

An equally significant development took place with regard to the stone arms adorned with metal grillwork that were part of the earlier design and that the National Capital Planning Commission had called "fussy." In the new design, these fifty-six arms, representing the states and territories, were transformed into fifty-six stone pillars, each 15 feet tall. "I wanted a pillar that I did not know a precedent for," St.Florian would say; what followed were pillars that each had an open slit in the center. Placed at 6-foot intervals around the plaza and moved farther back to the memorial's four interior corners, the pillars with their cut-out centers, allowed the Mall's north-south vista to remain unobstructed, but they also added their own interpretative meaning to the memorial. The open space in the middle of each pillar implicitly suggested, as St.Florian's original decapitated columns had, the tragic loss of life caused by war. Furthermore, the pillars reflected in an explicit way the war that was waged on America's home front: Attached to each pillar were alternating bronze oak and wheat wreaths, symbolizing, on the one hand, the military-industrial strength of the United States and, on the other hand, the role the United States, with its farms intact, played in helping to feed a hungry world during World War II.

The most dramatic change of all in St.Florian's preliminary design was reserved for the memorial's western side, now called the Sacred Precinct. In the design concept stage this area of the memorial had included waterfalls, a curvilinear wall with an inscription on it, and a vaguely defined Light of Freedom. But there was nothing truly special about it. Now, as St.Florian told the National Capital Planning Commission, the Sacred Precinct had been turned into the most meaningful part of the memorial. Its central element was a reminder of the war's dead and missing, a cenotaph adorned by a wreath. Then behind the cenotaph, rising up from the floor of the memorial, was a second reminder of the war's cost, a broken plane of basalt stone with a crater in its center. The dark, fissured stone with its crater was intended to reflect how brutal the "seismic upheaval" of the war had been, and in combination with the cenotaph, it constituted the tragic half of the Sacred Precinct. By contrast, the other two elements in the Sacred Precinct focused on the meaning of the victory won by America and its allies. In the center of the crater, St.Florian introduced a Light of Freedom that was designed to burn day and night and to reflect the triumph of light over darkness. Then directly behind the flame and the crater, he placed the curvilinear wall and waterfalls that in his earlier design marked the western edge of his memorial. In the new plans, the wall and the waterfalls continued to perform that function, but now their link to the Light of Freedom and cenotaph gave them a deeper symbolic importance. The wall with its inscription had become the background for the cenotaph, crater, and flame that lay before it.[27]

The reaction of both the Commission of Fine Arts and the National Capital Planning Commission to St.Florian's presentation of his preliminary design was very positive, with the Commission of Fine Arts approving the new design unanimously and the Planning Commission approving it by a nine-to-two vote. Chairman of the Commission of Fine Arts J. Carter Brown described the design as "extraordinarily improved" from what he had seen a year earlier, and in a May 25, 1999, letter to the National Park Service, Brown went on to observe that it was "an eloquent and effective statement worthy of the subject and site." The National Capital Planning Commission in its *Report to the National Park Service and American Battle Monuments Commission* used similar language, describing itself as "pleased with the results" of St.Florian's work and noting the degree to which the memorial's "major elements have been redesigned and refined."[28]

But the approval of the two commissions was again not without qualifications. In their testimony before the commissions, opponents of the memorial had complained about the number of architectural elements now filling the new Sacred Precinct, and the reports of both commissions focused on this area. J. Carter Brown, who thought the Sacred Precinct presented a "real opportunity for visual poetry," worried that with all the changes to it, this part of the memorial had too much going on. He thought that St.Florian's cenotaph competed for attention with the Light of Freedom and that the cenotaph might also be confused with an actual tomb by visitors to the memorial coming from Arlington Cemetery. "The Commission believes that the Sacred Precinct should be as severely simple as possible," Brown warned. By contrast, the National Capital Planning Commission was more terse in its observations about the Sacred Precinct. But in enumerating all the elements that now filled the precinct and by insisting that "this area still needs additional design," the National Capital Planning Commission made the same point as the Commission of Fine Arts. The Sacred Precinct would have to be made less cluttered by the time St.Florian submitted his final design.[29]

For St.Florian, the call from the two commissions that he do more work on the Sacred Precinct was not unexpected. As his memorial design had evolved, he had continually reworked crucial areas. His arches with the baldacchinos inside them were an example of such revision, and so were his hollowed-out pillars, which had first been decapitated stone columns. The Sacred Precinct was no different in its development, and the drawings that St.Florian did for this area—but did not bring to the Commission of Fine Arts or National Capital Planning Commission meetings—show him constantly experimenting. His Light of Freedom, for example, appears in his drawings both mounted on a raised base of its own and in an urn on top of the memorial's western wall, and in another drawing, instead of the cenotaph that the two commissions saw, a sculptural representation of a folded American flag appears in the center of the Sacred Precinct.

As he began work on his final design, the challenge for St.Florian was, as he put it, to remain loyal to his desire "to commemorate the sacrifices of the war at the western wall" and "to find a meaningful symbolic representation" for doing so. The problem with the symbols that he had presented to the Commission of Fine Arts and to the National Capital Planning Commission was not simply that they crowded each other but that they were also reminiscent of nearby Arlington National Cemetery and two very familiar icons—the eternal flame at President Kennedy's grave and the marble Tomb of the Unknowns.

Believing that the Sacred Precinct should be changed and finding a way to change it were two different matters, however, and it was not until the fall of 1999 that St.Florian finally had a breakthrough. The inspiration came, as his drawings show, in an unexpected way. St.Florian had been working on creating for the floor of the Sacred Precinct a Field of Honor that would consist of gold stars, reminiscent of the stars that families hung on banners in their windows during World War II to signify the death of a loved one. The problem was, as Haydn Williams observed in a conversation with St.Florian, having visitors to the National World War II Memorial walk on the stars contradicted the star's symbolism and made it seem as if one were stepping on the graves of the dead. The stars had to go some place else. But where? St.Florian, in consultation with the ABMC's World War II Memorial Site and Design Committee, solved the problem by elevating the stars to eye level and placing them on the Freedom Wall itself. But in placing the stars on the Freedom Wall, St.Florian did not just provide an answer to his star problem. He also answered the much greater problem of how to simplify the Sacred Precinct and make it less crowded. It was more than enough to have a 9-foot Freedom Wall with 4,000 gold stars, one for roughly every one hundred of the over 400,000 Americans who died in World War II, dominating the western side of the memorial. Nothing else was needed. All the other elements in the Sacred Precinct could be eliminated.[30]

When he appeared before the Commission of Fine Arts on July 20, 2000, and the National Capital Planning Commission on September 21, 2000, to present his final design, St.Florian did not, however, just focus on the changes that he had made to the Sacred Precinct. He also addressed the "refinements" that he had made in other areas of the memorial. His point to both commissions was that the memorial they were seeing in this third and last stage of the approval process was one that built upon the designs they had approved earlier. There was every reason for this memorial to seem familiar. The changes St.Florian and the design team had made were primarily intended to make the preliminary design of a year ago more focused and "unsparing."

What these refinements in architecture and landscape meant in practice, St.Florian went on to point out, was the following: The memorial's two arches had gone from 41 feet to 43 feet in order to make them more proportional, and the fountains at their bases had been enlarged and reshaped. A shaded garden area for contemplation had been added to the northwest corner of the site, and the grass panels on the eastern entranceway of the memorial had been enlarged. The primary elm walkways surrounding the memorial had been switched from asphalt to their historic brushed concrete. The waterfalls flanking the Freedom Wall had been strengthened by being simplified from three-tier to one-tier falls. The dedication stone of the memorial had been moved closer to the edge of the Rainbow Pool to provide more space for ceremonies. The inner openings of the memorial's fifty-six pillars had received a semicircular treatment to improve their transparency and appearance, and the classical guilloche motif on the balustrade linking these pillars had been changed to a rope motif in order to better symbolize the unity of the country during World War II.

St.Florian now believed that the big questions about the design of the National World War II Memorial—whether it fit its site and kept open the Mall's central vista—had at last been settled. "The Mall is the violin. We are providing the accompanying instruments," he assured the National Capital Planning Commission in concluding his testimony. The only addition of significance that St.Florian still wanted to keep open for consideration was a sculpture that would encompass a Light of Freedom (to be determined later, on the basis of a series of competitive submissions) for the reconstructed Rainbow Pool. With the Sacred Precinct now reduced to a single dominant element—a Freedom Wall with a Field of Stars—St.Florian believed that the National World War II Memorial could take on a central piece of sculpture without seeming too busy.[31]

For the opponents of the National World War II Memorial, St.Florian's assurance that his final design was based upon previously approved designs was the last thing they wanted to hear. When the site for the National World War II Memorial was being chosen in 1995, the memorial's opponents were badly organized, but after the unveiling of the memorial design in 1997, they became a significant force. They had come a long way from their meetings in the office of Senator Bob Kerrey, who along with his aide Michael Marinello, had helped organize early memorial opposition. After 1997 the National World War II Memorial opponents regularly appeared at the meetings of the Commission of Fine Arts and the National Capital Planning Commission and continually pressed their case on the op-ed pages of the nation's leading newspapers.

Now, with approval of the final design of the National World War II Memorial close at hand, the opponents were feeling desperate. At this point there was no reason for the opponents of the National World War II Memorial, who had become increasingly vocal with each new design submission, to hold back anything, and at the July 20 meeting of the Commission of Fine Arts, which lasted nearly six hours, and at the September 21 meeting of the National Capital Planning Commission, which lasted ten hours, they delivered testimony so damning of the memorial design that it left little room for thinking that they would ever reconcile themselves to the memorial unless it were completely redesigned. Architect Kent Cooper criticized the memorial for allowing the individual sacrifice it commemorated to be "swallowed by glitter." Judy Scott Feldman, the chairwoman of the National Coalition to Save Our Mall, described the memorial as being dominated by "increasingly imperial and triumphal" symbols. Washington, D.C., congressional delegate Eleanor Holmes Norton labeled the memorial a "confused set of half-baked notions," and former National Capital Planning Commission member Ann Loikaw concluded her testimony by dismissing the memorial as "a granite and marble Stonehenge that lacks any kind of celestial underpinnings."[32]

For the Commission of Fine Arts, which under the influence of J. Carter Brown, its chairman since 1971, had been supportive of the National World War II Memorial from the start, the criticism of the final design by its opponents had little effect. If anything, the opponents' rhetoric was off-putting to a commission trying to get a National World War II Memorial built. In a unanimous decision the members of the Commission of Fine Arts gave the final design their approval. It was a different story with the twelve-member National Capital Planning Commission, which, in contrast to the Commission of Fine Arts, consists of not only presidential appointees but appointees by the secretary of the interior, the secretary of defense, the Senate Committee on Governmental Affairs, the House Committee on Governmental Reform, the General Services Administration, as well as the mayor of Washington and the District of Columbia Council. A much more diverse group of individuals, the National Capital Planning Commission was not influenced by its chairman, Harvey Gantt, the way the Commission of Fine Arts was by J. Carter Brown. In the end, the National Capital Planning Commission approved the final design of the National World War II Memorial by a slim seven-to-five majority, with all four representatives of Washington plus presidential appointee Margaret Vanderhye casting no votes and making it clear how dissatisfied they were with the National World War II Memorial.[33]

In giving their approval to the final design, the two commissions still deferred certain decisions into the future. The detailing of the Field of Stars on the Freedom Wall, the memorial's night lighting, its inscriptions, the relief panels at the memorial's ceremonial east entrance would all be approved in the coming years by the ABMC commissioners appointed by President George W. Bush in August 2001, while the proposal for a Light of Freedom sculpture for the Rainbow Pool, despite a variety of submissions, including one from Frank Stella and another from Ray Kaskey, would be removed from active consideration. But even with these deferred decisions, by the fall of 2000 the battle over the National World War II Memorial at last seemed to have reached an end as far as its major architectural elements were concerned. By law, Secretary of the Interior Bruce Babbitt still needed to sign on to what the two commissions had approved, but in a Clinton administration supportive of the National World War II Memorial and reluctant, given the president's history with the draft, to take on the military, there was no question that Secretary of the Interior Babbitt would give his approval when it came time for him to make a decision on the final design of the memorial.[34]

J. Carter Brown's optimistic 1997 remark that St.Florian's National World War II Memorial design had a "certain inevitability" about it had not, it turned out, proven to be a predictor of the approval process that the memorial underwent between 1997 and 2000, but by the same token the approval battles had made a difference in the final architecture and its meaning. The fights over the National World War II Memorial's architecture had not been an empty exercise in wrangling. The diehard opponents of the memorial failed to carry the day, but their opposition to the memorial design had influenced its evolution. As George Hartman, the associate architect for the National World War II Memorial and a veteran of the Washington architecture scene, would later observe, "It has gone from too much architecture to about the right amount." Hartman was not being self-serving. Since 1997, the memorial's footprint had become smaller, its transparency greater, and with its Freedom Wall, its hollowed-out pillars, and the baldacchinos in its arches, the National World War II Memorial had acquired an elegiac quality that it did not have at the beginning of the approval process.[35]

In addition, the National World War II Memorial's final realization benefited enormously from the job done by Leo A Daly in coordinating the design and engineering elements of the memorial. In the media's coverage of the National World War II Memorial story, Leo A Daly did not get the kind of attention that Friedrich St.Florian as design architect did. But Daly's work, which included the firm's production of contract specifications and drawings, as well as a broad range of supervisory responsibilities, was crucial in making it possible for a highly complicated memorial design to be brought to completion as conceived.[36]

# 7

# ENDGAME

For the American Battle Monuments Commission, winning final design approval for the National World War II Memorial on September 21, 2000, was not the only good news as the fall began. The ABMC was now also able to look at its bank account and know that it was going to have enough money to build the National World War II Memorial the way it wanted without asking Congress for a handout.

That within the American Battle Monuments Commission there should have been, even for a short time, worry over fund-raising is hard to imagine today, given the more than $194 million the ABMC finally raised. But in the 1990s there was good reason for the ABMC to worry about getting the private contributions it needed and to fear falling victim to the financial problems that have plagued so many Washington monuments. By comparison with the Vietnam Veterans Memorial and the Korean War Veterans Memorial, the National World War II Memorial was going to be very expensive, and to make matters worse, a contemporary World War II memorial, the Battle of Normandy Foundation's Wall of Liberty, scheduled for construction on a 25-acre site near Utah Beach, was by 1994 in deep financial trouble, despite donations from World War II veterans and backing from John F. Kennedy's former press secretary, Pierre Salinger.[1]

When he took over as chairman of the American Battle Monuments Commission, retired army general Fred Woerner immediately recognized the financial challenge that building the National World War II Memorial presented. "The chief concern I had," he remembered thinking, "was not getting the site, not getting the design, not building the memorial. It was the money." Woerner's fears reflected the early assessment that he was given of the situation faced by the American Battle Monuments Commission. In the outline of a briefing he gave to the ABMC commissioners on September 29, 1994, on getting a National World War II Memorial built, Colonel Kevin Kelley, then the ABMC World War II Memorial Project officer, noted, "Money is a critical factor in this process; $20 million is an initial estimate, but that is by no means set in concrete. The actual amount could be more or less."

Jess Hay, a member of the National World War II Memorial Advisory Board and finance chairman for the Democratic Party from 1977 to 1979, recalls that the information he and others were initially given was anything but encouraging and that there were a "number of voices" on both the World War II Memorial Advisory Board and the American Battle Monuments Commission who felt that given the difficulty of raising money for the Korean War and Vietnam War veterans memorials, it was appropriate to think of a World War II memorial in the cost range of $25–30 million. "The first consultant who was retained by the Advisory Board did a survey across the country and came back with the conclusion that the maximum that could be raised was $35 million," Hay remembers. In addition, as late as the mid-1990s, the American Battle Monuments Commission was not structured to carry on a major fund-raising campaign. It did not have a chief fund-raiser or staff equal to the task, and until the fall of 1996, it had not even signed a contract with Burson-Marsteller, the public relations and advertising firm that would do the public service advertisements for the National World War II Memorial Campaign.[2]

Only in 1997 did the American Battle Monuments Commission begin to make the moves that finally allowed it to mount a successful fund drive for the National World War II Memorial. And only after

1997 did it become clear that within the American Battle Monuments Commission and the World War II Memorial Advisory Board, those such as Jess Hay, Helen Fagin, Haydn Williams, and former New York governor Hugh Carey, who as early as spring 1995 felt a campaign closer to $100 million, the estimated cost of replicating the Lincoln Memorial, was what the ABMC should be aiming for, had made an accurate assessment of the money that could be raised for a National World War II Memorial.

In 1997 the ABMC's first key step in putting itself in position to raise $100 million was persuading Bob Dole to accept the national chairmanship of the National World War II Memorial Campaign. At the January 17, 1997, unveiling of the National World War II Memorial at the White House, Dole, who was given a Medal of Freedom at the unveiling by President Clinton, expressed his interest in getting involved in the National World War II Memorial Campaign when he was approached by the American Battle Monuments Commission. But it was not until the spring, after he had returned from a Florida vacation and had more discussions with the ABMC and its secretary, retired U.S. Army Major General John Herrling, that Dole finally made the commitment. It was a move that gave the National World War II Memorial Campaign immediate visibility, and on March 19, when Dole announced that he was leading a fund drive to raise $100 million, the National World War II Memorial Campaign had its true beginning.[3]

Dole knew, however, that even with his political connections, he did not have the ties to the corporate world that were needed to raise $100 million, and his next step was to recruit Federal Express CEO Fred Smith to serve as co-chairman of the National World War II Memorial Campaign. Smith, a Vietnam veteran, whose father and three uncles had fought in World War II, was someone who took pride in having a "very strong family connection with World War II," and he was exactly the right choice for the campaign. Smith and Dole had known each other for years, having been introduced by former Tennessee Senator Howard Baker, and it did not take Smith long to make up his mind to serve as co-chairman of the National World War II Memorial Campaign.[4]

With Dole and Smith firmly committed to the World War II Memorial Campaign, the American Battle Monuments Commission then made a third dramatic move to acquire outside help. The commission asked Tom Hanks to become its official public spokesman. The AMBC had originally thought it should draw its spokesman from the World War II generation and in 1997 had carried on discussions that did not work out with two World War II–era newsmen, Walter Cronkite and David Brinkley. But in 1998 with the release of Steven Spielberg's hit film *Saving Private Ryan,* the ABMC's belief that it had to have a spokesman from the World War II years changed. Hanks's convincing performance immediately made him the ideal cross-generational representative for anything to do with the National World War II Memorial, and when John Herrling wrote Hanks about becoming spokesman for the National World War II Memorial Campaign, Hanks's answer was immediate and positive. Later, when Bob Dole called him, Hanks was equally responsive. Their conversation, as Dole recalls it, was very short. "I'm your man. What do you want me to do?" Hanks replied before Dole could begin the pitch that he thought Hanks would need to commit himself to working on the National World War II Memorial Campaign.[5]

The American Battle Monuments Commission now had commitments from the three figures who would become the public face of the National World War II Memorial Campaign, and by the end of 1998, the ABMC was able to complete a series of equally crucial internal moves, the most important of which was hiring a highly experienced professional fund-raiser, James Aylward, as executive director of the National World War II Memorial Project. Aylward recognized the problems that he was up against. In contrast to a college with an alumni base or a museum with art patrons, the tax-supported American Battle Monuments Commission did not have donors who had been contributing to it year in and year out. The ABMC had to build up public awareness of the National World War II Memorial before it could hope to succeed in raising $100 million or more. It was a task for which Aylward, who knew the ins and outs of corporate giving, was well suited, and in 1998 he and the American Battle Monuments Commission were given a boost not only by the popularity of *Saving Private Ryan* but by the best-seller status of NBC News anchor Tom Brokaw's book of profiles of World War II vets, *The Greatest Generation.* Suddenly World War II was part of the public consciousness in a way that it had not been in either 1994 for the fiftieth anniversary of D-Day or 1995 for the fiftieth anniversary of the end of the war.[6]

The potential appeal of a well-run National World War II Memorial Campaign became evident early in 1999, when on January 10, Tom Hanks made an appearance on the nationally televised program *People's Choice Awards* to accept an award for favorite motion picture actor. Hanks used his acceptance speech to promote the National World War II Memorial as "a place where we can honor forever a generation that defined an era and preserved our way of life" and asked viewers to call the National World War II Memorial's 800 number and pledge their contributions. It was a speech that the American Battle Monuments Commission had no idea was coming, and within one hour 19,000 calls swamped the ABMC's National World War II Memorial phone banks, transforming what up until then had been a minor part of the National World War II Memorial Campaign into a vital part of it that two years later had taken in more than 400,000 calls.[7]

As it evolved, the American Battle Monument Commission's National World War II Memorial Campaign was, however, anything but hit or miss in practice. The reaction to Tom Hanks's *People's Choice Awards* speech may have caught the ABMC by surprise, but the ABMC's radio, print, and television public service advertising campaign featuring Hanks was meticulously organized by the communications firm Burson-Marsteller, and the campaign had the personal backing of Advertising Hall of Fame legend Ed Ney, a World War II navy veteran, then both chairman of Burson-Marsteller's worldwide board of advisors and honorary chairman and director of the Ad Council, the public service advertising organization established in 1942 to rally support for World War II. At the heart of the public service advertising campaign were three TV spots, shot by director Joe Pytka, that featured Hanks reminding viewers that "incredibly there is still no national memorial" to honor the World War II generation. Concluding with the tagline, "It's time to say thank you," the Hanks ads, distributed by the Ad Council, ran for two years and reached millions of households in a campaign that turned out to be a bargain. The American Battle Monuments Commission paid the Ad Council $847,000 and Burson-Marsteller $373,000 for their work, and for this investment of $1,220,000, the ABMC got back an estimated $90 million in media-donated free airtime and print space.[8]

An equally systematic approach was taken to organize veteran support by John "Skip" Shannon, a Vietnam veteran and retired lieutenant colonel, who went to work for the American Battle Monuments Commission in 1997. Shannon not only went to the groups, the American Legion and Veterans of Foreign Wars, for which the ABMC knew the National World War II Memorial would have appeal, but he also met with the state directors of veterans affairs across the country and tapped into their ability to reach out to state legislatures for contributions. The result was a campaign in which the state legislatures contributed a dollar—and sometimes more—to the National World War II Memorial for each veteran from their state who fought in World War II. As for Bob Dole and Fred Smith, their calls to CEOs around the country reflected the most tightly organized campaign of all those that the American Battle Monuments Commission undertook to win support for the National World War II Memorial. Long before Dole and Smith ever made their calls, the ABMC staffers not only prepared the way by contacting company officials but also researched the kinds of charity donations a company had made in the past. Dole and Smith knew which calls were likely to bear fruit long before they made them, and when they did encounter resistance, they were a formidable pair. A CEO who made the mistake of telling Dole that giving to the National World War II Memorial did not fit into his company's plans found that on the other end of the line he had a veteran and former presidential candidate willing to remind him, "Well, World War II didn't fit my plans or sixteen million other plans, but because we were there, you're making a lot of money."⁹

The results bear out how successful the American Battle Monuments Commission's fund-raising strategy was. From 1993 to 1998 the ABMC brought in $36.2 million, $26.4 million from its own fund-raising efforts and $9.8 million from the government. But between 1998 and 2003, the year the American Battle Monuments Commission's revenues climbed to $194.1 million, the ABMC took in an astonishing $157.9 million, with most of that money coming during three peak fund-raising years. In 1999, the year the Tom Hanks "It's time to say thank you" ads debuted, the ABMC took in $42.2 million. In 2000, the figure was a whopping $68.8 million, and in 2001, it was $28.4 million, with $22.4 million of that coming from the ABMC's fund-raising and an additional $6 million coming from government revenues.¹⁰

The big contributors made donations that guaranteed a solid base for the ABMC's fund-raising efforts. Wal-Mart donated $14,751,360; the Veterans of Foreign Wars, $6,031,349; the American Legion, $4,579,783; SBC Corporation, $3 million; the National Funeral Directors Association $2,471,864; and Federal Express, the Lilly Foundation, and the Commonwealth of Pennsylvania each contributed $2 million. But equally revealing was the breadth of the financial support for the National World War II Memorial. Although on a percentage basis, corporations were predictably the largest contributors to the National World War II Memorial Campaign, accounting for 27.2 percent of all funds collected, they were far from the whole story. Direct mail to individuals accounted for 22.3 percent of all donations, and contributions from grassroots fund-raising and the Internet/1-800 number together topped 9 percent, leading to widespread personal involvement that generated enormous attention, as in the highly publicized story of Zane Fayos, a ten-year-old schoolboy who sent the National World War II Memorial a check for $195. Vets gave at their posts as well as in response to direct-mail solicitations. Wal-Mart customers gave through fund drives held at local stores, and Waffle House diners gave at the end of a meal when they paid their checks. For the American Battle Monuments

Commission, which was now also able to set aside some of the money it had raised to help with the future maintenance of the National World War II Memorial, the result was not only a greater-than-expected number of contributors but a savings in the outreach programs that the ABMC had to do, which allowed the ABMC to limit its fund-raising and administrative expenses to 22 percent of the total funds received.[11]

Resolution of the design and money problems surrounding the National World War II Memorial did not, however, put the American Battle Monuments Commission in a position in which all it had to worry about in the fall of 2000 was actually getting the memorial built. The fall of 2000 marked the start of a bitter endgame in which new attacks on the National World War II Memorial came close to delaying its construction for years. Only after Congress and the courts became involved were these threats to the National World War II Memorial defused.

The clearest indication of the trouble that lay ahead for the American Battle Monuments Commission was reflected in the escalation of criticism in 2000 and 2001 during the period before and after the Commission of Fine Arts and the National Capital Planning Commission gave their final design approval. To be sure, the National World War II Memorial did at this time have a number of important advocates, including J. Carter Brown and Harry Robinson III, the chairman and vice chairman of the Commission of Fine Arts, who both spoke out in support of the memorial.[12]

On July 15, 2000, in an article titled "A Fitting Memorial in Every Way," *Washington Post* architecture critic Benjamin Forgey came out in favor of the memorial, saying it "extends the Mall's references and enriches its meanings," and the next day the *Washington Post,* which in 1997 had been highly critical of the World War II Memorial, added its support with an editorial (based in part upon a viewing of a model of the National World War II Memorial at the Washington office of Leo A Daly, where a briefing was conducted by Friedrich St.Florian and Haydn Williams) praising the memorial for respecting the Mall's sight lines and "creating a significant and evocative space of its own." A few months later, on the day the National Capital Planning Commission made its final decision on the National World War II Memorial, Witold Rybczynski, the widely read architecture historian and author of *Perfect House* and *A Clearing in the Distance: Frederick Law Olmsted and America in the Nineteenth Century,* threw his support to the memorial in a *Wall Street Journal* article in which he concluded, "It will be a classic shrine: earnest, unabashedly patriotic, and yes, slightly old-fashioned." The following spring, as the battle over the National World War II Memorial became still more heated, Robert Campbell, the architecture critic of the *Boston Globe,* who had been on the Architect-Engineer Evaluation Board for the World War II Memorial design competition, entered the fray by attacking what he called the "distortions" surrounding the memorial that were advanced by the memorial's opponents. There was in this period even praise for the memorial from a powerful former critic. In 1997 Richard Longstreth, the editor of *The Mall in Washington, 1791–1991* and one of the best-known authorities on Washington architecture, had written National Capital Planning Commission Chairman Harvey Gantt a letter saying that the proposed World War II Memorial would "hideously violate" the order of the Mall. But three years later, after he had seen models of St.Florian's final design of the memorial, Longstreth reversed himself, and in an op-ed (intended for the *Washington Post* but never published by the paper) that he made available to the American Battle Monuments Commission, Longstreth observed of the revised National World War II Memorial and its relationship to the Mall, "It holds great potential to be a magnificent addition that ranks high among commemorative monuments."[13]

The problem with the praise that the National World War II Memorial won in this period was that time and again it was overshadowed by the criticism that appeared in a number of leading papers and journals. In a letter she wrote to Haydn Williams in 1997, former *New York Times* architecture critic Ada Louise Huxtable, who sat on the National World War II Memorial Design Jury, observed of the initial opposition to the memorial, "In situations like this, criticism can turn into opposition for its own sake, taking on a life of its own, burying reason and good will entirely." Three years later, counter-criticism like Huxtable's had a hard time gaining center stage, and the result was that the National World War II Memorial took a bashing in some of the country's most prestigious journals and papers.[14]

The *New York Times,* which in 1997 opposed the memorial with an editorial titled, "Hallowed Ground in Jeopardy," led the critical charge in 2000 with a "Don't Mar the Mall" editorial, in which it observed of St.Florian's design, "The latest version suffers from the same fundamental defects that led this page to oppose a slightly more grandiose version in 1997." In 2001, *Times* art critic Michael Kimmelman continued the attack with an essay, "Turning Memory into Travesty," in which he dismissed the National World War II Memorial as a "lousy work of modern art," and a few months later, *Times* architecture critic Herbert Muschamp followed up Kimmelman's essay with a front-page article, "New War Memorial Is a Shrine to Sentiment." In a word play upon President Dwight Eisenhower's famous description of America's "military-industrial complex," Muschamp panned the memorial as "a monument to the military-entertainment industry complex."[15]

In the *New Yorker,* former *New York Times* architecture critic Paul Goldberger was equally harsh, using a "Talk of the Town" column to describe the National World War II Memorial as "at once fussy and desolate," and in the *Washington Post,* columnist Jonathan Yardley, an outspoken opponent of the memorial, labeled the final design "pompous and ponderous," insisting that the World War II veterans "deserve better." On the West Coast the memorial also got a rough reception. The *Los Angeles Times,* which opposed the memorial with an editorial titled, "Wrong Thing, Wrong Place," gave its critics all the space they needed to trash the memorial. On the same day that the paper editorialized against the memorial, in a long accompanying article *L.A. Times* art critic Christopher Knight attacked the memorial and its builders for "despoiling one of the most powerful public spaces in America," and two months later in another lengthy article, *L.A. Times* architecture critic Nicolai Ouroussoff outdid Knight, saying of the memorial, "The degree of this disaster cannot be overstated." During this period even journals that rarely agreed on anything found themselves agreeing on their dislike of the National World War II Memorial. In the progressive *Nation* the memorial was a "monstrosity." In the skeptically liberal *New Republic* it was a product of an "ultracautious bureaucratic process." In the conservative *Weekly Standard* it was an example of "ersatz classicism."[16]

Behind these escalating attacks on the National World War II Memorial during 2000 and 2001 was no single, unifying idea so much as a series of widely varying ideas, linked by the belief that allowing the memorial to be built as planned was a grievous mistake. In their opposition to the memorial, a number of critics returned to the issue, formally settled in 1995, that building the memorial at the Rainbow Pool site was a mistake. Abandoning the notion that the memorial, now greatly reduced in size, would actually block the vista between the Washington Monument and the Lincoln Memorial, the critics took up a much subtler idea: namely, that just placing the World War II Memorial at the Rainbow Pool would adversely affect the memorials around it. "Monuments—especially ones with a high emotional quotient—don't do well cheek by jowl," Paul Goldberger observed in the *New Yorker* before going on to criticize the National World War II Memorial for not giving the memorials around it enough breathing space. In the *New York Times* Michael Kimmelman made the same point, then went one step farther by asserting that the improper spacing of the National World War II Memorial was a historical as well as an aesthetic intrusion. "The major problem with putting the memorial on the Mall," Kimmelman wrote, "is that it disrupts the link between monuments dedicated to the leaders of the two defining events in the nation's history: the Revolution and the Civil War." A "glorious open space" was being sacrificed for a memorial that was "insufficiently meaningful" to appear on the Mall.[17]

Although much of the criticism focused on the siting of the memorial, even more faultfinding was heaped on the design of the National World War II Memorial. Three separate complaints took center stage. The first complaint charged that as it evolved, the design of the National World War II Memorial had become too self-effacing. The memorial needed to be put in a place where, as an editorial in *USA*

*Today* noted, it can be "freed from the need to minimize itself." It was an idea that architect Robert Ivy explored in much more detail in *Architectural Record,* where he observed that the Mall made certain demands of anything built on it. "Unless the memorial rises to a heroic level, it will only distract from the ensemble of earth and sky," Ivy wrote. A year later in a *Weekly Standard* essay, Catesby Leigh carried Ivy's idea to its logical conclusion when he wrote that the National World War II Memorial was too modest for its own good. "It fears to intrude; it wants to be a monument without imposing on the existing landscape," Leigh insisted.[18]

The second major design complaint went in the opposite direction from the first. It charged that the National World War II Memorial had become too traditional during the long approval process and had lost touch with the modern world in which it was being built. At the heart of this complaint was the notion that especially by comparison with Maya Lin's Vietnam Veterans Memorial, the World War II Memorial was an inferior monument, which had avoided risk by sticking with a time-honored modern, or stripped, classicism. In his front-page *New York Times* article Herbert Muschamp took up this position when, after speaking of three architects, I. M. Pei, James Ingo Freed, and Maya Lin, who he believed had successfully challenged the status quo in postwar Washington, he characterized the National World War II Memorial as an example of "the hazard of relying on period styles to evoke memories of past events." The result, Muschamp concluded, was a memorial that amounted to a sentimental "period style" project, about which the best that could be said was that it was "well-designed propaganda."[19]

The third design complaint about the National World War II Memorial was, by contrast, very different from the other two in the nature of the criticism it leveled. This complaint carried with it the kind of moral weight that Eleanor Holmes Norton earlier introduced into the memorial debate when she argued that placing a war memorial at the Rainbow Pool undermined the historical civil rights events associated with the Lincoln Memorial. The third design complaint charged that the National World War II Memorial was in essence anti-American; that is, it imitated the fascist architecture of Nazi Germany and violated the values for which America had fought World War II. The argument was one that, given Friedrich St.Florian's Austrian birth and Germanic accent, often seemed like nothing so much as a architectural McCarthyism. But despite this taint, the analogy with Hitler architect Albert Speer that Deborah Dietsch earlier made in an *Architecture* magazine editorial was still powerful in 2000 and 2001. The analogy could be made casually, as Paul Goldberger did when he referred to the arches of the National World War II Memorial as "watered-down Albert Speer." The analogy could be made sardonically, as Michael Kimmelman did when he wrote that "even those who aren't reminded of Hitler's favorite architect when they look at the design" will find it sterile. Or the analogy could be made very soberly, as Nicolai Ouroussoff did in the *Los Angeles Times,* when he observed that the stripped-down neoclassicism and geometry of the National World War II Memorial "unwittingly recall the architecture of 1930s-era fascism." Whatever form the analogy took did not seem to matter. It always garnered enormous attention and even provoked the normally reticent Friedrich St.Florian to complain to a *New York Times* reporter, "This is quite a deliberate attack and clearly the most hurtful for me personally because I'm Austrian born."[20]

There were holes—often big ones—in these attacks on the National World War II Memorial. To begin with, the decision to place the National World War II Memorial at the Rainbow Pool was far from an assault on a popular Mall site. It was a way of a transforming a rundown, much-ignored Mall site into one that now framed the vista between the Washington Monument and Lincoln Memorial and became an important destination in its own right. Equally important, when it came to location, it was difficult to think of another place on the Mall that so clearly made the link between World War II, the Revolutionary War, and the Civil War as periods when America's very existence as a democracy was in jeopardy. As architect Hugh Hardy, who served on both the Design Jury and the Architect-Engineer Evaluation Board, noted, keeping the National World War II Memorial off the central spine of the

Mall would have been the equivalent of saying that instead of having continuity, the story of America ended in the mid-nineteenth century.[21]

The same kind of case could also be made in defense of the design of the National World War II Memorial. The charge that because the memorial was modest, it was not equal to the war it represented was hard to fathom, especially when the charge was made by those who had initially criticized the memorial for being too intrusive. A small memorial, such as Augustus Saint-Gaudens's nineteenth-century bronze relief of Civil War hero Robert Gould Shaw and his black troops marching into battle, has never been considered inadequate because it occupies only a fraction of the Boston Common, and on the Mall, Maya Lin's Vietnam Veterans Memorial has been widely praised for being, in Paul Goldberger's words, "respectfully invisible from a distance" and by virtue of such modesty compelling when viewed close up.[22]

By the same logic, it was difficult to figure out why the decision to design the National World War II Memorial by employing a modern classical style borrowed from the past was so intensely criticized. The battle was reminiscent of the one that took place in the 1930s when the modernists attacked neoclassical architect John Russell Pope for his Pantheon-inspired Jefferson Memorial. Now, as then, critics seemed to ignore the degree to which classicism is the architectural language at the center of the Mall, making continuity an integral issue for any architect who builds there.[23]

Finally and most seriously, there was the charge that the World War II Memorial design was reminiscent of the Nazi architecture of Albert Speer. Helen Fagin, a Holocaust survivor, a member of the World War II Memorial Site and Design Committee, and someone with extraordinary sensitivity in this area, angrily disputed the political basis of this charge from the time it first surfaced, insisting the comparison was "really hitting below the belt." But the fascism charge was also weak on purely architectural grounds. In terms of scale there was nothing fascistic or even imperial about St. Florian's memorial. His arches, said by critics to resemble triumphal arches built for conquering armies, were the last thing a Napoleon or a Hitler would want. With a baldacchino inside each, the arches encourage contemplation, not exultation, on the part of anybody entering them, and by virtue of a base that is just over 23 feet on each side, the arches can accommodate only a handful of people at a time, not a marching army.

At 43 feet in height, the arches are not only dwarfed by the towering elms around them but are one-fourth the height of France's Arc de Triomphe (164 feet high and 148 feet wide) and one-eighth the height of the massive 325-foot-high and 285-foot-wide Triumphal Arch that Albert Speer proposed building for Hitler in Berlin. The fascist analogy also failed at a deeper historical level, as Richard Striner, a history professor at Washington College in Maryland and co-author of the 1984 Smithsonian Institution Press study, *Washington Deco,* noted in a heated exchange of letters (which did not remain private) with Judy Scott Feldman during 1999, when both were members of the influential Committee of 100 on the Federal City, a Washington architectural and planning watchdog group devoted to making sure the district remained true to the famous turn-of-the-century McMillan Plan. To suggest that the National World War II Memorial was fascistic, Striner argued, was to adopt a very myopic perspective. The fascist comparison ignored the degree to which modern or stripped classicism was a worldwide, rather than just a German, phenomenon. Modern classicism was at the heart of the architectural scene on both sides of the Atlantic during the 1930s, particularly in liberal, New Deal Washington, D.C., where, with the completion of Paul Cret's Folger Shakespeare Library and Federal Reserve Board Building and Waddy B. Wood's Department of Interior, stripped classicism was embodied in some of the city's most important public buildings.[24]

For the opponents of the National World War II Memorial, the flaws in their arguments were not nearly so important as the support that their arguments won them. As a result of the help they got from those sympathetic to them in the media and in the architecture community, plus the publicity generated by thirty-second ads of their own, which ran briefly on network television, the memorial opponents found they did not have to stay on the defensive when it came to the National World War II

Memorial endgame, even though the approval process was seemingly over by the fall of 2000. As the politically conservative columnist Charles Krauthammer observed in a *Washington Post* op-ed about the challenges facing the National World War II Memorial opposition in 2000, "Some causes are hopeless and yet still worth pursuing to the bitter end."[25]

At the National Capital Planning Commission meeting of September 21, 2000, Judy Scott Feldman, faced with the likelihood that at the end of the day the National Capital Planning Commission would join the Commission of Fine Arts in approving the final design, gave notice in her testimony of how the key battles would be fought in the post-approval period. Referring back to a letter that she had sent both the National Capital Planning Commission and the Commission of Fine Arts a week earlier, Feldman spoke of the "legal ramifications" of the National World War II Memorial receiving final approval from these agencies. It was a threat of court action but hardly an idle one. Feldman, a former professor of art history, had initially gotten involved in the National World War II Memorial battle by working with the Committee of 100, but over time she had become the best-known, as well as the most media-savvy, memorial critic, consistently arguing that although the World War II veterans deserved a memorial, this particular memorial and its proposed site were all wrong. By September 2000, Feldman was speaking out as a member of the National Coalition to Save Our Mall, the group she had helped found and would, as chair and president, build into a 1,500-member, tax-exempt organization with a 7-member board of directors and, thanks to a $100,000 grant from the Nason Foundation of Cleveland, a solid financial base.[26]

Feldman had always believed that the National World War II Memorial approval process had been conducted without sufficient regard to what the law said could and could not be done on the Mall, and in the summer of 2000, her doubts about the fairness of the memorial approval process were fueled by two incidents. The first incident involved the delayed release by the National Park Service of two 1999 studies, a *Cultural Landscape Report* on West Potomac Park and the Lincoln Memorial grounds and a *Revised National Historic Places Nomina-*

*tion* for East and West Potomac Parks. The studies, which Feldman had not been able to obtain until July, 2000, declared that the Reflecting Pool and Rainbow Pool were "contributing features to the historic landscape" of the Lincoln Memorial, and in Feldman's eyes proved that locating the National World War II Memorial at the Rainbow Pool was a violation of the 1986 Commemorative Works Act requirement that a memorial be built in such a way as to not encroach upon an already existing memorial.

Whether building on the grounds of the Lincoln Memorial was the equivalent of encroaching on the Lincoln Memorial itself, as Feldman claimed, was questionable, but what was not questionable was the problem the delayed release of the two studies caused. In his statements to the press, John Parsons of the National Park Service only made matters worse in the explanations he gave. At times Parsons seemed unmindful of how the delayed release of the reports might be taken. "I guess I just didn't place that much importance on it," he told *USA Today.* At other times he appeared deeply aware of the reports' implications. "I know it looks strange having these documents come out just before the hearing," he told the *Washington Post.* And at still other times Parsons went out of his way to downplay the significance of the Rainbow Pool, insisting, "It is not dedicated to any individual or event."[27]

A second incident that arose at this time and also raised questions about whether environmental law had been properly followed was no less complicated. This incident involved the Advisory Council on Historic Preservation, a federal agency that under the National Historic Preservation Act is authorized to review federal projects with regard to historic preservation issues. On July 25, 2000, John Fowler, the executive director of the Advisory Council on Historic Preservation wrote Bruce Babbitt, the secretary of the Department of the Interior, that the Advisory Council had been given such short notice on participating in consultations on the National World War II Memorial that it could not do so and still "be productive." The Advisory Council would therefore only provide comments on the National World War II Memorial to the National Park Service.

Whether the Advisory Council on Historic Preservation had really been given the short notice it claimed was, as with the implications of the National Park Service studies, open to question. The American Battle Monuments Commission certainly believed that the Advisory Council on Historic Preservation was being less than candid on the short-notice question, and in a letter to the Advisory Council, Haydn Williams of the ABMC angrily noted that what the council found objectionable about the National World War II Memorial in 2000 was "not significantly different" from what the council "commented favorably upon" years before. Certainly, after years of highly publicized hearings on the site and design of the National World War II Memorial, the Advisory Council's assertion that it never had a real chance to make its views known was hard to accept. A September 18, 1997, letter from the Advisory Council to the National Park Service reveals that it declined to review the National World War II Memorial while the memorial was undergoing design changes, and a June 5, 1998, letter from the Advisory Council to the American Battle Monuments Commission shows that it thanked the ABMC for an "informative briefing" and scheduled another ABMC briefing for a June 25, 1998, Advisory Council meeting at Mount Vernon.

But whatever the truth was, given the Advisory Council on Historic Preservation's interpretation of events, it was clear that the legal issues surrounding its claim were not going away any time soon. Indeed, on September 5, 2000, the stakes got higher when, following an August 28 meeting devoted to the National World War II Memorial, Cathryn Slater, the chairwoman of the Advisory Council on Historic Preservation, wrote to the Department of Interior again complaining about a lack of "early consultation" with the National Park Service and declaring that the council believed that St. Florian's proposed National World War II Memorial would have "serious and unresolved adverse effects" on the historic character of the Mall. The *Washington Post* had no doubts about how potentially serious the Advisory Council claim was, and two days later the *Post* began its story on Slater's letter to the Department of the Interior by observing, "The Advisory Council on

Historic Preservation slammed the controversial World War II Memorial in an official report."²⁸

For the opponents of the National World War II Memorial, the question that remained was, Did complaints like these have the power to undo the final site and design approval given to the National World War II Memorial? There was only one way to find out, and on October 2, 2000, the National Coalition to Save Our Mall, the World War II Veterans to Save the Mall, the Committee of 100 on the Federal City, and the D.C. Preservation League filed suit in the United States District Court in Washington, D.C., against Bruce Babbitt in his official capacity as secretary of the Department of the Interior, the Department of the Interior, Robert Stanton in his official capacity as director of the National Park Service, J. Carter Brown in his official capacity as chairman of the Commission of Fine Arts, Harvey Gantt in his official capacity as chairman of the National Capital Planning Commission, the National Capital Planning Commission, and the American Battle Monuments Commission.²⁹

The six-count suit by the opponents of the National World War II Memorial was filed by Andrea Ferster, an experienced historic preservation attorney in solo practice in her own Washington public interest law firm, with clients that included the Rails-to-Trails Conservancy and the National Trust for Historic Preservation. In the suit, *National Coalition to Save Our Mall, et al. v. Bruce Babbitt, Secretary of the Interior, et al.*, the defendants were charged with violating provisions of the Commemorative Works Act, the National Environmental Policy Act, the National Historic Preservation Act, and the Federal Advisory Committee Act. The plaintiffs asked for declaratory and injunctive relief that would prevent construction of the National World War II Memorial until such time as there was compliance with the laws they charged had been violated.³⁰

For anyone familiar with the battles that had been raging over the National World War II Memorial, there were no surprises in the long list of specific accusations brought against the defendants. The suit repeated charges that the memorial opponents had been making for years and concluded, "The design of the World War II Memorial, as approved by Defendants, will encroach upon the grounds of the Lincoln Memorial and obstruct the important axial vista from the steps of the Lincoln Memorial across the length of the Reflecting Pool and the Rainbow Pool to the Washington Monument, both of which are important parts of existing commemorative works."[31]

How the District Court would view these charges was the great unknown at this point. It was easy, for example, to imagine the District Court deciding that a memorial 6 feet below grade with its most important features well to the side of the Mall's central axis would not in fact block the vista between the Lincoln Memorial and the Washington Monument. But given the host of charges the suit leveled, it was also easy to imagine that some might stick. In any case, it was clear that although the American Battle Monuments Commission had gone through a lengthy approval process, it still had significant issues to resolve. The ABMC was not going to be able to make up for lost time and throw all its energies into the construction phase of the National World War II Memorial, as it had anticipated. When asked by a reporter how long she thought it might take to resolve the suit, Andrea Ferster replied, "The process could take several months to several years." There was no public statement on how long litigation might take from the U.S. Department of Justice, which in its December 15 answer to the complaint, denied that the plaintiffs were entitled to the relief they requested. But years later, William Aileo, the counsel for the American Battle Monuments Commission, would look back and recall that despite being confident that that ABMC would win in court, he worried about the prospect of delay and what it would mean for the aging veterans of World War II. "We were well aware," Aileo would say, "of how long litigation can take, and this would have taken a substantial amount of time, eighteen months at the shortest."[32]

A month later the American Battle Monuments Commission's focus was on a different matter—the long-awaited groundbreaking ceremony for the National World War II Memorial. Five years earlier the site dedication ceremony had taken place on a cold and rainy November 11, but on this Veterans Day the sunny and blustery weather was perfect, and everything the American Battle Monuments Commission had scheduled for the day—including the flight of Challenger, a trained bald eagle who was released to fly over the crowd during the ceremony—came off as planned. The ABMC was able to announce that it had more than met its fund-raising goals and in its official brochure listed a host of sponsors ranging from Wal-Mart to Major League Baseball.[33]

Even the speeches that highlighted the afternoon's official ceremony were gripping. Bob Dole described how his World War II generation was moving from "the shade to the shadows" and needed the National World War II Memorial built now before none of them was around "to bear witness to our part in history's greatest conflict." Tom Hanks, rather than giving a talk of his own, read a 1943 column by war correspondent Ernie Pyle on the death of an army captain very much like the captain Hanks played in *Saving Private Ryan*. Luther Smith, one of the last surviving Tuskegee Airmen, told the story of the crash of his P-51 Mustang over Germany and the months he spent in Stalag 18A prison camp. And President Clinton, who had spoken at both the 1995 dedication of the National World War II Memorial site and the 1997 unveiling of the winning memorial design, quoted remarks he had made in 1994 at Normandy on the fiftieth anniversary of D-Day. "We are the children of your sacrifice," he told the veterans in the crowd, "and we thank you forever."[34]

There was, however, no ignoring the lawsuit that threatened to block the construction of the National World War II Memorial. Rather than risk being served with an injunction if it scheduled actual digging on the Mall, the American Battle Monuments Commission had played it safe, wanting to make sure its groundbreaking ceremony was not delayed for the thousands of World War II veterans expected to attend. When it came time for officials to begin the groundbreaking itself, what they stuck their shovels into was a 100-foot-long box filled with dirt that the ABMC had had trucked in. The irony of the event did not escape notice in the press. Neil Feldman, the husband of Judy Scott Feldman, the head of the National Coalition to Save Our Mall, was quoted by a reporter as triumphantly noting, "They just want to have a ceremony— but it doesn't mean anything. They can't put anything into the ground," and in its account of the Veterans Day ceremonies, the *New York Times* described the symbolic groundbreaking with the headline, "Ground-breaking, of Sorts, for a Contested War Memorial."[35]

Over the next six months the legal issues involved in *National Coalition to Save Our Mall, et al. v. Bruce Babbitt, Secretary of the Interior, et al.* grew even more complicated. In its December 15, 2000, answer to the memorial opponents' suit, the Justice Department had replied that until such time as a permit was issued to begin construction on the National World War II Memorial, the court lacked jurisdiction over the matter. But early in 2001 all that changed, when on January 23 the National Park Service issued a permit for the American Battle Monuments Commission to begin construction on the National World War II Memorial. The immediate response by the plaintiffs' lawyer, Andrea Ferster, was to go back into court on February 15 and seek a preliminary injunction to prevent the ABMC from entering into any contracts or construction activities on the memorial, and on March 8, after learning that the American Battle Monuments Commission and National Park Service intended to prune the roots of fourteen elm trees in connection with the construction of the National World War II Memorial, Judge Henry H. Kennedy Jr. of the U.S. District Court in Washington, D.C., issued a ten-day temporary restraining order to stop the pruning.[36]

As it turned out, the temporary restraining order was unnecessary. At this same time, as a result of its role in the legal proceedings surrounding the National World War II Memorial, the Justice Department discovered that Harvey Gantt, the former chairman of the National Capital Planning Commission, had cast votes on National World War II Memorial design issues in 1999 and 2000 after his term had expired. Nobody thought that Gantt had deliberately voted when he should not have. In the past, chairmen of the National Capital Planning Commission traditionally served, even when their terms expired, until they were replaced by a new chairman. But without anyone realizing it, the language allowing this practice had been inadvertently dropped when the enabling legislation for the National Capital Planning Commission was amended in 1973. Thus, at three different meetings—June 3, 1999, September 21, 2000, and December 14, 2000—Harvey Gantt had participated in key National Capital Planning Commission decisions on the National World War II Memorial when he should not have.[37]

The question for the National Capital Planning Commission was what to do next, especially since the commission decision approving the final design for the National World War II Memorial had come on a close seven-to-five vote. There was no precedent at hand for solving such a problem, and on March 1, 2001, when it met in executive session, the best the National Capital Planning Commission could do was vote to consider what future action to take about the decisions it had made when Gantt was illegally serving as its chairman. For the two sides in the National World War II Memorial lawsuit, now titled, because of a change in administration, *National Coalition to Save Our Mall, et al. v. Gale Norton, Secretary of the Interior, et al.*, the legal maneuvering also changed. There was now no immediate need for a preliminary restraining order. The Justice Department was very anxious to see the National Capital Planning Commission deal with the validity of its decisions on the National World War II Memorial, and in a motion to stay proceedings and suspend scheduling by Silas R. DeRoma, the Department of Justice attorney litigating for the defendants, it was announced that the American Battle Monuments Commission would not award any contract for construction of the National World War II Memorial until thirty days after the National Capital Planning Commission had resolved the dilemma surrounding Harvey Gantt's votes to approve the memorial.[38]

On March 13, 2001, the stay issued by Judge Henry H. Kennedy went into effect, and three weeks later, at its April 5 meeting, the National Capital Planning Commission announced in a written statement issued by commission chairman Richard Friedman that it would deal with the questions that had arisen over the legality of Harvey Gantt's votes in two stages. On June 13 and 14 the National Capital Planning Commission would hold public meetings "to review its previous actions on the National World War II Memorial," and to make sure the June meetings were conducted as openly as possible, the commission would use its May 3 monthly meeting to establish the procedures for the June meetings. For the opponents of the National World War II Memorial, it was the best news in a year. "It was a very good decision," Judy Scott Feldman of the National Coalition to Save Our Mall told the *Washington Post.* "I am particularly pleased they want to do this in two separate meetings." However, neither Feldman nor the American Battle Monuments Commission anticipated that the May 3 National Capital Planning Commission meeting would also prove so momentous that it would set in motion the steps that would finally end the battle over the National World War II Memorial.[39]

The May 3 National Capital Planning Commission meeting was presided over by its new, Clinton-appointed chairman, Richard Friedman, the president and CEO of a Cambridge, Massachusetts, real estate and investment firm, who brought to the commission views about the National World War II Memorial that were very different from Harvey Gantt's. In contrast to Gantt, who believed that "St.Florian's design was respectful of the Mall" and had improved over the years, Friedman was more skeptical. "My personal predilection was somewhat different than Harvey Gantt's," Friedman would later acknowledge. "I never voted on the World War II Memorial, but had it been called to a vote, I would have had a problem with the design."[40]

From the start, the May 3 National Capital Planning Commission meeting reflected the differences between the two chairmen. In a series of votes, the most important of which were unanimous, the commission opened up for reconsideration every key decision it had made about the site and design of the National World War II Memorial. Faced with the choice of reconsidering only the decisions made at the three key meetings at which Harvey Gantt should not have been present or reconsidering all of the memorial decisions it had made since 1995, the commission opted for the latter, voting to give itself the maximum scope possible at its June 13 and 14 public meetings. Then the National Capital Planning Commission followed this far-reaching decision with a second crucial decision. At the June 13 and 14 meetings, the National World War II Memorial applicant, the American Battle Monuments Commission, would not, as it had in the past, have unlimited time to state its case. It would be limited to thirty minutes of speaking time at the start of the meeting, exactly what the coalition opposed to the memorial would have for stating its case.

With the scope and form of the June 13 and 14 meetings now established, the National Capital Planning Commission next set out to change the way it would gather information about the memorial. It voted to assemble a group of architecture experts to offer their views of the National World War II Memorial at a May 23 meeting that would prepare the way for the June 13 and 14 discussions. This group of architects would, however, be different from those who had appeared before the National Capital Planning Commission in the past. The group would be composed of those who did not have a partisan interest in the memorial debate and who had not served on the National World War II Memorial Design Jury, which would eliminate, for example, two of the memorial's most prestigious defenders, architects Hugh Hardy and David Childs. Finally, in response to a request from the House of Representatives District of Columbia Subcommittee, the National Capital Planning Commission voted to ask the National Park Service to construct a mock-up of the National World War II Memorial, similar to those the National Park Service had built in the past for other memorials. It was a request that fell short of the full-scale mock-up the District of Columbia Subcommittee wanted; the National Park Service reported that its consultants estimated it would cost $3 million and take five months to build such a mock-up. The commission's caution on the mock-up was barely noticed, however, given the three dramatic measures it had already passed.[41]

The next day's *New York Times* and *Washington Post* both featured stories that emphasized the radical turn the National World War II Memorial process had taken. In its front-page story, the *Post* described the National Capital Planning Commission as "reopening a bitter debate that had seemed closed just a few months ago," and in the lead to its story, the *Times* observed, "The plan to build a World War II Memorial on the Mall was sent back to the drawing board." For proponents of the National World War II Memorial, the National Capital Planning Commission's sweeping decisions came as a surprise. In a May 5 article, *Washington Post* architecture critic Benjamin Forgey, who had come to believe the National World War II Memorial should be built as designed, angrily criticized the National Capital Planning Commission for using the contested Gantt votes as a "pretext" for reviewing all of its positive votes on the National World War II Memorial. For the members of the National Coalition to Save Our Mall, on the other hand, Richard Friedman's assertion about the memorial, "We are going to review it from square one," was encouraging. "We have a chance now," a happy Neil Feldman told the press.[42]

In contrast to the opponents of the National World War II Memorial, who were jubilant about the National Capital Planning Commission's May 3 decisions, Margaret Vanderhye was worried. A Clinton appointee to the National Capital Planning Commission, Vanderhye had finished her term in January 2001 and was sitting in on the May 3 meeting as a consultant. She had finally come to oppose the final design of the National World War II Memorial, believing that what was needed was a "simple and direct" memorial that would harmonize with the Mall landscape. But on May 3 when the National Capital Planning Commission voted to reopen the entire National World War II Memorial issue, Vanderhye was not happy. She believed that the case for simplifying the existing design of the memorial had been dealt a fatal blow. "We missed a tremendous opportunity. It was like watching a train crash in slow motion," she would remember thinking. At that moment, Vanderhye was sure that the final decision-making authority on the memorial would be taken from the National Capital Planning Commission by

Congress if the commission did not put some parameters on what it was prepared to reconsider.[43]

Vanderhye's political instincts were right. In Congress, where comparatively few in the House or the Senate shared Vanderhye's critical view of the National World War II Memorial, the National Capital Planning Commission's May 3 decisions came as a shock and a challenge. In the commission's decision to go back to square one in its deliberations, the majority of the House and Senate saw not democracy in action but a small minority taking advantage of the memorial approval process that had already gone on too long. "It's up to Congress to save the memorial," Arizona Congressman Bob Stump, a World War II veteran who had enlisted in the navy at sixteen, told the *Washington Post* in an interview in which he described the memorial opponents as a small group who had managed to drag the memorial back through "a mind-numbing bureaucracy." In the Senate, Alaska Republican Ted Stevens, another World War II veteran, was equally outspoken, noting that in contrast to the "small group of opponents" who had blocked approval of the National World War II Memorial, the supporters of the memorial included a half million individual Americans, hundreds of corporations and foundations, state legislatures, and 450 veterans groups. Most members of Congress found that the fine points in the debate over the National World War II Memorial had never reached the voters in their states. It was getting the memorial built that mattered to their constituents. As Bob Dole later observed, "You get ten miles out of town, and nobody's heard of the criticism. The question is, When are you guys going to finish it?"[44]

Less than a week after the May 3 National Capital Planning Commission meeting, some of the commissioners, aware of the firestorm they had created, tried to offer reassurances in *Washington Post* interviews that their decision was not as radical as it seemed. The vote "does not say the commission will necessarily consider the site," Pat Elwood observed. Changing a location chosen in 1995 "would have some unfair impacts," Arrington Dixon, another memorial opponent, conceded, and in what seemed like a barely concealed plea for intervention, National Capital Planning Commission Chairman Richard Friedman declared, "I personally would be delighted if Congress took the matter up and clarified it, but that is not up to us."[45]

But it no longer mattered what the National Capital Planning Commission wanted. In the Senate there was already a bill, S. 580, to expedite the construction of the National World War II Memorial, which Arkansas Senator Tim Hutchinson had introduced on March 20, 2001, influenced in part by a conversation he had had on a flight back to Washington with Bob Dole on the problems the National World War II Memorial was having in getting approval. The bill, which had been referred to the Committee on Governmental Affairs, had had no further action taken on it since then, but it provided a good foundation for locking in place the memorial approval process that had already occurred. "The decision to construct the World War II Memorial at the dedicated Rainbow Pool site, and the decisions regarding the design for the World War II Memorial are final and conclusive, and shall not be subject to further administrative or judicial review," Hutchinson's bill stated.[46]

On May 3, in the House of Representatives, Congressman Bob Stump, taking Hutchinson's bill as his model, introduced his own bill, H.R. 1696, to expedite construction of the National World War II Memorial. He did not have to wait long to get results. Twelve days later, on May 15, after quickly moving through the Committee on Resources and the Committee on Veterans' Affairs, H.R. 1696 came before the full House, where a motion to suspend the rules and pass the bill by voice vote was agreed to. The bill then won House approval by a vote of 400 to 15 and was sent on to the Senate, where the bill moved equally quickly. It was referred to the Committee on Energy and Natural Resources, discharged by unanimous consent on May 21, and sent to the Senate floor, where S. 745, a more precise version of H.R. 1696 proposed by Senator John Warner, another World War II veteran, was passed by unanimous consent and sent back to the House for its approval. The next day, May 22, on a motion from Representative Bob Stump, the House suspended its rules and by a voice vote agreed to use the text of Senator Warner's bill in H.R. 1696.[47]

All that was required now for the bill to become law was for President Bush to sign it, and there was little doubt that he intended to do so. On the day the Senate passed Senator Warner's National World War II Memorial bill, the president had urged, "It is more important than ever that we move quickly to begin construction if those who served are to see the nation's permanent expression of remembrance and thanks." Five days after receiving the bill that the House and Senate had approved, President Bush signed it into law on Memorial Day, May 28, in a ceremony in the East Room of the White House, promising a gathering of veterans, members of Congress, and ABMC commissioners, "I will make sure the monument gets built."[48]

The bill that President Bush signed into law was very much like the bills that preceded it. Its aim was to make sure construction of the National World War II Memorial moved forward without further challenges or delays in the approval process. Just three sections long, Public Law 107–11 left little to chance. Section 1 ordered that "notwithstanding any other provision of law," the National World II Memorial approved by the Commission of Fine Arts on July 20 and November 16, 2000, and by the National Capital Planning Commission on September 21 and December 14, 2000, be constructed "expeditiously at the dedicated Rainbow Pool site." Section 2 ordered that elements of the memorial design and construction not yet approved "be considered and approved in accordance with the requirements of the Commemorative Works Act." Section 3 declared that the site and design approvals described in Section 1 "shall not be subject to judicial review."[49]

The reactions of the beneficiaries of Congress's action on the National World War II Memorial were mixed. Early on, Friedrich St.Florian had felt uneasy about the Hutchinson bill, and in an interview with the *Boston Globe* he admitted, "I would prefer to let democracy run its course." The same doubts were expressed by the Commission of Fine Arts, which had been working very hard to complete the approval process. In a May 9 letter commenting on H.R. 1696 and S. 580, the secretary of the Fine Art Commission, Charles Atherton, noted that as far as the commission was concerned, Congress's termination of further judicial review of the National World War II Memorial process would be both "regrettable" and a contradiction of the rights World War II was fought to protect. On the other hand, for many who supported the National World War II Memorial, especially those with long experience in Washington politics, Congress's intervention was welcome. Bob Dole, who made no secret of helping to instigate Congress's action, was confident that intervention was the right choice and that the protestors had had their day in court. "I didn't sign on to make this my last career move," he would say of his role in the National World War II Memorial Campaign. Frank Moore, a member of the American Battle Monuments Commission and long-time aide to Jimmy Carter, was also relieved at Congress's intervention. He worried that once the National World War II Memorial case got into the courts, anything could happen. "These things have momentum," he would say of the headway made by the opponents to the memorial.[50]

For the opponents of the National World War II Memorial, who had been feeling so hopeful after the National Capital Planning Commission's May 3 meeting, the intervention by Congress was a huge disappointment. In less than a month they had gone from feeling that they had a good chance to prevent the construction of the latest version of the National World War II Memorial to finding that they had few options. Andrea Ferster, who ardently believed in the lawsuit she was bringing, was particularly disappointed. As she would later observe, "We thought this was a clear case of the decision-making process being illegal." However, the memorial opponents were not prepared to give up their fight to do whatever they could to stop the National World War II Memorial from going ahead as planned. In early June the opponents got a momentary boost when a news story asserted that Tompkins Builders—one of the two companies awarded a share of the $56 million contract for the memorial construction—was owned by a German company that had used concentration camp labor during World War II. The World War II Veterans to Save the Mall, a small group that is part of the National Coalition to Save Our Mall, immediately swung into action with a press release that said, "We are sickened by the announcement that a contract to build the World War II Memorial has been signed with a company tied to Nazi slave labor camps. This is the latest chapter in a dishonest process that is casting a shadow over what was until now a proud legacy."

The Nazi story was not one with legs, however. The link of Tompkins Builders to the use of forced labor in the Nazi era was so indirect as to be virtually nonexistent. Tompkins was established as an American company in 1911, acquired by J. A. Jones Incorporated of Charlotte, North Carolina, in the middle 1960s, and then in 1979, J. A. Jones was bought by Philipp Holzmann AG, a German construction company, which, it turned out, did agree, like a number of German companies, to contribute to a $4.5 billion fund established to compensate Nazi-era slave and forced laborers. Days after the story broke, the federal government's own General Services Administration reaffirmed its support of Tompkins Builders (the General Accounting Office would do the same later on), and Rabbi Andrew Baker, director of international affairs for the American Jewish Committee dampened protest still further by saying that German firms contributing to the forced labor fund deserved credit, not punishment, for doing so.[51]

After Memorial Day 2001, the only real chance for success that the memorial opponents had was somehow to convince courts to limit the broad latitude that Public Law 107–11 gave the American Battle Monuments Commission for going ahead with the construction of the National World War II Memorial. It was a difficult position to be in. On May 29, 2001, one day after President Bush signed Public Law 107–11, Justice Department attorney Silas R. DeRoma was back before District Court Judge Henry H. Kennedy, arguing that the new law made moot the issues before the court in *National Coalition to Save Our Mall, et al. v. Gale Norton, Secretary of the Interior, et al.* The Justice Department's client, the American Battle Monuments Commission, DeRoma declared, was preparing to authorize the General Services Administration to award a contract by June 6 and wanted the court to lift the stays issued earlier, which limited the commission's actions.[52]

Andrea Ferster's response was to file what would turn out to be the first of a series of legal briefs—in this case, one supporting a second application for a temporary restraining order on construction of the National World War II Memorial—in which she argued that Public Law 107–11 did not rule out major elements in the suit she had brought on behalf of the National Coalition to Save Our Mall, the World War II Veterans to Save the Mall, the Committee of 100, and the D.C. Preservation League. On substantive issues, Ferster contended that Public Law 107–11 did not withdraw the court's jurisdiction over the plaintiff's claims that the National Park Service had violated the National Environmental Policy Act by refusing to prepare an Environmental Impact Statement in 1998, and even more important, Ferster went on to say, Public Law 107–11, when expansively read, created an obstacle to continued litigation, which violated the principles of separation of powers contained in Article III of the Constitution by giving Congress the power to rule out judicial review.[53]

It was an argument that Ferster did not make much headway with either on her own before Judge Kennedy or later, when with William T. Mayton, a professor of constitutional and administrative law at Emory University Law School in Atlanta and a former assistant counsel to the Watergate Committee, she went before a federal appeals court and challenged Public Law 107–11 on constitutional grounds alone. On June 7, Judge Henry H. Kennedy refused to issue the temporary restraining order that Ferster had requested, and on August 16, Judge Kennedy dealt her case a second blow when he dismissed the entire lawsuit brought by the groups that Ferster represented, observing in his opinion that "the plain language of Public Law 107–11 provides clear and convincing evidence that Congress intended to preclude court review" of all agency decisions on the location and design of the National World War II Memorial and that in doing so Congress "merely exercised its authority" to decide what agency decisions are subject to judicial review. A similar rejection of Ferster's argument followed in the U.S. Court of Appeals for the District of Columbia, where, during the October 10 oral arguments phase of the appeal, the outcome of the case was foreshadowed when one of the three judges hearing the case, referring back to the "notwithstanding any other provision of the law" clause of Public Law 107–11, pointedly told William Mayton, "I'm not sure what you think that notwithstanding language in the statute means," and then went on to observe, "If we read it literally, you lose." On November 6, 2001, the three-judge panel denied the appeal Ferster and Mayton brought before it, with senior circuit court judge Stephen F. Williams delivering a unanimous opinion in which he declared that Public Law 107–11 withdrew all subject matter jurisdiction from the courts and did not in the relief it provided violate separation of powers as defined by Article III of the Constitution.[54]

It was the last time that Ferster, who in 2001 would start putting "Rainbow Pool Memorial Ale" labels on the beer she made for friends at a Washington microbrewery, would get to argue the case before a court. On February 6, 2002, the U.S. Court of Appeals for the District of Columbia turned down without explanation a December 21, 2001, petition from Ferster for the court to hear *National Coalition to Save Our Mall, et al. v. Gale Norton, Secretary of the Interior, et al.* with all of its judges present, and eight months later, on October 7, the Supreme Court took similar action on a May 3, 2002, petition by Ferster for a writ of certiorari to the U.S. Court of Appeals for the District of Columbia Circuit with a one-sentence note, "Petition for a writ of certiorari to the United States Court of Appeals for the District of Columbia Circuit is denied."[55]

*National Coalition to Save Our Mall, et al. v. Gale Norton, Secretary of the Interior, et al.* was now officially dead. The Commission of Fine Arts and the National Capital Planning Commission still had some decisions to make in regard to the embellishments and inscriptions, but these were relatively minor decisions compared to those that had already been made. On August 27, 2001, while the various appeals were still going on, construction on the National World War II Memorial began as work crews started preparing the site and set up tree protection. By 2002, the biggest challenge the American Battle Monuments Commission faced was one that it welcomed: making sure its memorial fulfilled the confident reply made by J. Carter Brown two years before his death to a memorial skeptic, "Just wait until you go and see it."[56]

# 8

## Constructing More Than the Eye Can See

On the wall across from his desk in the Tompkins Builders trailer at the National World War II Memorial site, project manager Ken Terry could always look up and see his grandfathers in their World War II military uniforms staring down on him. For Terry, the pictures were a daily reminder of why the World War II Memorial meant so much to him and why he believed, "I have a personal stake in this memorial." His paternal grandfather, Captain Mabry "Red" Terry, who spent twenty-five years in the U.S. Marine Corps before retiring, was captured by the Japanese when they overran Wake Island shortly after the bombing of Pearl Harbor and endured four years in a prison camp. His maternal grandfather, Colonel Nicholas Bruno, who retired from the U.S. Army after a thirty-six-year career, was commissioned a second lieutenant in 1941 and spent his war years in New Guinea and the Philippines, commanding an anti-aircraft battery.[1]

The pictures that Ken Terry kept on his office wall were not just indicative of the way he felt about the National World War II Memorial. They reflected a much wider belief on the part of the men and women working day to day on the memorial that this was a job too important to ever forget. As Victor McCoy, a Grunley-Walsh Construction superintendent put it, decades from now you could always bring a son or a daughter down to the Mall and say, "I had a part of that."[2]

As crews finished up their particular part of the work in building the National World War II Memorial and were replaced by new crews, their last day on the job was marked by a farewell party. Like the Friday potluck lunches that became a National World War II Memorial tradition during construction, the farewell parties were not formal affairs. Those leaving got a certificate signed by Senator Bob Dole and chairman of the American Battle Monuments Commission, retired U.S. Marine Corps Commandant P. X. Kelley. But there were not a lot of speeches, and there was nothing fancy about the food that got served at the farewell dinners. The point of these events was nonetheless clear both to those who were leaving the project and those who were remaining. Like the builders of its monumental neighbors, the Washington Monument and the Lincoln Memorial, the builders of the National World War II Memorial had played a part in U.S. history.[3]

The publicity surrounding the National World War II Memorial added to the sense that working on the memorial was special. The controversy during the approval process about the potential environmental damage was well known by everyone who went to work on the memorial. Most were skeptical about what they had read. They had done enough construction work in and around Washington to believe that a memorial could be built at the Rainbow Pool without threatening the foundations of the Washington Monument hundreds of yards away or sending pollutants into the nearby Tidal Basin. At the same time, they were aware that the criticism surrounding the National World War II Memorial was not going away any time soon.[4]

After construction on the National World War II Memorial began, the National Coalition to Save our Mall was relentless in attacking the memorial on its Web site. In one posting, "Mud Pit," the coalition showed a photo of construction in its early stages and claimed that the workers had not found bedrock (which was 35–45 feet below grade) but only muck. In another posting, "Eye in the Sky," the coalition showed a photo of the time-lapse camera that took a picture each day to record the construction of the memorial and claimed that the camera was a security camera being used for surveillance. In a third posting, "Construction Begins," the coalition showed a street-level photo of construction equipment and the 8-foot-high stockade fence surrounding the memorial and declared that the fence and construction equipment illustrated how the memorial (which would actually be 6 feet below grade and have its vertical structures on the sides of the Mall's central axis) was going to block the Mall's east-west vista. For both workers and the staff of the American Battle Monuments Commission, these Web postings were infuriating, but they were also a reminder of how little leeway they had. If what they had not done wrong could be exploited, any error they did commit was sure to be publicized.[5]

For the agencies, companies, and workers responsible for making sure construction of the National World War II Memorial did not cause environmental damage, coping with the pressure of completing a historic project that was sure to be scrutinized, even if done to perfection, was nothing new. Three governmental agencies with seasoned, expert staffs—the General Services Administration, the National Park Service, and the Corps of Engineers—were all involved in providing support and advice for the National World War II Memorial when it came to questions on construction and the environment. In the private sector, the companies responsible for building the memorial were also highly experienced. The construction manager, Gilbane Building Company, and the construction contractor, Tompkins/Grunley-Walsh Joint Venture, were firms with long histories. Together Tompkins Builders and Grunley-Walsh Construction had 135 years of construction experience in and around Washington, and the construction and renovation they had participated in included work on the Washington Monument, the Franklin D. Roosevelt Memorial, and the National Air and Space Museum. As James Walsh, the chairman of William V. Walsh Construction, the company his father founded, would say of the problems involved with building the National World War II Memorial, "It was nothing we had not seen before. Nothing about it scared me."[6]

In taking on the challenge of the National World War II Memorial, Walsh Construction, like the other contractors involved, nonetheless made a point of assigning its best and most reliable workers to the project. The heads of every construction company that worked in and around Washington knew that in building in West Potomac Park, they were building on landfill that had historically caused difficulties for architects and engineers. Ninety years earlier, when construction on the Lincoln Memorial began shortly after Lincoln's birthday in 1914, the only way builders could sink the piers on which the memorial would rest into the bedrock below was with men working under atmospheric pressure in huge caissons. The builders of the National World War II Memorial would not have to put their workers through such a risky ordeal, but they, too, would allocate a huge portion of construction time to working below ground on the invisible part of the memorial before they ever got above ground.[7]

The figures on the material used to build the National World War II Memorial provide a good indication of just how much time and effort had to be spent on the work below ground. By the time the memorial was done, 1,620 truck loads of concrete were used to build its foundations and support; 5.5 miles of pipe were laid for its fountains, drainage system, and utilities; and 20,800 cubic yards of crushed stone and gravel went under it.

The National World War II Memorial's thirty-month construction schedule reflected the extent of the work that was conducted beneath the grade. It was divided into twelve phases: (1) mobilization and site preparation; (2) utility relocation; (3) slurry wall work; (4) piling installation; (5) structural concrete work; (6) stone work; (7) comfort station construction; (8) information station construction; (9) artwork and inscriptions; (10) landscaping; (11) commissioning to check if everything works as designed; and (12) substantial completion of project and instructions for the National Park Service on how to maintain the memorial. Not until February 2003, eighteen months after the start of construction, would workers get around to phase six, stone work, and begin work on elements that would be visible to the public in the completed memorial.[8]

In constructing the invisible, underground parts of the National World War II Memorial that future visitors would never see, there was, moreover, no effective way to take shortcuts. The great medieval church builders, especially those erecting churches to honor the Virgin Mary, were obsessed with detail because, as Henry Adams wrote in *Mont-Saint Michel and Chartres,* "Mary's taste was infallible; her knowledge like her power had no limits." The builders of the National World War II Memorial had no such divine figure in mind when they began their work, but they were engaged in constructing a memorial that like the Lincoln Memorial and the Washington Monument was an expression of American "civil religion," of values that were seen by the nation as transcendent in nature. For the National World War II Memorial builders, as for the medieval church builders, there could be no thought of letting details slide. As James Walsh put it, "If there is any sacrifice in quality, it is not worth it."[9]

On August 27, 2001, site preparation on the National World War II Memorial began with workers surveying the Rainbow Pool area, taking photos of it, and setting up a stockade fence around its periphery. There was nothing unusual about these early steps, but before the 170 days of site preparation were over, there would be plenty of surprises to go around. In addition to finding the buried foundation of one of the temporary navy buildings that decades earlier occupied the Mall, workers discovered electric lines in places that nobody had known about and cracks in the Rainbow Pool storm-water drainage pipes that were allowing unfiltered groundwater to seep into them and eventually into the Tidal Basin. It was a situation that was the reverse of the one that memorial opponents had originally claimed. Instead of threatening to destabilize a Mall site that was working efficiently, the National World War II Memorial workers were entering a site that could be stabilized only if key areas of it were rebuilt. The discovery in 2002 that the supportive timber pilings on which the old Rainbow Pool was thought to rest were nowhere to be found only added to the feeling that the Rainbow Pool site was in need of far more work than anyone had imagined.[10]

The construction problems that could be readily handled were dealt with early on. The Rainbow Pool was split into two holding pools and used as a catch basin for groundwater and storm water, which were released into the Tidal Basin only after being run through sediment filters and tested for contamination by an independent certified agent, which then passed on the test results to the Environmental Protection Agency and District of Columbia. The old utility lines were replaced with new ones, which this time were properly mapped before being put in place. The soil that was dug up during excavation was carted away to a soil recycling facility in Baltimore, and a decision was made not to reuse any of it but to replace all old soil with clean fill. Finally, the storm-water and drainage pipes, which were discovered to be in such poor condition, were replaced with new ones, and a backup pumping system was added to the new pumping system to deal with any problems that might be caused by future breakdowns.[11]

For the most serious construction problems the National World War II Memorial faced, there were no quick fixes. The key to the underground and unseen National World War II Memorial was the time-consuming and costly installation of a slurry wall, steel pilings, and two vaults with water treatment systems in them.

Work on the slurry wall began in March 2002, after the site preparation and utility relocation phases of construction were completed. Building the slurry wall was an enormously complicated and laborious undertaking but one with a tremendous payoff. The slurry wall, which was to be 1,354 feet in circumference, followed the footprint of the memorial and provided the memorial site with a bathtub-like seal that prevented outside groundwater from seeping in, and work done on the memorial site from having unintended effects on the water table elsewhere on the Mall.

In comparison with the slurry walls built at the World Trade Center site in New York and for the Central Artery/Tunnel Project in Boston, the slurry wall at the National World War II Memorial site was modest in scale. Building it was slow going, however, and the mass excavation at the National World War II Memorial site could not get started until the slurry wall was finished.

The preparatory work for the National World War II Memorial slurry wall began in January 2002 with the installation of split guide walls, 2 feet apart from each other, around the memorial site. Then in March the slurry wall construction itself started as a giant crane with a hydraulic clamshell excavator attached to it was brought in for deep digging. The clamshell was 2 feet wide, exactly the desired thickness of the slurry wall, and was used to excavate soil down to the bedrock below. To prevent the trench from collapsing in on itself, slurry—a mixture of water and bentonite clay—was then poured in, and the process continued until the clamshell met resistance from bedrock, which at the National World War II Memorial site was typically 35 to 45 feet below grade.

The first phase of the slurry wall construction was now over, and the second phase began when a chisel was attached to the end of the crane and used to drill another 2 to 3 feet into the bedrock. It was now possible to make preparations for the final step—pouring the concrete that would form the panels making up the slurry wall. What had been done earlier with the slurry was now essentially reversed. A giant steel rebar cage, designed to reinforce the concrete, was lowered into the trench. Then concrete was poured into the bottom of the trench through a steel tremi tube, a pipe-like device with a funnel at its top, and as the slurry was displaced by the heavier concrete, it was pumped out and put through a filter system.

The result, after the concrete reached the top of the trench, was a section of slurry wall 2 feet thick and typically 20 feet long that was keyed into the bedrock that once formed the floor of the Potomac River. The process would then have to be repeated over and over with seventy panels as the slurry wall rose around the National World War II Memorial footprint. The concrete in each panel required a week to harden properly, and while this hardening, or curing, was going on, it was not possible to put a new panel next to a just-completed one, lest the shock from the digging interfere with the curing. The only choice work crews had was to install the next panel at another point along the wall and wait until June, when all the panels were done, to get the continuous seal for the memorial that the slurry wall was designed to provide.[12]

The next crucial phase in the building of the unseen National World War II Memorial could now begin, and following the destruction of the Rainbow Pool between June 18 and June 21, 2002, mass excavation of the memorial site began and continued until July 22. The discovery in this period that the wooden piles thought to be supporting the Rainbow Pool were nonexistent came as a surprise, but it was not a surprise that encouraged anyone to think that the new memorial could be built without the installation of piles, and on July 25 a pile-driving process, which would last through the fall and winter and would not finish until February 2003, got underway.

Like the installation of the slurry wall, the piling could not be rushed. The steel H piles, known as HP 14x89 and shaped like a capital H, got their designation from the fact that each was 14 inches deep at its cross section and weighed 89 pounds per linear foot. Able to bear 131 tons of weight each, the piles were difficult to install, even in the soft ground of the Mall. With a diesel-powered pile hammer doing the work, driving each pile down until it reached its point of refusal in the bedrock below was a slow process, and with 598 piles to be installed, it was six months before most of the H piles were in the ground.

There was, however, an important difference between the installation of the H piles in 2002–2003 and the earlier installation of the slurry wall. No other digging could be done while the slurry wall was being installed because of the potential effect on the water table in adjacent areas of the Mall. But with the driving of the H-piles there was nothing to worry about as far as the rest of the Mall was concerned. The piles were installed 20 feet apart from each other in grids, and while piling was going on in one grid, additional excavation, if called for, could go on elsewhere at the memorial site. The result was that while more than 2.6 miles of new H piles were being put into the ground to give the Rainbow Pool site more support than it had ever had, work also got underway on the third important component of the unseen National World War II Memorial—the underground vaults that contained the equipment for the operation of the memorial's fountains as well as its water treatment system.[13]

Work on the memorial's tunnels and vaults began on September 3, 2002, with the start of excavation on the storm water and electricity vault and continued into the summer of 2003 when work on the memorial's underground tunnels ended. What made this process so time-consuming was the complex nature of these underground facilities. The old Rainbow Pool had been a technically primitive operation. It had no underground rooms. The only controls for its fountain were in boxes located at ground level. By contrast, the National World War II Memorial was designed to be a modern, high-tech facility dependent on a series of fail-safe environmental and fountain controls.

Square footage tells the story. The below-ground area of the National World War II Memorial takes up 17,770 square feet. It has a 30-foot-deep fountain vault, which is 4,370 square feet, and a second vault, a 32-foot-deep storm water and electricity vault, which is 4,190 square feet. In addition, linking these vaults and running the length and width of the memorial is a 25-foot-deep tunnel system that occupies 9,210 square feet.

The idea behind building such a large underground area into the National World War II Memorial was to ensure not only that there was enough room to hold all the needed equipment but that in the future, workers would have enough space to get at the equipment. Rather than being crammed next to each other, the two vaults were located at opposite ends of the memorial, and to avoid installation problems, three-dimensional drawings showing the placement of wiring and plumbing were produced before anything was put in.

The fountain vault, located below the western ceremonial end of the National World War II Memorial, was designed to contain all the mechanical and electrical equipment for the fountains, including pumps, gauges, overflow holders, and pressure adjustment switches. From these controls the height of the fountain spray can be automatically adjusted for wind conditions, but even more important, also present in this vault, which because of its delicate equipment has two ship's doors to seal it off in case of flooding, are a filter system and automatic backwash that monitor and treat the dirt load in the memorial's fountains.

The storm water and electrical vault, located at the eastern end of the memorial, has a similar but broader focus. Everything in it has been built to ensure that the National World War II Memorial operates in an environmentally friendly way. On its bottom level, the storm water and electrical vault contains a sediment chamber and pump room; on its middle level is a control room with access hatches to the sediment and pump rooms below; and on its top level are a transformer room and a switch room. The vault's storm water system can remove 80 percent of the suspended solids and floating oil from rainwater, and its groundwater system, which has a second pumping system for backup in case problems develop with the first pumping system, can take in fifty gallons of groundwater per minute and remove the contaminants from it.[14]

Looking back on this underground construction on the National World War II Memorial during the summer of 2003, Darrell Brown, the project director for the General Services Administration, remarked, "There is so much more here than will ever meet the naked eye." It was a description that would also apply to much of the above-ground work on the memorial. To assemble just one 17-foot memorial pillar required seven stone pieces, sealed on the outside with mortar and grout and held on the inside with stainless steel bars fitted into center holes. To make sure that the trees replacing the dying and unhealthy elms around the memorial were planted in exactly the right spot, the original drawings of Frederick Law Olmsted Jr. were consulted by the National Park Service's regional horticulturist before he ordered planting. To make sure none of the stars on the Freedom Wall could be removed by souvenir hunters, the individual stars were attached with special tamper-proof bronze bolts rather than simply screwed into fixtures in the wall.

Finally, to make sure that the memorial's inscriptions, which the members of the American Battle Monuments Commission chose after careful research or wrote themselves, had a sculptural quality that blended with the memorial as a whole, their design and execution were assigned to Nick Benson, the head of the John Stevens Shop of Newport, Rhode Island, which since it was founded in 1705 has produced America's leading stonecutters. Benson, whose father was responsible for the inscriptions on the Franklin D. Roosevelt Memorial and whose grandfather purchased the John Stevens Shop in 1927, is a third-generation stone carver (his work can be seen at the National Gallery of Art in Washington as well as at Harvard and Yale universities), who relied on hand chiseling to make all his final cuts for the inscriptions on the National World War II Memorial. In the work that Benson, his job foreman, Joe Moss, and their assistants did on the National World War II Memorial, they used sandblasting (to a depth of three-sixteenths of an inch) only to get their lettering in the memorial's granite started. After that, they employed a hydraulic, bullnose chisel to go down an additional three-sixteenths of an inch and complete the memorial's special, hand-drawn lettering, which Benson created by combining Roman classical lettering with the block lettering characteristic of *Life* magazine in the 1940s. The result, achieved by making each individual letter slightly deeper at its top and bottom, is that the National World War II Memorial inscriptions do not appear in outline, as uniform sandblasted inscriptions do. What memorial visitors encounter instead are inscriptions, stained with a tinted lithochrome lacquer and done in a bold stroke, that, because they possess varying depths, cast shadows and have a three-dimensional, sculptural quality, consistent with the rest of the National World War II Memorial art work.[15]

Like visitors to the Lincoln Memorial, who, on entering its central chamber, stand in awe before Daniel Chester French's colossal statue of Lincoln without thinking about the 122 cylinders that form the Lincoln Memorial's subfoundation, visitors to the National World War II Memorial can also be expected not to consider how the unseen National World War II Memorial makes possible the seen memorial. When in a 1988 essay, "An Imagined Walk Through the National World War II

Memorial," Helen Fagin, a member of the World War II Memorial Site and Design Committee, tried to picture for her fellow committee members the completed memorial, the scene she imagined was one in which the "special aura" of the National World War II Memorial, not the complexity of its construction, held the attention of visitors. The paradox of a successful memorial is that it does not call attention to its hidden architecture and engineering.[16]

Visitors to the National World War II Memorial will certainly take in, however, all that has happened since the stonework on the memorial began in February 2003. The old Rainbow Pool, as architect Hugh Hardy observed in testimony before the National Capital Planning Commission, was a place visitors generally stopped at only on their way to other sites. That is not true any more. The National World War II Memorial has transformed the Rainbow Pool site into a destination in its own right. The Rainbow Pool itself, approximately 15 percent smaller than the original pool, is still at the center of the site, but with its new eighteen-inch-deep black concrete bottom, surrounded by a sloping wall of Academy Black granite and light-gray Mount Airy granite coping, the pool is much more visually defined than it was before. It now adds an important calming element to a site that is two-thirds softscape (trees, water, and grass) and one-third hardscape (concrete and stone).

The calming element is needed. For the three main components of the National World War II Memorial—the ceremonial entrance at its east end, the pillars and arches at its north and south sides, and the Freedom Wall with its Field of Stars at its western end—make a series of visual and emotional demands on the memorial visitor that build in intensity.[17]

For visitors entering the National World War II Memorial through its ceremonial entrance, the historical sense of World War II that they get at this point is the most explicit one they will experience on the entire site. The memorial's announcement stone, which is integrated into the entrance paving, acknowledges the view visitors have at this moment of the Lincoln Memorial to their west and the Washington Monument towering behind them to their east. "Here in the presence of Washington and Lincoln, one the eighteenth-century father and the other the nineteenth-century preserver of our nation," the announcement stone inscription declares, "we honor those twentieth-century Americans who took up the struggle during the Second World War and made the sacrifices to perpetuate the gift our forefathers entrusted to us: a nation conceived in liberty and justice."[18]

However, the most important element at this ceremonial entrance, which guides visitors down into the memorial plaza with its sloping walk, is the set of twenty-four relief panels, both high and low, that Ray Kaskey and the sculptors in his studio crafted for the memorial's northern and southern balustrades. Just as the announcement stone speaks directly to the historical context in which the National World War II Memorial appears on the Mall, Kaskey's relief panels speak directly to the historical narrative the National World War II Memorial commemorates.

For Kaskey, getting chosen to work on the Mall was, as he put it in a *Washington Post* interview, "the biggest thing that will happen to me." Best known before he began his work on the National World War II Memorial for Portlandia, his 36-foot-high copper sculpture of a goddess clad in a toga that sits atop the Michael Graves-designed Public Services Building in Portland, Oregon, Kaskey, like the late Frederick Hart, is one of the few contemporary sculptors to favor figurative work over abstraction. The relief panels that Kaskey created for the National World War II Memorial were not part of the original memorial design plans, but when in 1999 Friedrich St.Florian and the American Battle Monuments Commission decided that the entrance to the memorial should encompass more than grass and stone, it opened up an opportunity for Kaskey to do the only work in the memorial in which the human figure is dominant.

In the former truck garage by the railroad tracks in Brentwood, Maryland, that serves as his studio, Kaskey was already busy with other sculpture for the National World War II Memorial, and taking on the relief panels meant spending additional time doing research and planning in order to make storyboards for himself and the Commission of Fine Arts, which had right of approval over the memorial relief panels. For Kaskey, who operates his studio as an atelier and employs three sculptors—Aaron Sykes, Perry Carsley, and Joanna Blake—the new work was manageable because it could be divided up. Kaskey believed that it was essential for his relief panels to be as authentic as possible, and the only way he knew how to get the results that he wanted was enormously time-consuming. Kaskey based his preliminary sketches on composites of hundreds of World War II–era photographs he personally researched at the National Archives and Library of Congress, and then to ensure that the final reliefs looked authentic, Kaskey had World War II re-enactors come to his studio and pose in full battle dress while he and his assistants worked on the clay models that would ultimately be sent off to the foundry and cast in bronze.

The key to the historical experience that Kaskey wanted to capture was "the overall transformation of America caused by World War II," and what worried him most was the possibility that the material of war—guns, tanks, rifles—would come to dominate his reliefs. To prevent this from happening, Kaskey made sure that his relief panels (nearly 2 feet high and 5.5 feet long) were "isocephalic"—that is, the heads of the principal figures (each 18 inches tall) lined up horizontally. The human figure thus became the principal compositional element in every relief, and all other details were subordinated to it.

In addition, Kaskey made sure that when it came to actual subject matter, the war front did not dominate the home front in his panels. Visitors who enter the National World War II Memorial by its southern, or Pacific Front balustrade side, will see twelve relief panels titled: "Pearl Harbor," "Draft, Physical, Swearing In," "Embarkation," "Ship Building," "Agriculture," "Submarine Warfare," "Navy in Action," "Amphibious Landing," "Jungle Warfare," "Field Burial," "Liberation of POWs," and "V-J Day." Those who enter the memorial by its northern, or Atlantic Front balustrade side, will see twelve relief panels titled: "Lend Lease/War Declared," "War Bond Parade," "Mobilization of Women," "Men and Women at Work/Aircraft Construction," "Battle of the

Atlantic," "Air War/B–17 Crew," "Paratroopers," "D-Day," "Tanks in Combat," "Medics on the Battlefield," "Winter Combat/Battle of the Bulge," and "Americans and Russians Meet at the Elbe."

For memorial visitors who came of age in the 1940s, Kaskey's bronze relief panels will have a familiar quality. But what follows, whether one does or does not have firsthand knowledge of the history that Kaskey depicts, is a sense of how complex the story that the National World War II Memorial commemorates is and how jolting it was for Americans, wherever they were, to live through the years from Pearl Harbor to V-J Day.[19]

As visitors descend into the National World War II Memorial from its eastern entrance, they can either turn left and go south or turn right and go north. The pillars representing the states and territories they encounter to the south lead them to an arch commemorating victory in the Pacific-Asiatic theater of the war, and the pillars representing the states and territories they encounter to the north lead them to an arch commemorating victory in the Atlantic-European theater of war. But architecturally the two halves of the memorial, which reach out to each other like arms and have the configuration of a semicircle, are identical. There are different inscriptions on the inner rampart walls on the memorial's northern and southern sides, and different states and territories are represented by the two sets of twenty-eight pillars, but that is all that allows the visitor to distinguish the southern from the northern sides of the memorial. And it is truly a distinction without a significant difference. The narrative history related by the relief panels at the ceremonial entrance is over at this point. From here on, it is the evocativeness of the memorial's architecture and sculpture that defines the visitor's experience.

As the visitor descends from the entrance of the National World War II Memorial, it is St. Florian's 17-foot-high pillars that set the tone for what comes next. Made from the same light-gray Kershaw granite as the nearby benches and arches, the pillars are visually very different from the large decapitated columns in the memorial's winning design, but they lend themselves to parallel interpretation. In the most literal sense the pillars represent the states and territories whose names appear at their base. The oak and wheat bronze wreaths, each just over 4 feet in diameter, that alternate front and back on every pillar symbolize the industrial and agricultural strength of the country during the war, and the bronze rope that links the pillars to each other reflects how the states were unified in the war effort. But there is also a tragic element to these pillars. The opening in each pillar has a very functional purpose; it allows the pillar to be transparent and helps preserve the Mall's north-south vista. But at the same time, like the memorial's original decapitated columns, the pillars with their center openings (with missing stone) also suggest a deeper meaning: namely, that although the home front was peaceful, it was haunted by tragedy. Missing from the home front were the men and women serving overseas and dying in battle.[20]

For memorial visitors who respond to the layered meaning that the pillars carry, the transition to the arches that the pillars lead into and out of becomes a very natural one. Forty-three feet high and resting on a base that is just over 23 feet on each side, the two arches are the antithesis of a huge monumental arch like Napoleon's Arc de Triomphe, which took from 1806 to 1836 to complete, or classic imperial Roman arches, such as the Arch of Titus and the Arch of Constantine, which, with their decorative reliefs, celebrate conquest and power. St. Florian's arches are free from all but the most minimal ornamentation and war references. The inscription on the northern arch says Atlantic and on the southern arch Pacific, and surrounding the arches in a semicircle at their bases are inscriptions, just 4 inches high, that list without comment the key battles from World War II. To stand in each arch—and only a handful of people can fit in one at the same time—is to feel surrounded by an intimate enclosure, not an arch that a victorious army might parade through. In scale, the Roman arch that St. Florian's memorial resembles is the kind that historian William MacDonald in his *Architecture of the Roman Empire* calls the civic or passageway arch, and in modern terms the best comparison is with Sir Edwin Lutyens's brick-and-stone World War I memorial, constructed between 1927 and 1932 at Thiepval, France, in which a pyramid of multiple arches—surrounded by panels bearing the names of those killed at the 1916 Battle of the Somme—invites mourning and contemplation rather than exultation for anyone who enters the memorial from the French and British graveyards below it.[21]

The interior structure of the National World War II Memorial arches only deepens the sense of intimacy that their dimensions and form convey. Inside each arch is a baldacchino that Ray Kaskey designed. Like the baldacchinos that we find inside a church, Kaskey's are freestanding structures that rest on four columns. But with their secular and patriotic meaning, Kaskey's baldacchinos are also very different from their religious counterparts. Rather than being covered on top and crowned with a cross, as a church baldacchino traditionally is, each Kaskey baldacchino—which supports four bronze eagles holding a stainless steel ribbon with a bronze cladding in their beaks that is attached to a bronze laurel wreath—opens up to an oculus 11.5 feet in diameter, and instead of covering an altar, as a church baldacchino does, each Kaskey baldacchino covers a granite floor that contains a relief of the World War II Victory Medal (a figure of Liberation, looking to the dawn of a new day while holding the hilt and broken blade of a sword in her hands) and three inscriptions, "Victory on Land," "Victory at Sea," "Victory in the Air," accompanied by the dates "1941–1945."

For visitors to the memorial, the interior space of the Atlantic and Pacific arches becomes more human in scale and more personally demanding because of the baldacchino inside each. With the eagles on the top of the baldacchino columns rising to a height of 27 feet, 4 inches, and the baldacchino columns separated by just 11 feet, the 43-foot Atlantic and Pacific arches become a very intimate space—a "point of compression" as St. Florian put it—for anyone who enters them. It is virtually impossible to remain passively standing in the memorial arches. Because of the sunlight coming in through the oculus in each arch, daytime visitors cannot help looking skyward through the suspended bronze laurel wreath that frames the oculus above them. In this context, in which the sky and the manmade are visually linked and the eagles with their 13-foot wingspans provide a sense of shelter, it is not the religious transcendence of Christ that the baldacchinos announce (as in traditional churches) but the transcendence over the forces of darkness, represented by Nazi Germany and Imperial Japan, that the allied victory in World War II made possible.[22]

As memorial visitors emerge from the Atlantic and Pacific arches, there remains one last stopping point—the Freedom Wall with its Field of Stars at the western end of the National World War II Memorial. To get there, the visitor needs only to continue along the path created by the memorial's encircling pillars. Known in the earlier memorial design as the Sacred Precinct because it contained a Light of Freedom, two wreaths, a cenotaph, and a wall with an inscription on it, the western end of the National World War II Memorial now contains just one important architectural element—a curved Freedom Wall 75.5 feet long and just over 8 feet above plaza level with a Field of Stars consisting of 4,000 gold-plated stars, roughly one for every one hundred American World War II military dead.

The stars are reminiscent of the individual gold star a family would hang on a banner in a window when they lost a loved one during the war, and aesthetically, the stars, designed by Ray Kaskey, are the closest the National World War II Memorial comes to employing folk art. But there is nothing Norman Rockwell-like about the Field of Stars, nothing that puts the stars in a contradictory relationship with the austere classicism of the National World War II Memorial. Kaskey, who wanted the stars to appear as "a work of art instead of a piece of architectural embellishment," designed them so that they are not uniform in appearance and thereby suggestive of undifferentiated, mass deaths. There are seven star prototypes and five positions in which a star can be placed, and rather than being installed in even rows, the stars are lined up so that only every other star is at the same height. The differences in the stars—which are made of stainless steel, treated with a copper flash undercoat and a nickel bath, and then plated in 24-carat gold—are very discernable to any memorial visitor standing close to the Freedom Wall.

The paradox, as with the names carved into Maya Lin's Vietnam Veterans Memorial, is that the farther the visitor pulls back from the Field of Stars on the Freedom Wall to gain perspective, the harder it becomes to make out details. From a distance, the Field of Stars conveys the collective loss of the more than 400,000 American World War II dead and the toll those deaths took on grieving families. For visitors who want relief at this point, there is the calming Rainbow Pool behind them that they can turn to and exits through the two memorial arches. But there are no exits to West Potomac Park built into the Freedom Wall, no opportunity for anyone who gets close to the wall to avoid facing the tragedy it symbolizes.[23]

How visitors in the future will come to judge the National World War II Memorial cannot be predicted. The Vietnam Veterans Memorial was attacked as "a black gash of shame" before it was built, but after it was completed, the Vietnam Veterans Memorial quickly drew the support of many of the veterans who had attacked it as an anti-war memorial. The proposed construction of the Lincoln Memorial at the western end of the Mall was criticized by House Speaker and Illinois Republican Joe Cannon, who described the West Potomac Park location as "that God damned swamp," but by 1915, after construction was underway, Cannon reversed himself completely and acknowledged that he was glad he had lost his fight against the Lincoln Memorial.[24]

The truth is that memorials, especially those on the Mall, acquire an iconic and political life of their own that we cannot foresee. The austere and minimalist wall of the Vietnam Veterans Memorial has become a place where visitors leave flags, pictures, and flowers. The Lincoln Memorial was originally conceived of as a monument to the president who preserved the Union, not the president who freed the slaves. The memorial's opening ceremonies in 1922 were even segregated, with blacks confined to a "colored section." But with the passage of time, it is not the opening ceremonies or the Lincoln Memorial's axial link, via Memorial Bridge, to the Lee mansion in Arlington, Virginia, that we recall. We now think of the Lincoln Memorial in terms of a series of historic civil rights events. It is the place where on Easter Sunday in 1939 Marian Anderson sang because the Daughters of the American Revolution would not allow her, as a black woman, to rent their auditorium, Constitution Hall. It is the site of Martin Luther King's 1963 "I have a dream" speech.[25]

We do not, however, have to wait on history before we make *any* judgments about the impact of the National World War II Memorial on American life. To be sure, the memorials on the Mall that have in the past touched us most deeply are those that are defined by a single architectural form—the obelisk of the Washington Monument, the Greek temple of the Lincoln Memorial, the V-shaped walls of the Vietnam Veterans Memorial. But that record does not mean that in the twenty-first century we will not be touched by the multiple architectural forms that constitute the National World War II Memorial.

The National World War II Memorial will not, as its critics repeatedly charged, block the Mall's east-west vista. The construction of the memorial plaza 6 feet below grade and the location of the memorial's vertical elements far to the north and south of the Mall's center assure clear sight lines between the Washington Monument and the Lincoln Memorial. Nor will the memorial, despite its association with war, be a militarizing presence on the Mall. Like the Washington Monument, with its Revolutionary War link, and the Lincoln Memorial, with its Civil War link, the World War II Memorial is concerned with how a nation experiences, then transcends, war.

In the end the National World War II Memorial is an elegiac memorial in which two of its key elements—the semi-circle of pillars that frame the memorial and the baldacchinos within its arches—are reminiscent not of the martial but of sculptor-architect Gianlorenzo Bernini's seventeenth-century work at St. Peter's Church in Rome. The church features two of Bernini's greatest achievements: a colonnade that frames the piazza in front of St. Peter's and a baldacchino under Michelangelo's monumental dome that creates within the church an intimate space for worship. Visitors to the National World War II Memorial may not be moved to prayer, as the faithful are at St. Peter's, but within the context established by architect Friedrich St.Florian and sculptor Ray Kaskey—an artistic collaboration as close as that of Lincoln Memorial architect Henry Bacon and sculptor Daniel Chester French—it is dramatically clear how, through the references it makes to its monumental surroundings and to the sky, the National World War II Memorial works to reach beyond itself.[26]

We also do not need to wait on history to judge the impact of the National World War II Memorial on the Mall itself. In the most direct sense, that impact is visible in the work of landscape architect James van Sweden. In the original version of the memorial, van Sweden had proposed covering the memorial's two large berms with white roses. The berms are gone now and so are the white roses. But in their place, van Sweden produced a sweeping landscape plan consisting of 148 trees, 633 shrubs, 21,030 ground cover plants, and 42,650 bulbs of which anything that flowers has white blossoms. The memorial's 7.4 acres, which now feature an area of contemplation at the highest point, are vastly changed from the landscape that surrounded the original Rainbow Pool.[27]

Even more important is how the National World War II Memorial enlarges the vision of American history that the Mall conveys. To begin with, the memorial makes a value judgment about what has been missing from the Mall's central spine: a memorial that says the world war that America fought against totalitarianism in the 1940s was as important in the shaping of our national character as the Revolutionary War of the eighteenth century and the Civil War of the nineteenth century. In an era in which there has been great pressure in preservationist circles and among the commissions that control building on the Mall to declare that the cross-axis of land bounded by the Capitol and the Lincoln Memorial in one direction and the White House and the Jefferson Memorial in the other is a completed work of art, the National World War II Memorial makes the point that while we can legitimately worry about overbuilding on the Mall, we cannot pronounce the Mall closed without seeming to say that the greatness of the present can never equal the greatness of the past.[28]

By its very presence the National World War II Memorial also changes the way in which America's twentieth-century wars are viewed on the Mall. In its location on the center line of the Mall, rather than off to the side, the National World War II Memorial upstages both the Vietnam Veterans Memorial and the Korean War Veterans Memorial. The tragedy and hubris that Maya Lin's Vietnam Veterans Memorial speaks to with its somber black granite walls are not nullified by this placement, but what the decision to put the National World War II Memorial on a direct line between the Lincoln Memorial and Washington Monument does challenge is the idea, which ever since the 1960s has gained wide acceptance in political and academic circles, that the Vietnam War represents the culmination of modern American history. In the Mall's visual continuum it is World War II that is now officially linked to the Revolutionary War and Civil War, and by extension it is the classicism of the National World War II Memorial's design, not the stark modernism of Maya Lin's Vietnam Veterans Memorial, that is put forward as the architectural language most suited to expressing the values that lie at the root of American life.

These are remarkable accomplishments for a memorial that has just been completed, and they remind us that we are living in a period in which the re-evaluation of World War II has not come, as we might have expected, at the opportune historic moments presented by the fiftieth anniversary of D-Day in 1994 and the fiftieth anniversary of the war's end in 1995. The re-evaluation has come about as a result of the public response to an outpouring of books, films, and television programs about the war that appeared between 1997 and 2001 and included Stephen Ambrose's *Citizen Soldiers,* Tom Brokaw's *The Greatest Generation,* Steven Spielberg's *Saving Private Ryan,* James Bradley's *Flags of Our Fathers,* and the HBO series *Band of Brothers.* Very different from a film like *The Best Years of Our Lives,* a novel like *The Naked and the Dead,* a memoir like Paul Fussell's *Wartime,* all of which contain a strong ironic sensibility, what these current depictions of World War II have in common is that they concentrate on paying tribute to the World War II generation. Their aim is to honor that generation rather than put it under an historical microscope. The National World War II Memorial now joins in this turn-of-the-century homage, but by virtue of the sustained attention it will get over the years because of its place on the Mall between the Lincoln Memorial and Washington Monument, the National World War II Memorial has a chance to have a deeper, more lasting impact on American life than the books, films, and television programs with which it shares a common outlook.

For an America that in the wake of the September 11 attacks has felt threatened to a degree unknown in this country since the bombing of Pearl Harbor, such homage is more than just a final tribute to a parting generation. It is also an act of self-preservation, a way of reminding ourselves of our ability as a nation to come together in a crisis and, by extension, a way of linking ourselves with a generation that dealt successfully with years of crisis. "Earn it," says a dying John Miller, the army captain played by Tom Hanks in *Saving Private Ryan*, to the young Private Ryan, whom he and his squad have found at great cost to themselves so that Ryan may leave the war and return to his mother, who has already lost three sons in battle. Fifty-nine years later, the National World War II Memorial has become one more way of "earning it," of acknowledging all that has been made possible by the sacrifices of World War II. The sad part is that with its completion in 2004, fewer than 4 million of the more than 16 million G.I.'s who fought in World War II will have lived long enough to see the National World War II Memorial for themselves.[29]

# Interviews

Included here are interviews done by telephone as well as in person. In the case of group interviews, I have noted the affiliation of those with whom I spoke.

William Aileo
Brian and Katherine Ambroziak
Charles Atherton
James Aylward
Diana Balmori
Nick Benson
Sally Berk
Stanley Bernstein
Tersh Boasberg
Darrell W. Brown
J. Carter Brown
Davis Buckley
Robert Campbell
David Childs
Mike Conley
Kent Cooper
Leo A. Daly III
Deborah DeBernard, John Hart, Sean Imber, Al O'Konski, Darren Zehner (Leo A Daly firm)

Robert De Feo
Nick De Pace
Deborah Dietsch
David Dillon
Bob Dole
Durbin, Growden, and Sanderson families (Roger Durbin relatives)
Pat Elwood
Helen Fagin
Ed Feiner
Judy Scott Feldman
Henry Fernandez
Andrea Ferster
Pat Foote
Richard Friedman
Harvey Gantt
John Graves
Allan Greenberg
Hugh Hardy

George Hartman
Jess Hay
John Herrling
Peter Himler, Libby Schnee, Woody
  Woodruff (Burson-Marsteller)
Jaan Holt and Susan Piedmont-
  Palladino
Tim Hutchinson
Ash Jain
Lisa Jorgenson
Wayne Kaiser
Marcy Kaptur
Ray Kaskey
P. X. Kelley
Bob Kerrey
Rolland Kidder
Bill Lacy
Maureen Lagas
William R. Lawson
Denise Liebowitz
Richard Longstreth
Gregory McCarthy
Jim McCloskey
Joyce McCluney
Victor McCoy
Michael A. Manfredi and
  Marion Weiss
Michael Marinello
Elizabeth Merritt
Richard Moe
Sonny Montgomery
Frank Moore
Maureen Newman
William Newman
Edward Ney
Eleanor Holmes Norton

George Oberlander
Laurie Olin
Harold O'Neil
John O'Shaughnessy
Barry Owenby
John Parsons
Bob Peck
Brian Peper
Joe Persico
Kenneth Pond
Lawrence Rebel
Harry Robinson
Rena Sichel Rosen
Friedrich St.Florian
Rick Santos
Pamela Scott
John Shannon
Fred Smith
Luther Smith
Ray Smith
Richard Striner
Marta Teegen
Ken Terry
Margaret Vanderhye
James van Sweden
Robert Venturi and
  Denise Scott Brown
Kelly Vervish
Raphael Viñoly
Roman Viñoly
James Walsh
George M. White
Haydn Williams
Fred Woerner
Bernard J. Wulff and
  William C. Jackson

# ACKNOWLEDGMENTS

For help in the writing of this book, I would especially like to express my gratitude to Mildred Marmur, my agent, who year in and year out has remained loyal to one of New York's least profitable writers; my research assistants Melinda Rice and Lisa Harrell-Edge, who spent hours in front of the computer on my behalf; Judy Kicinski and the librarians of Sarah Lawrence College; Jennifer Reshen and the staff and students in Academic Computing at Sarah Lawrence College, who came to my rescue time and again; Friedrich St.Florian, who shared his architecture drawings and insight in a way that was an education in itself; Haydn Williams, who through his notes and memory made the history of the National World War II Memorial come alive; Mike Conley, who always came up with more and better information on the National World War II Memorial than I imagined existed; Barry Owenby, who continually kept the larger picture of what it meant to be building a National World War II Memorial in mind; Ken Terry, who was able to break down the most complicated memorial construction problem into understandable steps; Andrea Ferster, who proved a great environmental law teacher; Judy Scott Feldman, who was always willing to explain her opposition to the National World War II Memorial; Senator Bob Dole, who by his very presence summed up the feelings of an entire generation about World War II; Professor Richard Longstreth and Professor Richard Striner, who were kind enough to read chapters of the manuscript; my two editors at Basic Books, Vanessa Mobley and Chip Rossetti, who provided enormous insight; Peter Durbin, who started out as a source of information on his father, Roger Durbin, then took on the duties of a senior editor; Melissa Growden, who supplied a granddaughter's and historian's insight into Roger Durbin; Representative Marcy Kaptur and her congressional staff, who opened my eyes to the six-year ordeal of getting National World War II Memorial legislation passed; Pamela Scott, who shared with me her knowledge of the Mall and allowed me to read prior to publication her essay, "A City Designed as a Work of Art"; Sue Kohler and Susan Raposa of the Commission of Fine Arts, Denise Liebowitz and Mary Beth Murphy of the National Capital Planning Commission, Viki Reath of the General Services Administration, and Sian Imber of Leo A Daly, who were consistently helpful with my requests for information and interviews; Joan Baillon, who supplied much-needed background material and newspaper clippings on the Omaha World War II Memorial; the Woodrow Wilson International Center, for allowing me to be a Visiting Senior Scholar for two years; Sarah Lawrence College for a grant and time off, which aided in the writing of this book; and John Seidman, who read the manuscript from cover to cover with a brother's zeal and a critic's eye.

# NOTES

## INTRODUCTION

1. Daniel Webster, "The Bunker Hill Monument," in *The Works of Daniel Webster*, vol. 1 (Boston: Little and Brown, 1851), pp. 64, 77–78. Andrew Burstein, *America's Jubilee* (New York: Alfred A. Knopf, 2001), p. 29. Maurice G. Baxter, *One and Inseparable: Daniel Webster and the Union* (Cambridge: Harvard University Press, 1984), pp. 81–83.

2. Tom Brokaw, *The Greatest Generation* (New York: Random House, 1998), p. xxx. Steven Ambrose, "The Kids Who Changed the World," *Newsweek*, July 13, 1998, p. 2. Bob Dole, *Remarks at National World War II Memorial Groundbreaking Ceremony*, November 11, 2000.

3. Elisabeth Hess, "A Tale of Two Memorials," *Art in America*, April 1983, p. 121. Edward T. Linenthal, *The Unfinished Bombing: Oklahoma City in American Memory* (New York: Oxford University Press, 2001), p. 227. Kim A. O' Connell, "The Gates of Memory," *Landscape Architecture*, vol. 90 (September 2000), p. 69. John W. Reps, *Monumental Washington* (Princeton: Princeton University Press, 1967), p. 44. Charles L. Griswold, "The Vietnam Veterans Memorial and the Washington Mall," *Critical Inquiry*, vol. 12 (Summer 1986), p. 715. Christopher A. Thomas, *The Lincoln Memorial and American Life* (Princeton: Princeton University Press, 2002), pp. 104, 141. David Dillon, *The Franklin D. Roosevelt Memorial* (Washington, D.C.: Spacemaker Press, 1998), p. 35. Reuben M. Rainey, "The Garden as Narrative: Lawrence Halprin's Franklin Delano Roosevelt Memorial," in Joachim Wolshke-Bulmahn, ed., *Places of Commemoration: Search for Identity and Landscape Design* (Washington, D.C.: Dumbarton Oaks Research Library and Collection, 2001), p. 377.

4. Andrew M. Shanken, "Planning Memory: Living Memorials in the United States During World War II," *Art Bulletin*, vol. 84 (March 2002), p. 6. Karal Ann Marling and John Wetenhall, *Iwo Jima: Monuments, Memories, and the American Hero* (Cambridge: Harvard University Press, 1991), pp. 72, 93, 103–104, 115, 146–150, 164, 169,

3–11. James M. Goode, *The Outdoor Sculpture of Washington, D.C.* (Washington, D.C.: Smithsonian Institution Press, 1974), pp. 189–190.

5. "Dundee Golf Course to Be Memorial to Service Men," *Omaha World-Herald*, November 7, 1944, p. 1A. "Initial Gifts for Memorial Park Reach Total of $113,910," *Omaha World-Herald*, December 12, 1944, p. 1A. "Memorial Park Program Is Submitted to Public," *Omaha World-Herald*, February 4, 1945, p. 1A. "Memorial Park Work to Start Monday; Final Plans Set," *Omaha World-Herald*, September 30, 1945, p. 17A. World War II Memorial Park Association, *Report of the Executive Committee*, February 20, 1946. "War Park Accepted by City," *Omaha World-Herald*, May 28, 1946, p. 1A. "Foundation Poured for Memorial Shrine," *Omaha World-Herald*, September 22, 1946, p. 18A. Terry Henion, "Memorial Park: 40 Years of Beauty, Memories," *Sunday World-Herald Magazine of the Midlands*, May 29, 1988, pp. 11, 19. Joan Baillon, Memorial Completion, E-mail, August 26, 2003. Michael M. Riordan, Omaha Memorial Dimensions, E-mail, September 2, 2003.

6. Eric F. Goldman, *The Crucial Decade—And After: America 1945–1960* (New York: Vintage Books, 1960), pp. 48–50. James T. Patterson, *Grand Expectations: The United States, 1945–1971* (New York: Oxford University Press, 1996), pp. 8, 13–14.

7. Philip Johnson, "War Memorials: What Aesthetic Price Glory?" *Art News*, vol. 44 (September 1945), p. 9.

8. Andrew M. Shanken, "Planning Memory: Living Memorials in the United States During World War II," pp. 130–140.

9. Ibid., 130–142. Percival Goodman, "Real War Memorials," *New York Herald Tribune*, May 17, 1944, p. 18. Louis Bromfield, "Let's Have Living Memorials," *Recreation*, vol. 38 (November 1944), pp. 415, 441–442. John Scott Williams, "On War Memorials," *Art Digest*, vol. 20 (October 15, 1945), p. 32.

10. James E. Young, *The Texture of Memory: Holocaust Memorials and Meaning* (New Haven: Yale University Press, 1993). Jay Winter, *Sites of Memory, Sites of Mourning* (Cambridge: Cambridge University Press, 1993). Kirk Savage, "The Politics of Memory: Black Emancipation and the Civil War Monument," in John R. Gillis, ed., *Commemorations: The Politics of National Identity* (Princeton: Princeton University Press, 1994), pp. 127–149. Sanford Levinson, *Written in Stone: Public Monuments in Changing Societies* (Durham, N.C.: Duke University Press, 1998). Robert Ivy, "Memorials, Monuments, and Meaning," *Architectural Record*, vol. 190 (July 2002), pp. 85–87.

11. Young, *The Texture of Memory*, pp. 10–14.

12. Pamela Scott, "This Vast Empire: The Iconography of the Mall, 1791–1848," in Richard Longstreth, ed., *The Mall in Washington, 1791–1991* (New Haven: Yale University Press, 2002), p. 43. Allan Greenberg, "L'Enfant, Washington, and the Plan of the Capital," *Antiques*, vol. 40 (July 1991), p. 116. John W. Reps, *Monumental Washington: The Planning and Development of the Capital Center* (Princeton: Princeton University Press, 1967), pp. 5–21. Pamela Scott and Antoinette J. Lee, *Buildings of the District of Columbia* (New York: Oxford University Press, 1993), p. 76. Alan Lessoff, *The Nation and Its City: Politics, Corruption, and Progress in Washington, D.C., 1861–1902* (Baltimore: Johns Hopkins University Press, 1994), pp. 174–175. David C. Streatfield,

"The Olmsteds and the Landscape of the Mall," in Richard Longstreth, ed., *The Mall in Washington, 1791–1991* (New Haven: Yale University Press, 2002), p. 120.

13. Richard Guy Wilson quoted in Christopher Shea, "The Brawl on the Mall," *Preservation*, vol. 53 (January–February 2001), p. 40. Andrew Jackson quoted in Lessoff, *The Nation and Its City*, p. 90. Dian Olson Belanger, "The Railroad in the Park," *Washington History*, vol. 2 (Spring 1990), p. 5. Robert Belmont Freeman Jr., "Design Proposals for the Washington National Monument," *Records of the Columbia Historical Society*, vol. 73–74, pp. 167–169. Scott and Lee, *Buildings of the District of Columbia*, p. 101. Mark Twain and Charles Dudley Warner, *The Gilded Age* (New York: Signet Classic, 1969), p. 177. Joe Cannon quoted in Reps, *Monumental Washington*, p. 158.

14. Benjamin Forgey, "A Nasty Skirmish and a Hazy Future; WWII Memorial Back to Drawing Board," *Washington Post*, July 26, 1997, p. F1.

15. Interview with Marcy Kaptur, December 20, 2001. Interviews with Friedrich St.Florian, November 12, 2001, and February 18, 2002.

16. Interview with Bob Dole, June 18, 2002. Interview with Bob Kerrey, July 29, 2002. Interview with J. Carter Brown, November 13, 2001.

17. Interview with Judy Scott Feldman, January 8, 2002. Public Law 107–11, *An Act to expedite the construction of the World War II Memorial in the District of Columbia*, 107th Congress, May 28, 2001. Elaine Sciolino, "War Memorial Seems All but Certain on the Mall," *New York Times*, May 22, 2001, p. A14. Sewall Chan, "WWII Memorial Bill Signed," *Washington Post*, May 29, 2001, p. A1.

18. Monte Reel, "Preservation Law Puts Leash on Mall Projects," *Washington Post*, November 20, 2003, pp. 10–11. *Report of the Joint Task Force on Memorials*, August 2001, pp. 1–4. National Capital Planning Commission, *Memorials and Museums Master Plan*, December 2001, pp. 6–7. Elaine Sciolino, "Agencies Limit New Memorials on Coveted Washington Mall," *New York Times*, September 7, 2001, p. A14. Richard Longstreth, "Monumental Challenge," *Journal of the American Planning Association*, vol. 68 (Spring 2002), pp. 134–136. James Reston Jr., "The Monument Glut," *New York Times Magazine*, September 10, 1995, p. 48. Lincoln Memorial Commission, *Report*, December 15, 1912, p. 30.

19. Commission of Fine Arts. Richard Moe, Letter to J. Carter Brown, Chairman, Commission of Fine Arts, May 20, 1998. Eleanor Holmes Norton, Press Release, May 22, 2001. Michael Richman, "A Memorial with History on Its Side," *Washington Post*, August 27, 2000, p. G7. J. Carter Brown quoted in Shea, "The Brawl on the Mall," p. 39. See Rena Sichel Rosen, *Preserving the Mall: How the World War II Memorial Debate Can Inform Change*, Unpublished Master's Thesis, Graduate School of Architecture, Planning, and Preservation, Columbia University, May 22, 2002.

20. Steven McLeod Bedford, *John Russell Pope: Architect of Empire* (New York: Rizzoli, 1988), p. 222. Joseph Hudnut, "Twilight of the Gods," *Magazine of Art*, vol. 30 (August 1937), pp. 480–484. Roger K. Lewis, "Shaping the City; Trying to See the World War II Memorial from a Future Perspective," *Washington Post*, July 29, 2000, p. G4. Herbert Muschamp, "New War Memorial Is Shrine to Sentiment," *New York*

*Times,* June 7, 2001, pp. A1, A30. Catesby Leigh, "9/11 Memorial Needs a Heroic Touch," *Los Angeles Times,* December 9, 2003, p. 13.

21. Lewis, "Shaping the City," p. G4. Michael Kimmelman, "Turning Memory into Travesty," *New York Times,* March 4, 2001, Section 4, p. 5.

22. Robert Belmont Freeman Jr., "Design Proposals for the Washington National Monument," *Records of the Columbia Historical Society,* vol. 73–74 (1973–43), pp. 167–170. Thomas, *The Lincoln Memorial and American Life,* pp. 39, 118. Edward F. Conklin, *The Lincoln Memorial in Washington* (Washington, D.C.: United States Printing Office, 1927), pp. 17, 22, 24, 27, 31. Bedford, *John Russell Pope: Architect of Empire,* p. 222. Interview with Fred Woerner, July 18, 2002. Interview with Bob Dole, June 18, 2002. Mike Conley, American Battle Monuments Commission, *Fund Raising Totals,* E-mail, June 5, 2003. Interview with Mike Conley, February 9, 2004.

23. Interview with Jim McCloskey, May 29, 2002.

## Chapter One

1. Interview with Representative Marcy Kaptur, December 20, 2001. Interview with Dan Foote, aide to Marcy Kaptur, August 15, 2002. E-mail from Sue Rowe, aide to Marcy Kaptur, May 21, 2003.

2. Testimony of Representative Marcy Kaptur before the National Capital Planning Commission, July 31, 1997.

3. E-mail from Dan Foote, August 20, 2002.

4. Interview with Durbin, Growden, and Sanderson families, August 15, 2002.

5. Interview with Durbin family, August 15–16, 2002. "Roger T. Durbin," *Toledo Blade,* February 13, 2000.

6. Letter from Roger Durbin to Peter Durbin, August 15, 1944. (All Durbin quotations come from Roger Durbin Papers, courtesy of Peter Durbin.)

7. Interview with Durbin family, August 15–16, 2002. Remarks by Roger Durbin to 10th Armored Division Association, September 2, 1990.

8. Interview with Durbin, Growden, and Sanderson families, August 15-16, 2002.

9. Interview with Durbin, Growden, and Sanderson families, August 15–16, 2002.

10. Interview with Harold O'Neil, August 19, 2002.

11. Journées du Patrimoine en wallonie, www.skene.be/RW/aJLP99/99lux003.html. Memorial du Mardasson, www.chez.com/chezlecoiffeur/bast1.htm. Joe Cook, "Visit to WWII Monument Comforting," *Star-Beacon,* March 13, 1992.

12. Roger Durbin, World War II Memorial Site, April 2, 1998.

13. Interview with Representative Marcy Kaptur, December 20, 2001. Michael Barone, Richard E. Cohen, and Charles E. Cook, eds., *Almanac of American Politics* (Washington, D.C.: National Journal, 2001), 1212–1214. Jack Torry, "Ohio's Maverick Kaptur Runs as Senior Democratic Woman in House," *Pittsburgh Post-Gazette,* May 31, 1999, p. A13. Sue Rowe, Background on Marcy Kaptur, E-mail, June 12, 2003.

14. Interview with Representative Marcy Kaptur, December 20, 2001.

15. Ibid.

16. H.R. 3742. Committee on Veterans' Affairs, *Report,* 100th Congress, 2nd Session, July 7, 1988.

17. Congressional Research Service, *Legislative History of the World War II Memorial and World War II Commemorative Legislation,* April 16, 2002, pp. 5–6 (hereafter cited as *Leg. History*). Testimony of Marcy Kaptur at *Hearings Before the Subcommittee on House and Memorial Affairs of the Committee on Veterans' Affairs,* July 11, 1991.

18. Congressional Research Service, *Leg. History,* pp. 6–7.

19. Ibid., p. 7.

20. Ibid. *Hearings Before the Subcommittee on Consumer Affairs and Coinage, Committee on Banking, Finance, and Urban Affairs, House of Representatives,* April 4, 1990, pp. 1–5.

21. Congressional Research Service, *Leg. History,* p. 8. *Congressional Record,* June 30, 1992, pp. H 5672–75. Interview with Representative Marcy Kaptur, December 20, 2001. Bill McAllister, "Foundations Finances Seen in Poor Shape: Wall of Liberty Project May Not Be Completed," *Washington Post,* June 7, 1994, p. A14. Joe Smydo, "Plans for Normandy Memorial Alive, But Barely," *Pittsburgh Post-Gazette,* February 24, 2002, p. A3.

22. Congressional Research Service, *Leg. History,* p. 7.

23. Ibid., pp. 11–12. Congresswoman Marcy Kaptur, *History of the World War II Memorial Legislation,* n.d.

24. Public Law 102–414, *World War II 50th Anniversary Commemorative Coins Act,* 102d Congress, October 14, 1992. Interview with Mike Conley, February 9, 2004.

25. Kaptur, *History.* Congressional Research Service, *Leg. History,* pp. 8-10. Bill McAlliser, "Seeking a Fantastic Memorial to a 'Fantastic' War," *Washington Post,* July 10, 1992, p. A19.

26. Kaptur, *History.* Congressional Research Service, *Leg. History,* pp. 11–12.

27. Public Law 103–32, 103d Congress, May 25, 1993.

28. Interview with the Durbin, Growden, and Sanderson families, August 15–16, 2002.

29. Howard Schneider and N. Scott Vance, "Center of Mall Reserved for WWII Shrine," *Washington Post,* November 12, 1995, p. B6. Bill Clinton, Remarks at the Dedication of the World War II Memorial Site, November 11, 1995. Remarks by Roger Durbin, Celebrating the Stamp Unveiling, November 10, 1988.

30. Roger Durbin, World War II Memorial Site, April 2, 1988. Interview with Marian Durbin, August 16, 2002.

31. Roger Durbin, World War II Memorial Site, April 2, 1998. Roger Durbin, Letter to the editor, n.d.

32. Joseph Ellis, "Right Time, Wrong Place," *New York Times,* March 24, 1997, p. 15. Roger Durbin, Letter to the Editor, n.d.

33. Interview with Durbin, Growden, and Sanderson families, August 15–16, 2002.

34. Interview with Representative Marcy Kaptur, December 20, 2001.

## Chapter Two

1. Interview with Barry Owenby, January 6, 2003.

2. Pierre Charles L'Enfant, Letter to George Washington, August 19, 1791, reprinted in H. Paul Caemmerer, *The Life of Pierre Charles L'Enfant* (New York: Da Capo Press, 1970), p. 158.

3. Pierre Charles L'Enfant, Letter to George Washington, September 11, 1789, reprinted in Caemmerer, *The Life of Pierre Charles L'Enfant,* pp. 127–128.

4. John W. Reps, *Monumental Washington: The Planning and Development of the Capital Center* (Princeton: Princeton University Press, 1967), pp. 5–9. Frederick Gutheim, *Worthy of the Nation: The History of Planning for the National Capital* (Washington, D.C.: Smithsonian Institution, 1977), pp. 18–19.

5. Dumas Malone, *Jefferson and the Rights of Man* (Boston: Little, Brown, 1951), p. 371.

6. Pierre Charles L'Enfant, Letter to George Washington, September 11, 1789, p. 128. Allan Greenberg, "L'Enfant, Washington, and the Plan of the Capital," *Antiques,* July 1991, p. 114.

7. Thomas Jefferson, Letter to Major Pierre Charles L'Enfant, April 10, 1791, in Merrill D. Peterson, *The Portable Thomas Jefferson* (New York: Penguin Books, 1977), p. 453.

8. Pierre Charles L'Enfant, Letter to Thomas Jefferson, April 4, 1791, in Caemmerer, *The Life of Pierre Charles L'Enfant,* pp. 145–146. Pamela Scott, "This Vast Empire: The Iconography of the Mall, 1791–1848," in Richard Longstreth, ed., *The Mall in Washington, 1791–1991* (New Haven: Yale University Press, 2002), p. 43. Greenberg, "L'Enfant, Washington, and the Plan of the Capital," p. 116.

9. Pierre Charles L'Enfant, "Plan of the City," *Gazette of the United States,* January 4, 1792, reprinted in Caemmerer, *The Life of Pierre Charles L'Enfant,* p. 164. Pierre Charles L'Enfant, "Progress Report to George Washington," June 22, 1791, reprinted in Caemmerer, *The Life of Pierre Charles L'Enfant,* p. 152.

10. L'Enfant, "Progress Report," pp. 152, 153. Pierre Charles L'Enfant, Letter to George Washington, August 19, 1791, reprinted in Caemmerer, *The Life of Pierre Charles L'Enfant,* p. 157. L'Enfant, "Plan of the City," p. 164. Greenberg, "L'Enfant, Washington, and the Plan of the Capital," p. 118.

11. Pierre Charles L'Enfant, Letter to George Washington, August 19, 1791, p. 157. L'Enfant, "Progress Report," p. 154.

12. Scott, "This Vast Empire," p. 46. Thomas Jefferson, Letter to Pierre Charles L'Enfant, February 27, 1792, in Caemmerer, *The Life of Pierre Charles L'Enfant,* pp. 212–213.

13. Pierre Charles L'Enfant, Letter to Thomas Jefferson, February 26, 1792, in Caemmerer, *The Life of Pierre Charles L'Enfant,* pp. 210–212. George Washington, Letter to Pierre Charles L'Enfant, December 2, 1791, in Caemmerer, *The Life of Pierre Charles L'Enfant,* pp. 181–182. Constance McLaughlin Green, *Washington: Village and Capital, 1800–1878* (Princeton: Princeton University Press, 1962), p. 14. Reps, *Monu-*

*mental Washington,* pp. 5, 22. Thomas Jefferson, Letter to Daniel Carroll, March 1, 1792, in Saul K. Padover, ed., *Thomas Jefferson and the National Capital* (Washington, D.C.: United States Government Printing Office, 1946), p. 102.

14. Scott, "This Vast Empire," p. 46.

15. Reps, *Monumental Washington,* pp. 36–37.

16. Scott, "This Vast Empire," pp. 46–47.

17. Pamela Scott and Antoinette J. Lee, *Buildings of the District of Columbia* (Washington, D.C.: Oxford University Press, 1993), p. 70. Gutheim, *Worthy of the Nation,* p. 51. Scott, "This Vast Empire," p. 47.

18. Scott and Lee, *Buildings of the District of Columbia,* p. 70. Richard Longstreth, Letter, July 18, 2003. Andrew Jackson Downing, *A Treatise on the Theory and Practice of Landscape Gardening Adapted to North America* (Washington, D.C.: Dumbarton Oaks Research Library and Collection, 1991), p. 18.

19. Andrew Jackson Downing, "Explanatory Notes (To accompany the plan for improving the Public Grounds at Washington)," and Andrew Jackson Downing, Letter to Joseph Henry, February 23, 1852, in Wilcomb E. Washburn, "Vision of Life for the Mall," *American Institute of Architects Journal* 47 (March 1967), pp. 54–56. David Schuyler, *Apostle of Taste: Andrew Jackson Downing, 1815–1852* (Baltimore: Johns Hopkins University Press, 1996), p. 201.

20. Therese O'Malley, "A Public Museum of Trees: Mid-Nineteenth Century Plans for the Mall," in Richard Longstreth, ed., *The Mall in Washington, 1791–1991* (New Haven: Yale University Press, 2002), p. 72. Daniel Rieff, *Washington Architecture, 1791–1861: Problems in Development* (Washington, D.C.: U.S. Commission of Fine Arts, 1971), p. 46. Gutheim, *Worthy of the Nation,* p. 63. Mark Twain quoted in Frank Freidel and Lonnelle Aikman, *George Washington: Man and Monument* (Washington, D.C.: Washington National Monument Association, 1965), p. 48. Mark Twain and Charles Dudley Warner, *The Gilded Age* (New York: Signet Classic, 1969), p. 177.

21. Charles Dickens, *American Notes* (Baltimore: Penguin Books, 1972), pp. 163–164. Reps, *Monumental Washington,* p. 56. Frederick Gutheim, *The Federal City: Plans and Realities* (Washington, D.C.: Smithsonian Institution Press, 1976), p. 21. Richard Longstreth, Letter, July 18, 2003. Alan Lessoff, *The Nation and Its City: Politics, Corruption, and Progress in Washington, D.C., 1861–1902* (Baltimore: Johns Hopkins University Press, 1994), p. 89.

22. Lessoff, *The Nation and Its City,* pp. 90–91.

23. Freidel and Aikman, *George Washington: Man and Monument,* pp. 44–48.

24. Lessoff, *The Nation and Its City,* pp. 175–176. David C. Streatfield, "The Olmsteds and the Landscape of the Mall," in Richard Longstreth, ed., *The Mall in Washington, 1791–1991* (New Haven: Yale University Press, 2002), p. 120. Reps, *Monumental Washington,* p. 66.

25. Gutheim, *Worthy of the Nation,* p. 84. Reps, *Monumental Washington,* p. 66. Carol M. Highsmith and Ted Landphair, *Union Station: A Decorative History of Washington's Grand Terminal* (Washington, D.C.: Chelsea Publishing, 1988), pp. 17–21.

Dian Olson Belanger, "The Railroad in the Park," *Washington History*, vol. 2 (Spring 1990), pp. 5, 10-15.

26. Scott and Lee, *Buildings of the District of Columbia*, pp. 72–73.

27. David C. Streatfield, "The Olmsteads and the Landscape of the Mall," p. 119.

28. Reps, *Monumental Washington,* pp. 72–84.

29. Frederick Law Olmsted Jr., "Landscape in Connection with Public Buildings in Washington," in Glenn Brown, *Papers Relating to the Improvement of the City of Washington, District of Columbia,* 56th Congress, 2nd session, Senate Document 94 (Washington, D.C.: U.S. Government Printing Office, 1901), p. 28.

30. Reps, *Monumental Washington,* pp. 92–95.

31. Olmsted Jr., "Landscape in Connection with Public Buildings in Washington," p. 34. Reps, *Monumental Washington,* pp. 94-100.

32. *The Improvement of the Park System of the District of Columbia* (Washington, D.C.: Government Printing Office, 1902), p. 35–51.

33. Ibid., pp. 23, 43–44.

34. Frederick Law Olmsted Jr., quoted in Glenn Brown, *Memories, 1860–1930* (Washington, D.C.: W. F. Roberts, 1931), p. 261. *The Improvement of the Park System of the District of Columbia*, pp. 40–45.

35. *The Improvement of the Park System of the District of Columbia*, pp. 47–50.

36. Ibid., pp. 51–52.

37. Reps, *Monumental Washington,* pp. 107–109, 140.

38. Thomas S. Hines, *Burnham of Chicago: Architect and Planner* (Chicago: University of Chicago Press, 1979), pp. 149, 155.

39. Richard Longstreth, "Introduction: Change and Continuity on the Mall, 1791–199l," in Richard Longstreth, ed., *The Mall in Washington, 1791–1991* (New Haven: Yale University Press, 2002), p. 12. Frederick Law Olmsted Jr. quoted in Gutheim, *Worthy of the Nation,* p. 218.

40. Reps, *Monumental Washington,* pp. 146–149.

41. Christopher Thomas, *The Lincoln Memorial and American Life* (Princeton: Princeton University Press, 2002), pp. 31–40, 158.

42. Thomas, *The Lincoln Memorial,* pp. 36–42. Michael Richman, "A Memorial with History on Its Side," *Washington Post,* August 27, 2000, p. G7.

43. Reps, *Monumental Washington,* p. 162. Gutheim, *Worthy of the Nation,* p. 132.

44. *The Improvement of the Park System of the District of Columbia,* pp. 49–50. Sue Kohler, *The Commission of Fine Arts: A Brief History, 1910–1995* (Washington, D.C.: Commission of Fine Arts, 1995), pp. 68–69. Reps, *Monumental Washington,* pp. 176–177.

45. Reps, *Monumental Washington,* p. 173.

46. Streatfield, "The Olmsteds and the Landscape of the Mall," p. 138.

47. T. Sutton Jett, "Renaissance of the Grand Mall," *Parks and Recreation,* April 1966, p. 326. J. Carter Brown, "The Mall and the Commission of Fine Arts," in Richard Longstreth, ed., *The Mall in Washington, 1791–1991* (New Haven: Yale University Press, 2002), pp. 249–250.

48. Commission of Fine Arts, *Ninth Report,* 1921, pp. 25–26. David Brinkley, *Washington Goes to War* (New York: Ballantine Books, 1996), p. 119. Brown, "The Mall and the Commission of Fine Arts," pp. 251–254. *Constitution Gardens,* www.nps.gov/coga/index2.htm.

49. Brown, "The Mall and the Commission of Fine Arts," p. 249.

50. Ibid., p. 257.

51. Michael H. Koby and Ash Jain, "Memorializing Our Nation's Heroes: A Legislative Proposal to Amend the Commemorative Works Act," *Journal of Law and Politics,* vol. 17 (Winter 2001), pp. 117–118.

52. Statement of J. Carter Brown, March 18, 1986, *Hearing Before the Subcommittee on Public Lands, Reserved Water and Resource Conservation of the Committee on Energy and Natural Resources United States Senate,* March 16, 1986, pp. 38–39. *Commemorative Works Act,* Public Law 99–652, Section I, 99th Congress, November 14, 1986.

53. Koby and Jain, "Memorializing Our Nation's Heroes," pp. 116–117. Reuben M. Rainey, "The Garden as Narrative: Lawrence Halprin's Franklin Delano Roosevelt Memorial," in Joachim Wolshke-Bulmahn, ed., *Places of Commemoration: Search for Identity and Landscape Design* (Washington, D.C.: Dumbarton Oaks Research Library and Collection, 2001), p. 381. J. William Thompson, "The Power of Place," *Landscape Architecture,* vol. 87 (July 1997), p. 64.

54. Benjamin Forgey, "Washington's Monumental Excess," *Washington Post,* June 16, 1990, B01. James Reston Jr., "The Monument Glut," *New York Times Magazine,* September 10, 1995, p. 48.

55. Forgey, "Washington's Monumental Excess," p. B01.

56. Reston, "The Monument Glut," p. 48.

57. Al Horne, "A Monumental Proposal," *Washington Post,* May 8, 1997, p. C26. Bob Dart, "Monumental Problem Building," *Atlanta Journal-Constitution,* October 18, 1997, p. A10. Deborah K. Dietsch, "Remember This: Memorial Mania in America," *Architecture Boston,* 2000, pp. 24–26. Richard Longstreth, "Monumental Challenge," *APA Journal,* vol. 68 (Spring 2002), pp. 134–136. *Report of the Joint Task Force on Memorials,* August 2001, pp. 1–4. Koby and Jain, "Memorializing Our Nation's Heroes," p. 131. Monte Reel, "Preservation Law Puts Leash on Mall Projects," *Washington Post,* November 20, 2003, p. Z10.

## CHAPTER THREE

1. Public Law 107–11, *An Act to expedite the construction of the World War II Memorial in the District of Columbia,* 107th Congress, May 28, 2001.

2. Linda Wheeler, "World War II Memorial Site to Be Reconsidered," *Washington Post,* May 4, 2001, p. A1. Bob Stump, quoted in Linda Wheeler, "House Vote Backs World War II Memorial as Planned," *Washington Post,* May 16, 2001, p. A1. "World War II Memorial Saga May Be Near End," *Architectural Record,* vol. 189 (June 2001), p. 30.

3. National Center for Veterans Analysis and Statistics, Department of Veterans Affairs, October 24, 2003. Interview with Mike Conley, October 20, 2003. See also

Mike Anton, "Strains of Taps Over and Over," *Los Angeles Times*, November 11, 2002, p. A1.

4. Ada Louise Huxtable, "The Washington Monument, 1836–1884," *Progressive Architecture*, vol. 138 (August 1957), p. 142. Frederick Gutheim, "Who Designed the Washington Monument?" *AIA Journal*, vol. 15 (March 1951), p. 136. Garry Wills, *Cincinnatus: George Washington and the Enlightenment* (Garden City, N.Y.: Doubleday, 1984), pp. xix–xx. John Jay quoted in Kirk Savage, "The Self-Made Monument," in Harriet F. Senie and Sally Webster, eds., *Critical Issues in Public Art: Content, Context, and Controversy* (New York: HarperCollins, 1992), pp. 6–8.

5. Kirk Savage, "The Self-Made Monument," pp. 10–12.

6. Frank Freidel and Lonnelle Aikman, *George Washington: Man and Monument* (Washington, D.C.: Washington National Monument Association, 1965), p. 32. Milton W. Brown, *American Art to 1900* (New York: Abrams, 1977), p. 373.

7. Freidel and Aikman, *George Washington*, pp. 32–35. George Watterston quoted in Savage, "The Self-Made Monument," pp. 13–16. Robert Belmont Freeman Jr., "Design Proposals for the Washington National Monument," *Records of the Columbia Historical Society*, 1973–1974, p. 162.

8. John M. Bryan, *Robert Mills: America's First Architect* (New York: Princeton Architectural Press, 2001), p. 290. Savage, "The Self-Made Monument," pp. 16–17.

9. Robert C. Winthrop, *Oration on the Occasion of the Laying of the Cornerstone of the National Monument to George Washington* (Washington, D.C.: J. and G.S. Gideon, 1848), p. 35. Freidel and Aikman, *George Washington*, pp. 38–44.

10. Savage, "The Self-Made Monument," p. 18. Henry Adams, *The Education of Henry Adams* (New York: Modern Library, 1931), p. 44.

11. Savage, "The Self-Made Monument," p. 19. Huxtable, "The Washington Monument," p. 143. Freidel and Aikman, *George Washington*, pp. 48–53.

12. Huxtable, "The Washington Monument," p. 143. Henry van Brunt, "The Washington Monument," *American Art Review* (1880), p. 10. Freidel and Aikman, *George Washington*, p. 40.

13. Savage, "The Self-Made Monument," pp. 21–22. Freidel and Aikman, *George Washington*, p. 53.

14. Savage, "The Self-Made Monument," pp. 24–25.

15. Christopher A. Thomas, *The Lincoln Memorial and American Life* (Princeton: Princeton University Press, 2002), p. 5. *Improvement of the Park System of the District of Columbia* (Washington: Government Printing Office, 1902), pp. 51–52.

16. Thomas, *The Lincoln Memorial and American Life*, pp. 5–6.

17. James M. Goode, *The Outdoor Sculpture of Washington, D.C.* (Washington, D.C.: Smithsonian Institution Press, 1974), p. 86. David W. Bright, *Race and Reunion: The Civil War in American Memory* (Cambridge: Harvard University Press, 2001), pp. 26–27.

18. *Improvement of the Park System of the District of Columbia*, pp. 51–52.

19. Thomas, *The Lincoln Memorial and American Life*, pp. 17–19, 26–27.

20. Ibid., pp. 32–33.

21. Ibid., pp. 36–37. *Lincoln Memorial Commission Report*, 62nd Congress, 3rd Session, Senate Document 965, December 5, 1912, p. 8.

22. Appendix A, Report of the Commission of Fine Arts on the Site and Selection of a Designer for the Lincoln Memorial, July 17, 1911, in *Lincoln Memorial Commission Report*, pp. 22–23.

23. Thomas, *The Lincoln Memorial and American Life*, pp. 40, 50, 78–80.

24. Appendix E and Appendix G, *Lincoln Memorial Commission Report*, pp. 35–36, 39–41. Stephen McLeod Bedford, *John Russell Pope: Architect of Empire* (New York: Rizzoli, 1988), pp. 128–130. Thomas, *The Lincoln Memorial and American Life*, p. 63.

25. Thomas, *The Lincoln Memorial and American Life*, pp. 94–97, 157.

26. Charles Moore quoted in Sue Kohler, *The Commission of Fine Arts: A Brief History, 1910–1995* (Washington, D.C.: U.S. Government Printing Office, 1996), p. 73.

27. Ibid., p. 68.

28. Ibid., p. 68. Bedford, *John Russell Pope*, p. 215.

29. Bedford, *John Russell Pope*, pp. 216–217.

30. Ibid., pp. 217–220.

31. Ibid., p. 220.

32. John W. Reps, *Monumental Washington: The Planning and Development of the Capital Center* (Princeton: Princeton University Press, 1967), p. 173. "Facts from the Fine Arts Commission," *Magazine of Art*, vol. 31 (June 1938), p. 348.

33. "Facts from the Fine Arts Commission," p. 348. Kohler, *The Commission of Fine Arts*, p. 72. Bedford, *John Russell Pope*, p. 222.

34. Bedford, *John Russell Pope*, p. 222. William Lescaze, "America's Outgrowing Imitation Greek Architecture," *Architectural Record*, vol. 82 (August 1937), p. 55. Joseph Hudnut, "Classical Architecture Not Essential," *Architectural Record*, vol. 82 (August 1937), p. 55.

35. Bedford, *John Russell Pope*, p. 222. Kohler, *The Commission of Fine Arts*, p. 73. "Mr. Kimball on the Jefferson Memorial," *Magazine of Art*, vol. 31 (May 1938), p. 316.

36. Bedford, *John Russell Pope*, p. 222. Kohler, *Commission of Fine Arts*, p. 73. Franklin Delano Roosevelt, "Address at the Dedication of the Thomas Jefferson Memorial, Washington, D.C., April 13, 1943. Sidney Shalett, "Roosevelt, Hailing Jefferson, Looks to Gain in Liberty," *New York Times*, April 14, 1943, pp. 1, 16.

37. "Reagan Makes His First Visit to Vietnam Memorial on the Mall," *New York Times*, May 2, 1983, p. A15. Patrick Hagopian, "The Commemorative Landscape of the Vietnam War," in Joachim Wolschke-Bulmahn, ed., *Places of Commemoration: Search for Identity and Landscape Design* (Washington, D.C.: Dumbarton Oaks Research Library and Collection, 2001), pp. 316–317. Bernard Weinraub, "Carter Hails Veterans of Vietnam in Signing Bill for a War Memorial," *New York Times*, July 2, 1980, p. A14. J. Carter Brown, "The Mall and the Commission of Fine Arts," in Richard Longstreth, ed., *The Mall in Washington, 1791–1991* (New Haven: Yale University Press, 2003), p. 257. Joel Swerdlow, "To Heal a Nation," *National Geographic*, May 1985, p. 566. "Student Wins War Memorial Contest," *New York Times*, May 7, 1981, p. A20.

38. Swerdlow, "To Heal a Nation," p. 566. Kohler, *The Commission of Fine Arts,* p. 126.

39. Kohler, *The Commission of Fine Arts,* pp. 127–128. Karl Ann Marling and Robert Silberman, "The Statue Near the Wall," *Smithsonian Studies in American Art,* Spring 1987, p. 11. "Stop That Monument," *National Review,* September 18, 1981, p. 1064. Charles Krauthammer, "Memorials," *New Republic,* May 16, 1981, p. 43. Tom Carhart, "Insulting Vietnam Vets," *New York Times,* October 24, 1981, Section One, p. 23. James H. Webb Jr., "Reassessing the Vietnam Veterans Memorial," *Wall Street Journal,* December 18, 1981, p. 22.

40. Kohler, *The Commission of Fine Arts,* pp. 127–128. Elizabeth Hess, "A Tale of Two Memorials," *Art in America,* April 1983, p. 122. Louis Menand, "The Reluctant Memorialist," *New Yorker,* July 8, 2002, p. 59.

41. Hess, "A Tale of Two Memorials," p. 122. Hagopian, "The Commemorative Landscape of the Vietnam War," pp. 320–321. "Watt Raises Obstacle on Vietnam," *New York Times,* January 13, 1982, p. A12.

42. Benjamin Forgey, "Memorial Delayed," *Washington Post,* February 27, 1982, p. C1. Hess, "A Tale of Two Memorials," p. 125. Kohler, *Commission of Fine Arts,* p. 129.

43. Brown, "The Mall and the Commission of Fine Arts," p. 258.

44. Hagopian, "The Commemorative Landscape of the Vietnam War," p. 322. Kohler, *The Commission of Fine Arts,* p. 130.

45. Benjamin Forgey, "Vietnam Memorial Changes Clear Last Major Hurdle," *Washington Post,* October 14, 1982, A1. Jane Addams Allen, "Vietnam Memorial Gets a Spanish Face," *Washington Times,* January 1, 1989, pp. 1A, 12A. Menand, "The Reluctant Memorialist," p. 60. Tom Wolfe, "Art Disputes War: The Battle of the Vietnam Memorial," *Washington Post,* October 13, 1982, B3.

46. Irwin Molotsky, "Changes Set in Viet Memorial," *New York Times,* October 14, 1982, p. C17. Hess, "A Tale of Two Memorials," pp. 123–124. Frederick Hart, "Letter on Vietnam Memorial Controversy," *Art News,* vol. 71 (November 1983), p. 5. Rick Horowitz, "Maya Lin's Angry Objections," *Washington Post,* July 7, 1982, p. B1. Marling and Silberman, "The Statue Near the Wall," p. 14.

47. Betty Cuniberti, "Battle Heats Up Again Over Role of Women," *Los Angeles Times,* November 11, 1987, p. 1. Roxanne Roberts, "New Vietnam Memorial Readied on Mall," *Washington Post,* November 2, 1993, p. A1. J. Carter Brown, "The Mall and the Commission of Fine Arts," p. 260. Charles L. Griswold, "The Vietnam Veterans Memorial and the Washington Mall," *Critical Inquiry,* vol. 12 (Summer 1986), pp. 688–719. Jeffrey Karl Ochsner, "A Space of Loss: The Vietnam Veterans Memorial," *Journal of Architecture and Education,* vol. 50 (February 1997), pp. 158–171.

48. "The Battle of the War Memorial," *Art News,* vol. 90 (April 1991), pp. 40–41.

49. Ash Jain, "Memorializing Our Nation's Heroes: A Legislative Proposal to Amend the Commemorative Works Act," *Journal of Law and Politics,* vol. 17 (Winter 2001), p. 122. Jory Johnson, "Granite Platoon," *Landscape Architecture,* vol. 80 (January 1990), pp. 69–70.

50. Johnson, "Granite Platoon," pp. 69–71. Kohler, *The Commission of Fine Arts*, p. 166.

51. Kohler, *The Commission of Fine Arts*, pp. 167–168. Heidi Landecker, "Architects File Suit Over Changes in Korean War Memorial Design," *Architecture*, vol. 80 (February 1991), pp. 26–27.

52. Kohler, *The Commission of Fine Arts*, p. 168. "The Battle of the War Memorial," pp. 40–41. "Four Architects Suing Over War Memorial," *New York Times*, December 19, 1990, p. C22. Barbara Gamarekian, "Architects Clash Over Korean War Memorial," *New York Times*, December 15, 1990, Section 1, p. 17.

53. Sarah Booth Conroy, "Korea War Memorial Praised," *Washington Post*, February 22, 1991, p. B2. Benjamin Forgey, "The Korean Controversy," *Washington Post*, February 2, 1991, p. D1. Sarah Booth Conroy, "Korean War Memorial Design Fails Again," *Washington Post*, October 25, 1991, p. B2.

54. Sarah Booth Conroy, "Arts Panel Approves Korean War Memorial," *Washington Post*, January 17, 1992, p. C1.

55. Thomas Vonier, "A Wall, a Mural, and Then Some," *Progressive Architecture*, vol. 76 (August 1995), p. 25. Gregg Zoroya, "Korean War Repair," *USA Today*, September 4, 1998, p. 3D. Deborah Dietsch, "Compromised Commemoration," *Architecture*, vol. 84 (September 1995), p. 15. Menand, "Reluctant Memorialist," p. 62. James Reston Jr., "The Monument Glut," *New York Times Magazine*, September 10, 1995, p. 48.

56. Doug Struck, "Clinton Dedicates Memorial," *Washington Post*, May 3, 1997, p. A1. David Dillon, *The Franklin D. Roosevelt Memorial* (Washington, D.C.: Spacemaker Press, 1998), p. 22.

57. Dillon, *The Franklin D. Roosevelt Memorial*, pp. 22–26.

58. Wolf von Eckardt, "The Making of a Monument," *Washington Post*, April 26, 1980, p. C1. Testimony Before House Administration Subcommittee, June 8, 1962, in Dillon, *The Franklin D. Roosevelt Memorial*, p. 26. Frederick Gutheim, "Looking at Architecture," *Washington Post*, December 31, 1960, p. B1. Kohler, *The Commission of Fine Arts*, pp. 86–89.

59. Dillon, *The Franklin D. Roosevelt Memorial*, pp. 27–30. Reuben M. Rainey, "The Garden as Narrative: Lawrence Halprin's Franklin Delano Roosevelt Memorial," in Joachim Wolshke-Bulmahn, ed., *Places of Commemoration: Search for Identity and Landscape Design* (Washington, D.C.: Dumbarton Oaks Research Library, 2001), p. 382. Isabel Hyman, "Marcel Breuer and the Franklin Delano Roosevelt Memorial," *Journal of the Society of Architectural Historians*, vol. 54 (December 1995), pp. 447–449.

60. Kohler, *The Commission of Fine Arts*, p. 90. Dillon, *The Franklin D. Roosevelt Memorial*, p. 30. Hyman, "Marcel Breuer and the Franklin Delano Roosevelt Memorial," pp. 448–452.

61. Felix Frankfurter, "What FDR Wanted," *Atlantic Monthly*, March 1961, pp. 39–40. Rupert Cornwell, "FDR's Memory," *Independent*, July 7, 1996, p. 13. Benjamin Forgey, "Recognition for a President Who Confronted Fear Itself," *Washington Post*, April 27, 1977, p. G1. Kohler, *The Commission of Fine Arts*, p. 91. Dillon, *The Franklin*

*D. Roosevelt Memorial*, pp. 30–32. J. William Thompson, *Landscape Architecture*, vol. 87 (July 1997), p. 64.

62. Lawrence Halprin, *The Franklin Delano Roosevelt Memorial* (San Francisco: Chronicle Books, 1997), pp. 1, 6. Dillon, *The Franklin D. Roosevelt Memorial*, p. 30.

63. Rainey, "The Garden as Narrative," pp. 378, 385–387. Dillon, *The Franklin D. Roosevelt Memorial*, p. 34–35.

64. Halprin, *The Franklin Delano Roosevelt Memorial*, p. 23. Forgey, "Recognition of the President Who Confronted Fear Itself," p. G1. Charles Krauthammer, "The FDR Memorial Scam," *Washington Post*, May 9, 1997, p. A25. Roger Lewis, "Washington Monuments: Battles Over the Mall," *Architectural Record*, vol. 184 (January 1996), p. 18. Paul Richard, "The Memorial's Old Deal," *Washington Post*, April 27, 1997, p. G6.

65. Mary McGrory, "FDR Sits Corrected," *Washington Post*, May 1, 1997, p. A2. Nancy N. Kari and Harry C. Boyte, "Work of the People," *Public Art Review* (Fall-Winter, 1997), pp. 10–11.

66. Lawrence Halprin, "Halprin on the FDR Memorial," *Landscape Architecture*, June 2001, p. 7. Jack Rosenberg, "Protests Over FDR Memorial," *Art in America*, vol. 83 (July 1995), p. 19. Hugh Sidey, "Where's His Wheelchair?" *Time*, March 6, 1995, p. 105.

67. Online NewsHour, "FDR Memorial Opening," May 1, 1997, www./pbs.org/newshour/bb/remember/1997/fdr_5–1.html. Russell Baker, "Leave a Little Unchiseled," *New York Times*, April 26, 1997, Section One, p. 21. Marc Fisher, "Forcibly Updating History," *Landscape Architecture*, April 2001, p. 132. Sidey, "Where's His Wheelchair?" p. 105. Neely Tucker, "A Wheelchair Gains a Place at FDR Memorial," *Washington Post*, January 7, 2001, p. C1. Halprin, "Halprin on the FDR Memorial," p. 7.

68. Halprin, "Halprin on the FDR Memorial," p. 7.

## Chapter Four

1. Interview with General P. X. Kelley, October 21, 2002. Al Kamen, "Clinton Could Face Enemy at Omaha Beach," *Washington Post*, March 23, 1994, p. A19.

2. Interview with General P. X. Kelley, October 21, 2002. American Battle Monuments Commission, *Fiscal Year 2000 Report*, p. 24.

3. *Memorandum for Record, 117th ABMC Commissioners' Meeting, April 27, 1994.* Interview with General Fred Woerner, July 18, 2002.

4. Interview with Haydn Williams, May 15, 2003. Memorial Advisory Board list, April 28, 1994. *Record of Proceedings for 118th Meeting of American Battle Monuments Commission*, September 29, 1994. Interview with General Fred Woerner, July 18, 2002.

5. Interview with General Fred Woerner, July 18, 2002.

6. American Battle Monuments Commission, *Chronology*, May 28, 2001, p. 1. Haydn Williams, Background Interview, April 7, 2003.

7. Interview with Davis Buckley, January 10, 2002. American Battle Monuments Commission, *Chronology*, p. 2.

8. Davis Buckley Architects and Planners, *Site Selection Report for the World War II Memorial*, May 9, 1995, pp. 2–14.

9. Haydn Williams, Background Interview, April 7, 2003. Interview Haydn Williams, May 15, 2003.

10. Interview Haydn Williams, May 15, 2003. National Capital Memorial Commission, *Transcript of Commission Meeting*, May 9, 1995, pp. 27, 37, 49, 85, 95.

11. *Record of Proceedings for 119th Meeting of American Battle Monuments Commission*, May 12, 1995. Haydn Williams, Background Interview, April 7, 2003. Interview with Haydn Williams, May 15, 2003. National Capital Memorial Commission, *Transcript of Commission Meeting*, June 20, 1995, pp. 7, 8, 61, 63, 64, 66, 71.

12. National Park Service, *World War II Memorial Suggested Program Elements*, July 19, 1995, pp. 1–2. Haydn Williams, Background Interview, April 7, 2003. Commission of Fine Arts, *Transcript of Commission Meeting*, July 27, 1995, pp. 16–40.

13. Commission of Fine Arts, *Transcript of Commission Meeting*, July 27, 1995, pp. 54–55. Commission of Fine Arts, *Minutes of the Meeting*, July 27, 1995, p. 4. Interview with J. Carter Brown, November 13, 2001.

14. Commission of Fine Arts, *Minutes of the Meeting*, July 27, 1995, pp. 4–6.

15. Interview with Haydn Williams, June 20, 2002. National Capital Planning Commission, *Transcript of Commission Meeting*, July 27, 1995, p. 60. Kathleen Hall Jamieson, *Dirty Politics: Deception, Distraction, and Democracy* (New York: Oxford University Press, 1992), pp. 94–95.

16. Benjamin Forgey, "No Accord on WWII Memorial; Two Agencies Send Mixed Signals About Location," *Washington Post*, July 28, 1995, p. B3. Commission of Fine Arts, *Transcript of Commission Meeting*, July 27, 1995, p. 55. National Capital Planning Commission, *Transcript of Commission Meeting*, July 27, 1995, pp. 38–39.

17. National Capital Planning Commission. Hugh Carey and Haydn Williams, Letter to Harvey Gantt, J. Carter Brown, and John Parsons, August 3, 1995. Haydn Williams, Background Interview, April 7, 2003. Interview with Haydn Williams, April 11, 2003.

18. Interview with Haydn Williams, June 24, 2003. Commission of Fine Arts. Robert Stanton, Letter to J. Carter Brown, September 15, 1995.

19. Davis Buckley, *World War II Memorial Site Selection Report*, September 19, 1995, pp. 22–24.

20. National Capital Planning Commission, *Transcript of Commission Meeting*, October 5, 1995, p. 94. Haydn Williams, Background Interview, April 7, 2003, and Interview with Haydn Williams, November 7, 2003.

21. Commission of Fine Arts, *Transcript of Commission Meeting*, September 19, 1995, pp. 5–18. Commission of Fine Arts, *Minutes of the Meeting*, September 19, 1995, pp. 2–5.

22. National Capital Planning Commission, *Transcript of Commission Meeting*, October 5, 1995, pp. 96, 97, 102, 117.

23. Benjamin Forgey, "WWII Memorial Gets Choice Mall Site," *Washington Post*, October 6, 1995, p. B1. President Clinton, Remarks at the Dedication of the World War II Memorial Site, November 11, 1995. Howard Schneider and N. Scott Vance, "Center of Mall Reserved for World War II Shrine," *Washington Post*, November 12, 1995, p. B6. Mike Conley, E-mail on World War II Memorial Dedication, June 26, 2002.

24. Interview with Haydn Williams, May 13, 2003. American Battle Monuments Commission: General Fred Woerner, letter to ABMC Commissioners on committees, September 19, 1995. Neil B. Feldman, "Where Were We in '95?" *Washington Post*, June 11, 2000, p. B8. Linda Wheeler, "Dole Raps Critics of Memorial as Late," *Washington Post*, June 7, 2000, p. B3.

25. Interview with Sally Berk, May 20, 2002. Christopher Shea, "The Brawl on the Mall," *Preservation*, vol. 53 (January-February, 2001), p. 41. Commission of Fine Arts, *Minutes of the Meeting*, July 27, 1995, p. 1. Denise Liebowitz, public affairs officer, National Planning Commission. Letter on National Capital Planning Commission Agendas, April 7, 2003. National Capital Planning Commission, *Tentative Agenda Items*, September 14, 1995, p. 4. Benjamin Forgey, "Site-Seeking at the Mall," *Washington Post*, July 1, 1995, p. C1. Benjamin Forgey, "No Accord on WWII Memorial," *Washington Post*, July 28, 1995, p. B3. Benjamin Forgey, "New Mall Site Backed for WWII Memorial," *Washington Post*, September 20, 1995, p. A1. Benjamin Forgey, "WWII Memorial Gets Choice Mall Site," *Washington Post*, October 6, 1995, p. B1. Commission of Fine Arts, *Transcript of Meeting*, July 27, 1995, pp. 54–55. National Capital Planning Commission, *Transcript of Commission Meeting*, July 27, 1995, pp. 38–39, 46.

26. Commission of Fine Arts. J. Carter Brown, Letter to General Fred Woerner, July 30, 1997.

27. Interview with Senator Bob Kerrey, July 29, 2002. Interview with Mike Marinello, former aide to Senator Bob Kerrey, July 15, 2002. Janny Scott, "Planned Memorial Sets Off Its Own Battle in Washington," *New York Times*, March 18, 1997, p. C13.

28. National Capital Planning Commission. Senator Bob Kerrey, Letter to Harvey Gantt, chairman, National Capital Planning Commission, May 27, 1997.

29. Senator Bob Kerrey, "Concerns with the Selection of the Rainbow Pool Site," *Congressional Record*, June 25, 1997.

30. National Capital Planning Commission, *Transcript of Commission Meeting*, July 31, 1997, pp. 110–111. Roger Lewis, Deborah Dietsch, Senator Bob Kerrey, Dorn McGrath, The Committee of 100, and the Guild of Professional Tour Guides of Washington, D.C., *The World War II Memorial: Why the Rainbow Pool Site Is the Wrong Location, A White Paper*, 1997. (White Paper included in transcript of July 31, 1997, National Capital Planning Commission meeting.) Bob Kerrey and Strom Thurmond, Letter to the President, February 27, 1998.

31. American Battle Monuments Commission, *Chronology*, May 28, 2001, p. 3.

32. Bob Kerrey, *Statement Regarding the New World War II Design Concept*, May 13, 1998. Jake Thompson, "Kerrey Approves of Changes to World War II Memorial Design," *Omaha World-Herald*, May 14, 1998, p. 6. Interview with Bob Kerrey, July 29, 2002. Interview with Mike Marinello, July 15, 2002. See letters from the Senate and

House sent on July 9, 1998, to Harvey Gantt, Chairman of the National Capital Planning Commission and made part of National Capital Planning Commission, *Transcript of Planning Commission Meeting,* July 9, 1998.

33. U.S. Department of the Interior, National Park Service, *Cultural Landscape Report: West Potomac Park, Lincoln Memorial Grounds,* August 1999, p. 180. National Park Service, National Capital Region, *East and West Potomac Parks Historic District: Revised National Register of Historic Places Nomination,* July 16, 1999, pp. 9–11. Leonard J. Furbee, *The Reflecting and Rainbow Pools* (Washington, D.C.: U.S. Department of Interior, National Park Service, 1964), pp. 3–4. Commission of Fine Arts. Neil Feldman, Letter to Charles Atherton, executive secretary, Commission of Fine Arts, September 7, 2000. Neil Feldman, *Testimony to the National Capital Planning Commission,* September 21, 2000.

34. Advisory Council on Historic Preservation. Cathryn B. Slater, Letter to Bruce Babbitt, September 5, 2000.

35. Michael Richman, "A Memorial with History on Its Side," *Washington Post,* August 27, 2000, p. G7. Lincoln Memorial Commission, *Minutes,* January 28, 1922, Records of the Lincoln Memorial Commission, Records of the Office of Public Buildings and Public Parks of the National Capital, National Archives, p. 4.

36. National Park Service: Robert G. Stanton, *Memorandum to the Secretary of the Interior: Response to Comments from the Advisory Council on Historic Preservation Regarding the Proposed World War II Memorial,* September 13, 2000, p. 5. National Park Service, *Cultural Landscape Report: West Potomac Park, Lincoln Memorial Grounds,* August 1999, p. 178.

37. Christopher Thomas, *Memo to Judy Scott Feldman, Pam Scott, Michael Richman,* September 9, 2000. Interview with Richard Longstreth, July 8, 2002.

38. National Capital Planning Commission. Richard Moe, president of the National Trust for Historic Preservation, Letter to Harvey Gantt, chairman, National Capital Planning Commission, April 23, 1997. Judy Scott Feldman, *Testimony Before the National Capital Planning Commission on the Proposed World War II Memorial,* December 14, 2000.

39. Interview with Lisa Jorgenson, November 23, 2002. National Capital Planning Commission. Lisa Jorgenson, *Hydrology Concerns About the Proposed World War II Memorial Site,* June 4, 1998. Lisa Jorgenson, *Statement Before the National Capital Planning Commission on the Proposal for the World War II Memorial,* July 31, 1997. National Capital Planning Commission, *Transcript of Commission Meeting,* July 31, 1997, pp. 180–189. National Capital Planning Commission, *Transcript of Commission Meeting,* July 8, 1998, pp. 113–118.

40. An Engineering Report on the Possible Effects of the World War II Memorial Construction on the Washington Monument, Prepared by Charles Gavin, P.E., Gavin and Associates, Inc., August 29, 2001. National Coalition to Save Our Mall, *If the World War II Memorial Is Built Across the Mall, The Washington Monument May Fall Over,* August 30, 2001. National Park Service, *Environmental Assessment: The National World War II Memorial,* May 1998.

41. Environmental Protection Agency, E-mail to Ken Terry saying that ground water and storm water collected in Rainbow Pool will not exceed District of Columbia Water Standards and may be discharged into Tidal Basin, April 30, 2002. Environmental Protection Agency Fax to Ken Terry saying ground water collected at World War II Memorial site will not exceed District of Columbia Water Quality Standards and may be discharged into Tidal Basin, July 24, 2002. Interview with Barry Owenby, American Battle Monuments Commission director of Procurement and Contracting, June 21, 2002. Laurie A. Shuster, "Washington Monument's Foundation Not Threatened by Memorial," *Civil Engineering*, vol. 72 (January 2002), pp. 16–17.

42. Judy Scott Feldman, *Testimony Before the National Capital Planning Commission on the Proposed World War II Memorial*, December 14, 2000. National Capital Planning Commission: Law Office of Daniel Wemhoff, Letter to National Capital Planning Commission, September 24, 2000.

43. Eleanor Holmes Norton, News Release, September 6, 2000. Interview with Eleanor Holmes Norton, January 9, 2002. Eleanor Holmes Norton quoted in Richard Benedetto, "World War II Tribute Set in Stone," *USA Today*, May 23, 2001, p. A3.

44. National Capital Planning Commission, *Transcript of Commission Meeting*, September 21, 2000, pp. 46–53.

45. Ibid., pp. 43–46. National Park Service calculates distance from steps of the Lincoln Memorial to eastern edge of Reflecting Pool as 765 yards. E-mail from Mike Conley, July 9, 2003.

46. Jonathan Yardley, "Tunnel Vision: A Compromise for the Mall," *Washington Post*, September 11, 2000, p. C2.

47. Commission of Fine Arts, *Transcript of Commission Meeting*, July 27, 1995, p. 30.

## CHAPTER FIVE

1. Jory Johnson, "Granite Platoon," *Landscape Architecture*, vol. 80 (January 1990), pp. 69–70.

2. Roger Lewis, "Washington Monuments: Battles Over the Mall," *Architectural Record*, vol. 184 (January 1996), p. 17. Heidi Landecker, "Architects File Suit Over Changes in Korean War Memorial Design," *Architecture*, vol. 80 (February 1991), pp. 26–27. Barbara Gamarekian, "Architects Clash Over Korean War Memorial," *New York Times*, December 15, 1990, Section 1, p. 17. Benjamin Forgey, "Competition Set for War Memorial," *Washington Post*, April 17, 1996, p. C6.

3. Minutes of the Commission of Fine Arts, July 25, 1996, p. 3. National Capital Planning Commission, *Transcript of Commission Meeting*, July 25, 1996, pp. 13–14. Interview with Haydn Williams, May 13, 2003. General Services Administration, Public Building Service, *Design Excellence Program*, http://hydra.gsa.gov/pbs/pc/ds_files/excellen.htm, pp. 1–3. Interview with Ed Feiner, chief architect, General Services Administration, May 28, 2002. Interview with Brian Peper, project manager, General Services Administration, May 27, 2003. E-mail from Marilyn Farley, May 28, 2003.

4. Edward Wyatt, "There's Nothing So Closed as an Open Competition," *New York Times*, August 31, 2003, Section 2, p. 18. Interview with Haydn Williams, November 7, 2003. American Battle Monuments Commission. Haydn Williams, Memo to ABMC Commissioners, March 27, 1996. "National World War II Memorial Design," *Commerce Business Daily*, April 19, 1996.

5. Paul D. Spreiregen, "A Democratic Approach for Our World War II Memorial," *Washington Post*, May 5, 1996, p. C8.

6. American Battle Monuments Commission. Colonel Kevin C. Kelley, *Memo to Haydn Williams*, March 14, 1996. "National World War II Design," *Commerce Business Daily*, May 17, 1996.

7. Benjamin Forgey, "War Memorial Battle," *Washington Post*, May 21, 1996, p. B2. Interview with Jaan Holt and Susan Piedmont-Palladino, August 20, 2002.

8. Forgey, "War Memorial Battle," p. B2. Washington Area Architecture Group, *Petition of Protest*, May 16, 1996. Forgey, "War Memorial Battle," p. B2.

9. Interview with Haydn Williams, May 13, 2003. Forgey, "War Memorial Battle," p. B2. Roberta Hershenson, "The Fight for the World War II Memorial," *New York Times*, July 27, 1997, Section 13, p. 13. Interview with Bill Lacy, February 15, 2002.

10. Interview with Bill Lacy, February 15, 2002. Interview with Brian Peper, May 27, 2003.

11. Interview with Bill Lacy, February 15, 2002. Interview with Haydn Williams, May 13, 2003. Benjamin Forgey, "Battle Lines Redrawn: New Rules for Design of War Memorial," *Washington Post*, June 11, 1996, p. E2. General Services Administration: Bill Lacy, *Proposed Amendment to CBD Announcement*, May 26, 1996. General Services Administration: Bill Lacy, *Memorandum to the American Battle Monuments Commission and General Services Administration: CBD Announcement Recommendations*, May 28, 1996.

12. "National World War II Memorial Design," *Commerce Business Daily*, June 11, 1996.

13. General Services Administration. Bill Lacy, Letter to Haydn Williams, June 6, 1996. Interview with Haydn Williams, November 7, 2003. American Battle Monuments Commission. Haydn Williams, Memo to ABMC Commissioners, June 11, 1996. Interview with Jaan Holt, August 20, 2002. American Battle Monuments Commission, Preliminary Program Brochure.

14. Hugh Hardy, "Remarks at Round Table Discussion of World War II Memorial at National World War II Memorial Symposium," Rhode Island School of Design, April 26, 1977. General Services Administration. Bill Lacy, Letter to Bob Peck, General Services Administration Commissioner, June 12, 1996. Stanley Collyer, "Surgery on the Mall: World War II Memorial Site Still the Center of a Major Controversy," *Competitions*, vol. 7 (Summer 1997), p. 7.

15. Interview with Haydn Williams, May 13, 2003. Benjamin Forgey, "Designs on History," *Washington Post*, August 22, 1996, p. C1.

16. Haydn Williams, *Notes for World War II Memorial ABMC Stage II Orientation Session*, August 29, 1996, pp. 1–8.

17. "National World War II Memorial Design," *Commerce Business Daily*, August 23, 1996. American Battle Monuments Commission, *The National World War II Memorial Design Competition Program*, pp. 2–9.

18. Bill Lacy quoted in Forgey, "Designs on History," p. C1.

19. Rhode Island School of Design Department of Architecture, *The National World War II Memorial Competition: A Symposium*, April 26, 1997. Brian Peper, "The Public Display for the Entries," E-mail, June 6, 2003. Collyer, "Surgery on the Mall," p. 7. Forgey, "Designs on History," p. C1.

20. Deborah Dietsch, "Memorial Madness," *Architecture*, vol. 85 (July 1996), p. 15. Roger Lewis, "Proposed World War II Memorial Site Is Land Worth Fighting Over," *Washington Post*, August 17, 1996, p. E1. Benjamin Forgey, "Tactical Error: World War II Monument Site Is No Place for a Museum," *Washington Post*, September 7, 1996, p. C1.

21. Haydn Williams, "The Right Place for a Memorial," *Washington Post*, September 29, 1996, p. C8.

22. Interviews with Brian and Katherine Ambroziak, July 16, 2002, and May 12, 2003. Brian and Katherine Ambroziak, Material Submitted for World War II Memorial Competition. Bran and Katherine Ambroziak, Notes on World War II Memorial Proposal, July 18, 2003.

23. Interview with Diana Balmori, July 25, 2002. Diana Balmori, Material Submitted for World War II Memorial Competition. Rhode Island School of Design Department of Architecture, *Transcript of The National World War II Memorial Competition Symposium*. Diana Balmori, E-mail, December 1, 2003.

24. Interview with Rafael Viñoly, December 2, 2002. Interview with Ramon Viñoly, July 31, 2002. Rafael Viñoly Architects, *National World War II Memorial, Washington, D.C.*, July 21, 2002. Statement by Rafael Viñoly Architects in booklet published by Rhode Island School of Design Department of Architecture for *The National World War II Memorial Competition: A Symposium*.

25. Interview with Marion Weiss and Michael A. Manfredi, July 29, 2002. Marion Weiss and Michael A. Manfredi, *Site Specific: The Work of Weiss/Manfredi Architects* (Princeton: Princeton Architecture Press, 2000), pp. 38–43. Statement by Marion Weiss and Michael A. Manfredi in booklet published by Rhode Island School of Design Department of Architecture for *The National World War II Memorial Competition: A Symposium*.

26. Interview with Bernard Wulff and William Jackson, March 29, 2002. Material submitted by Bernard Wulff and William Jackson for World War II Memorial Competition. Statement by Bernard Wulff and William Jackson in booklet published by the Rhode Island School of Design Department of Architecture for *The National World War II Memorial Competition: A Symposium*. Interview with Bernard Wulff, December 1, 2003.

27. "World War II Design Winner Tells of Challenge and Triumph," *Architectural Record*, vol. 85 (March 1997), p. 31. Benjamin Forgey, "A Just Victory for WWII Memorial Design," *Washington Post*, May 3, 1997, p. C1.

28. Benjamin Forgey, "World War II Memorial Design Unveiled," *Washington Post*, January 18, 1997, p. A1. Interview with Friedrich St.Florian, February 18, 2002. Notes from Friedrich St.Florian on World War II Memorial Dimension, E-mail, June 12, 2003.

29. Interview with Haydn Williams, May 13, 2003.

30. J. Carter Brown quoted in Forgey, "World War II Memorial Design Unveiled," p. A1. Interview with Hugh Hardy, October 5, 2002. Interview with Laurie Olin, November 21, 2002.

31. Interview with Friedrich St.Florian, November 12, 2001.

32. Interview with David Childs, September 12, 2002. Interview with Haydn Williams, May 13, 2003.

33. Forgey, "World War II Memorial Design Unveiled," p. A1.

34. James Bennet, "With Ballots Still Warm, Clinton Pays Homage to Dole," *New York Times*, January 18, 1997, Section 1, p. 12. Peter Baker, "Bob Dole, Every Inch a Winner; Two Political Opponents Score a Mutual Victory at Emotional Award Ceremony," *Washington Post*, January 18, 1997, p. D1.

35. Remarks by the President and Senator Robert Dole at Presentation of Medal of Freedom to Senator Dole, January 17, 1997, from Clinton Presidential Materials Project of the National Archives.

36. Interviews with Haydn Williams, April 10, 2002, November 7, 2003, and August 28, 2002. Interview with Bob Dole, June 18, 2002. National World War II Memorial, *Review by Fiscal Year*, March 31, 2002.

## CHAPTER SIX

1. Sarah Bayliss, "The Man Behind the World War II Memorial," *Boston Globe*, August 26, 2001, p. L1. Interview with Friedrich St.Florian, February 18–19, 2002.

2. Interview with Friedrich St.Florian, February 18–19, 2002.

3. Ibid. Eric Pfanner, "What's Doing in Graz," *New York Times*, March 16, 2003, Section 5, p. 13.

4. Herbert Muschamp, "A Gift from Vienna That Skips the Schlag," *New York Times*, April 19, 2002, pp. E33–38. *Friedrich St.Florian: Projects 1961–1976* (Austin: University of Texas at Austin Art Museum, 1976). *Friedrich St.Florian, Architect* (Providence, Rhode Island, n.d.). Interview with Friedrich St.Florian, February 18–19, 2002.

5. *Friedrich St.Florian, Architect*. Interview with Friedrich St.Florian, February 18–19, 2002.

6. Interview with Friedrich St.Florian, February 18–19, 2002.

7. Interview with Friedrich St.Florian, February 18–19, 2002. Benjamin Forgey, "Leaving a Mark on Washington: The War Memorial Designer," *Washington Post*, April 6, 1997, p. G1.

8. *Friedrich St.Florian: Projects, 1961–1976*. Interview with Friedrich St.Florian, February 18–19, 2002.

9. Interview with Friedrich St.Florian, February 18–19, 2002. *Friedrich St.Florian, Architect.*

10. Interview with J. Carter Brown, November 13, 2001. The list of the 407 entrants who did not make the World War II Memorial competition finals is available from the General Services Administration.

11. Interview with Friedrich St.Florian, November 12, 2001. Elizabeth Greenwell Grossman, *The Civic Architecture of Paul Cret* (Cambridge: Cambridge University Press, 1996), pp. 168–179, 220. Patricia Cummings Loud, *The Art Museums of Louis Kahn* (Durham, N.C.: Duke University Press, 1989), pp. 28–33. American Battle Monuments Commission, *National World War II Memorial Design Competition*, August 29, 1966, pp. 5, 8.

12. Bayliss, "The Man Behind the World War II Memorial," p. L1.

13. Forgey, "World War II Memorial Design Unveiled," *Washington Post*, January 18, 1997, p. A1. Commission of Fine Arts, *Minutes of the Meeting*, July 24, 1997, p. 8.

14. Commission of Fine Arts, *Transcript of the Meeting*, July 24, 1977, pp. 49–66. National Capital Planning Commission, *Transcript of the Commission Meeting*, July 31, 1977, pp. 65–81.

15. Commission of Fine Arts, *Transcript of the Meeting*, July 24, 1997, pp. 132–145. National Capital Planning Commission, *Transcript of the Commission Meeting*, July 31, 1997, pp. 169–175. American Battle Monuments Commission. Haydn Williams, Letter to David M. Childs, August 13, 1997.

16. Linda Wheeler, "WWII Memorial Goes Back to the Drawing Board," *Washington Post*, July 25, 1997, p. A1. Linda Wheeler, "Capital Planning Commission Also Rejects Memorial Design," *Washington Post*, August 1, 1997, p. A15. Bill Van Siclen, "Panel: Design of World War II Memorial Needs Work," *Providence Journal-Bulletin*, July 25, 1997, p. A5. Benjamin Forgey, "Tactical Error; World War II Monument Site Is No Place for a Museum," *Washington Post*, September 7, 1996, p. C1. Commission of Fine Arts: J. Carter Brown, Letter to General Frederick Woerner Jr., July 30, 1997.

17. Interview with J. Carter Brown, May 13, 2001.

18. Commission of Fine Arts, *Transcript of the Meeting*, July 24, 1997, pp. 176–179. Commission of Fine Arts, *Minutes of the Meeting*, July 24, 1997, pp. 22–24.

19. "Hallowed Ground in Jeopardy," *New York Times*, July 4, 1997, p. A18. "Not This Design," *Washington Post*, July 27, 1997, p. C8. "The Monument and the Mall," *Cleveland Plain Dealer*, July 31, 1997, p. 10B.

20. Interviews with Friedrich St.Florian, November 12, 2001, and February 18, 2002. Commission of Fine Arts. J. Carter Brown, Letter to General Fred Woerner, July 30, 1997.

21. Interview with Friedrich St.Florian, November 12, 2001. Interviews with Haydn Williams, June 20, 2002, and November 7, 2003.

22. Interview with Haydn Williams, August 28, 2003. American Battle Monuments Commission.Haydn Williams, Letter to Bob Kerrey, September 18, 1997. Commission of Fine Arts, *Transcript of the Meeting*, May 21, 1998, pp. 8–12. National Capital Planning Commission, *Transcript of the Commission Meeting*, July 9, 1998, pp. 30–42. Judy Packer-Tursman, "Revision Scales Back WWII Memorial," *Pittsburgh Post-Gazette*, May 12, 1998, p. A1.

23. National Capital Planning Commission. Ted Stevens, Daniel Inouye et al., Letter to Harvey Gantt, Chairman, National Capital Planning Commission, July 9, 1988. National Capital Planning Commission. Marcy Kaptur, Henry Hyde et al., Letter to Harvey Gantt, Chairman, National Capital Planning Commission, July 9, 1998. Jake Thompson, "Kerrey Approves of Changes to WWII Memorial Design," *Omaha World-Herald*, May 14, 1998, p. 6. Linda Wheeler, "World War II Memorial: A Lower Profile," *Washington Post*, May 13, 1998, p. B1. Packer-Tursman, "Revision Scales Back WWII Memorial," p. A1.

24. Commission of Fine Arts, *Transcript of the Meeting*, May 21, 1998, pp. 12–14, 36. National Capital Planning Commission, *World War II Memorial: Report to the National Park Service and the American Battle Monuments Commission*, July 9, 1998, p. 8. John W. Fountain, "New Design for WWII Memorial Approved," Washington Post, July 11, 1998, p. C4.

25. Commission of Fine Arts. J. Carter Brown, Letter to Haydn Williams, American Battle Monuments Commission, May 26, 1998. National Capital Planning Commission, *World War II Memorial: Report to the National Park Service and the American Battle Monuments Commission*, July 9, 1998, pp. 8–9.

26. American Battle Monuments Site and Design Committee, Letter to Friedrich St.Florian, July 23, 1998. Interview with Friedrich St.Florian, February 18, 2002.

27. Commission of Fine Arts, *Transcript of the Meeting*, May 20, 1999, pp. 5–11. National Capital Planning Commission, *Transcript of the Commission Meeting*, June 3, 1999, pp. 24–42. Interview with Friedrich St.Florian, February 18, 2002. Friedrich St.Florian, The Pillars, E-mail, September 3, 2003.

28. Commission of Fine Arts, *Minutes of the Meeting*, May 20, 1999, p. 7. Commission of Fine Arts. J. Carter Brown, Letter to Terry R. Carlstrom, Regional Director, National Capital Region, National Park Service, May 25, 1999. National Capital Planning Commission, *World War II Memorial: Report to the National Park Service and the American Battle Monuments Commission*, June 3, 1999, pp. 5–6.

29. Commission of Fine Arts. J. Carter Brown, Letter to Terry R. Carlstrom. National Capital Planning Commission, *World War II Memorial: Report to the National Park Service and the American Battle Monuments Commission*, p. 6.

30. Interview with Friedrich St.Florian, February 18, 2002. Friedrich St.Florian, Drawings and computer renderings of World War II Memorial prior to completion.

31. Commission of Fine Arts, *Transcript of the Meeting*, July 20, 2000, pp. 57–69. National Capital Planning Commission, *Transcript of the Commission Meeting*, September 21, 2000, pp. 15–25.

32. Interview with Senator Bob Kerrey, July 29, 2002. Interview with Michael Marinello, July 15, 2002. Jacqueline Newmyer, "Panel Allows WWII Memorial Plan to March On," *Los Angeles Times*, July 21, 2000, p. F21. Linda Wheeler, "WWII Memorial's Design Gets Commission Approval," *Washington Post*, September 22, 2000, p. B1. Commission of Fine Arts, *Transcript of the Meeting*, July 20, 2000, pp. 149, 133. National Capital Planning Commission, *Transcript of the Commission Meeting*, September 21, 2000, pp. 47, 119.

33. Linda Wheeler, "WWII Memorial's Design Gets Commission Approval," *Washington Post*, September 22, 2000, p. B1.

34. Commission of Fine Arts. J. Carter Brown, Letter to Haydn Williams and American Battle Monuments Commission, July 27, 2000. National Capital Planning Commission, *World War II Memorial: Report to the National Park Service and American Battle Monuments Commission*, September 21, 2000, pp. 1–7. Interview with Haydn Williams, August 22 and 23, 2002.

35. Interview with George Hartman, January 10, 2002. J. Carter Brown quoted in Forgey, "World War II Memorial Design Unveiled," p. A1.

36. General Services Administration, Architect-Engineer Contract for the World War II Memorial Project, November 7, 1997. (Obtained through Freedom of Information Act request from the General Services Administration.) Interview with Leo A. Daly III, October 11, 2002. Interview with Deborah DeBernard, John Hart, Sean Imber, Al O'Konski, Darren Zehner, October 11, 2002. Interview with George M. White, January 6, 2003. Christine S. Kelly, contracting officer, General Services Administration, National Capital Region, Letter with enclosures to Deborah DeBernard, director of operations and vice president, Leo A Daly, on contractual role and responsibilities of Leo A Daly for National World War II Memorial Project, July 22, 2003. (Obtained through Freedom of Information Act request from the General Services Administration.)

## Chapter Seven

1. Mike Conley, World War II Memorial Revenue by Fiscal Year, E-mail, June 12, 2003. Reuben M. Rainey, "The Garden as Narrative: Lawrence Halprin's Franklin Delano Roosevelt Memorial," in Joachim Wolshke-Bulmahn, ed., *Places of Commemoration: Search for Identity and Landscape Design* (Washington, D.C.: Dumbarton Oaks Research Library, 2001), p. 377. Bill McAllister, "Foundations Finances Seen in Poor Shape," *Washington Post*, June 7, 1994, p. A14. American Battle Monuments Commission, *Record of Proceedings*, May 12, 1995. Interview with Mike Conley, February 9, 2004.

2. Interview with Fred Woerner, July 18, 2002. American Battle Monuments Commission: Colonel Kevin Kelley, *Outline of a Briefing to Commissioners on WWII Memorial*, September 29, 1994. Interview with Jess Hay, April 18, 2002. Libby Schnee, Letter on Burson-Marsteller World War II Memorial Campaign, E-mail, April 2, 2003.

3. Interview with Jess Hay, April 18, 2002. Interview with Fred Woerner, July 18, 2002. Curt Anderson, "Dole Defends Planned Site of World War II Memorial," *Chicago Sun-Times*, March 20, 1997, p. 18. Haydn Williams, Interview on 1995 Financial Discussions, September 9, 2003. Interview with John Herrling, April 19, 2001.

4. Interview with Bob Dole, June 18, 2002. Interview with Fred Smith, May 6, 2002.

5. Interview with John Herrling, August 19, 2002. Interview with Bob Dole, June 18, 2002.

6. Interview with Fred Woerner, July 18, 2002. Interview with John Herrling, August 19, 2002. Interview with Jim Aylward, March 28, 2002.

7. Interview with John Herrling, August 19, 2002. Rick Atkinson, "The Battle Over the Big One," *Talk*, November 1999, p. 224. Interview with Mike Conley, May 31, 2002.

8. Interview with Peter Himler, Libby Schnee, and Woody Woodruff, April 26, 2002. Interview with Ed Ney, May 2, 2002. Interview with Mike Conley, May 31, 2002. "News Roundup," *Brandweek*, March 29, 1999. Jane L. Levere, "Advertising," *New York Times*, July 1, 2002, p. C8. Mike Conley, ABMC Expenses, E-mail, July 7, 2003.

9. Interview with John "Skip" Shannon, November 5, 2002. Interview with Jim Aylward, March 28, 2002. Interview with Bob Dole, June 18, 2002.

10. Mike Conley, World War II Revenue by Fiscal Year, E-mail, July 7, 2003. Interviews with Mike Conley, August 18, 2003 and February 9, 2004.

11. Ibid. American Battle Monuments Commission, *World War II Memorial Cumulative Revenue from FY 93 to August 2003*, E-mail from Mike Conley, October 22, 2003. Interview with Rick Santos, American Legion, June 6, 2002. Interview with Ray Smith, American Legion, June 27, 2002. Terry Lefton, "The Game," *Brandweek*, May 17, 1999. Zane Fayos, Letter to Tom Hanks, April 12, 1999. Bob Dole, Mention of Zane Fayos at White House Remarks, June 29, 2000. American Battle Monuments Commission: Haydn Williams and Design Consultants Committee, *Year-End Report and Recommendations*, December 31, 2001. Mike Conley, ABMC Expenses, E-mail, July 7, 2003.

12. J. Carter Brown, "Why This Design Is a Winner," *Washington Post*, June 6, 2001, p. A27. Harry G. Robinson III, "Right Place, Right Memorial," *Washington Post*, July 23, 2000, p. B8.

13. Benjamin Forgey, "A Fitting Memorial in Every Way," *Washington Post*, July 15, 2002, p. C1. "Build the WWII Memorial," *Washington Post*, July 16, 2002, p. B6. Interview with Haydn Williams, February 10, 2004. Witold Rybczynski, "A Fitting Memorial to Those Who Won World War II," *Wall Street Journal*, September 21, 2000, p. A26. Robert Campbell, "World War II Vets Wait for Monumental Battle to End," *Boston Globe*, April 5, 2001, p. D1. National Capital Planning Commission: Richard Longstreth, Letter to Harvey B. Gantt, chairman, National Capital Planning Commission. Richard Longstreth, "The Right Solution," Unpublished op-ed, November 27, 2000. Interview with Richard Longstreth, July 8, 2002.

14. Ada Louise Huxtable, Letter to Haydn Williams, July 24, 1997.

15. "Hallowed Ground in Jeopardy," *New York Times*, July 4, 1997, p. A18. "Don't Mar the Mall," *New York Times*, September 24, 2000, Section 4, p. 14. Michael Kimmelman, "Turning Memory into Travesty," *New York Times*, March 4, 2001, Section 4, p. 5. Herbert Muschamp, "New War Memorial Is Shrine to Sentiment," *New York Times*, June 7, 2001, pp. A1, A30.

16. Paul Goldberger, "Not in Our Front Yard," *New Yorker*, August 7, 2000, pp. 27–28. Jonathan Yardley, "The Battle of the Mall," *Washington Post*, July 3, 2000, p.

C2. "Wrong Thing, Wrong Place," *Los Angeles Times*, July 19, 2000, p. B8. "Desecrating a Landmark to Build a Memorial," *San Francisco Chronicle*, October 8, 2000, p. 3/Z1. Christopher Knight, "Planned Memorial Would Damage Prime Piece of Real Estate," *Los Angeles Times*, July 19, 2000, p. F1. Nicolai Ouroussoff, "World War II Memorial: Sound the Retreat," *Los Angeles Times*, September 20, 2000, pp. F6-7. Jon Wiener, "Save the Mall," *Nation*, November 13, 2000, p. 19. Joseph Fishkin, "*Monumental* Error," *New Republic*, September 25, 2000, pp. 14–16. Catesby Leigh, "Our Monuments, Our Selves," *Weekly Standard*, March 5, 2001, p. 27.

17. Goldberger, "Not in Our Front Yard," pp. 27–28. Kimmelman, "Turning Memory into Travesty," Section 4, p. 5.

18. "World War II Memorial Misplaced," *USA Today*, July 20, 2000, p. 14A. Robert Ivy, "Keep Off the Grass," *Architectural Record*, vol. 188 (October 2000), p. 19. Leigh, "Our Monuments, Our Selves," p. 27.

19. Muschamp, "New War Memorial Is Shrine to Sentiment," pp. A1, A30.

20. Deborah K. Dietsch, "Capital Offense," *Architecture*, vol. 86 (March 1997), pp. 62–63. Goldberger, "Not in Our Front Yard," pp. 27–28. Kimmelman, "Turning Memory into Travesty," Section 4, p. 5. Ouroussoff, "World War II Memorial," pp. F6–7. Friedrich St.Florian quoted in Elaine Sciolino, "War Memorial Seems All but Certain on the Mall," *New York Times*, May 22, 2001, p. A14.

21. Interview with Hugh Hardy, October 5, 2002.

22. Goldberger, "Not in Our Front Yard," pp. 27–28.

23. Steven McLeon Bedford, *John Russell Pope: Architect of Empire* (New York: Rizzoli, 1988), p. 222.

24. National Capital Planning Commission, *Transcript of Meeting*, July 31, 1997, p. 54. Peter Adam, *Art of the Third Reich* (New York: Henry N. Abrams, 1988), p. 265. Interview with Richard Striner, August 26, 2002. Interview with Judy Scott Feldman, January 8, 2002. Richard Striner, Letter to Judy Scott Feldman, August 6, 1999. Judy Scott Feldman, Letter to Richard Striner, August 14, 1999. Richard Striner, Letter to Judy Scott Feldman, August 20, 1999. (Copies of the Feldman-Striner letters were specifically sent to the same four people: Tersh Boasberg, Richard Longstreth, Dorn McGrath, and J. Carter Brown.)

25. Linda Wheeler, "WWII Memorial's Site in Middle of Mall Is Under Attack," *Washington Post*, June 6, 2000, p. B1. Linda Wheeler, "WWII Memorial Foes Plan Another Volley," *Washington Post*, July 19, 2000, p. B1. Charles Krauthammer, "The WWII Memorial: Inadequate and Out of Place," *Washington Post*, July 28, 2000, p. A25.

26. National Capital Planning Commission, *Transcript of Meeting*, September 21, 2000, p. 73. National Capital Planning Commission. Judy Scott Feldman, Letter to Harvey Gantt, Chairman, National Capital Planning Commission, September 12, 2000. Judy Scott Feldman, E-mail, June 17, 2003. Judy Scott Feldman, E-mail, July 8, 2003.

27. Commission of Fine Arts. Neil Feldman, Letter to Charles Atherton, September 7, 2000. National Park Service, *Cultural Landscape Report: West Potomac Park. Lincoln Memorial Grounds*, August 1999, p. 169. National Park Service, *East and West*

*Potomac Parks Historic District: Revised National Register of Historic Places Nomination*, July 16, 1999, p. 11. Brian Sharp, "New Assault on WWII Memorial," *USA Today*, July 20, 2000, p. 6A. John Parsons quoted in Linda Wheeler, "WWII Memorial Foes Plan Another Volley," *Washington Post*, July 19, 2000, p. B8.

28. Advisory Council on Historic Preservation: John Fowler, executive director, Letter to Bruce Babbitt, secretary, Department of the Interior, July 25, 2000. American Battle Monuments Commission: Haydn Williams, Letter to Cathryn B. Slater, chairwoman, Advisory Council on Historic Preservation, September 22, 2000. Advisory Council on Historic Preservation: Don L. Klima, director office of planning and review, Letter to John Parsons, National Park Service, September 18, 1997. Advisory Council on Historic Preservation: John Fowler, Letter to Colonel John Brown, American Battle Monuments Commission, June 5, 1998. Advisory Council on Historic Preservation: Cathryn B. Slater, Letter to Bruce Babbitt, secretary, Department of the Interior, September 5, 2000. Linda Wheeler, "Federal Panel Criticizes WWII Memorial," *Washington Post*, September 7, 2000.

29. *National Coalition to Save Our Mall et al. v. Bruce Babbitt, Secretary of the Interior, et al.*, Complaint for Declaratory and Injunctive Relief, October 2, 2000.

30. Interview with Andrea Ferster, May 25, 2002. Andrea Ferster, E-mail, June 30, 2003. *National Coalition to Save Our Mall, et al. v. Bruce Babbitt, Secretary of the Interior, et al.*, Complaint for Declaratory and Injunctive Relief, October 2, 2000.

31. *National Coalition to Save Our Mall, et al. v. Bruce Babbitt, Secretary of the Interior, et al.*, Complaint for Declaratory and Injunctive Relief, October 2, 2000.

32. Andrea Ferster quoted in Kavita Kumar, "Groups Sue Over WWII Memorial," *Atlanta Journal and Constitution*, October 3, 2000, p. 5A. Interview with William Aileo, November 22, 2002.

33. American Battle Monuments Commission, *National World War II Memorial Groundbreaking Ceremony*, November 11, 2000.

34. American Battle Monuments Commission, *Transcript of World War II Memorial Groundbreaking Ceremony Speeches*, November 11, 2000.

35. Interview with Barry Owenby, August 18, 2003. Antonio Glib, "Permit Delays WWII Site," *Pittsburgh Post-Gazette*, November 11, 2000, p. A11. Jeff Gerth, "Groundbreaking of Sorts, for a Contested Memorial," *New York Times*, November 12, 2000, Section 1, p. 21.

36. *National Coalition to Save Our Mall, et al. v. Bruce Babbitt, Secretary of the Interior, et al.*, Answer, December 15, 2000, p. 16. *National Coalition to Save Our Mall, et al. v. Gale Norton, Secretary of the Interior, et al.*, Plaintiff's Motion for a Preliminary Injunction, February 15, 2001. Bill Miller, "Groups Seek Injunction on WWII Memorial," *Washington Post*, February 16, 2001, p. B9. Judge Henry H. Kennedy, Temporary Restraining Order for Plaintiffs in *National Coalition to Save Our Mall, et al. v. Gale Norton, Secretary of the Interior, et al.*, March 8, 2001.

37. Sciolino, "War Memorial Seems All but Certain," p. A14. Bill Miller, "Plans for WWII Memorial on Hold; Officials Question Legality of Vote Approving Design," *Washington Post*, March 9, 2001, p. B1.

38. *National Coalition to Save Our Mall, et al. v. Gale Norton, Secretary of the Interior, et al.*, Motion to Stay Proceedings and Suspend Scheduling Order, March 9, 2003.

39. *National Coalition to Save Our Mall, et al. v. Gale Norton, Secretary of the Interior, et al.*, Motion to Vacate Stay and Dismiss, May 29, 2001. Linda Wheeler, "Planners to Reconsider WWII Memorial Question," *Washington Post*, April 6, 2001, p. A10. National Capital Planning Commission, Press Release, Statement by NCPC Chairman Richard Friedman, April 5, 2001.

40. National Capital Planning Commission, *Commission Member Biographies*. Interview with Harvey Gantt, February 11, 2002. Interview with Richard Friedman, February 17, 2002.

41. National Capital Planning Commission, *Transcript of Commission Meeting*, May 3, 2001, pp. 135–138, 146–147, 148–149, 160, 182, 189–190. Interview with Barry Owenby, August 18, 2003.

42. Linda Wheeler, "World War II Memorial Site, Design to be Reconsidered," *Washington Post*, May 4, 2001, p. A1. Elaine Sciolino, "Panel Votes to Review Plan for World War II Memorial," *New York Times*, May 4, 2001, p. A14. Benjamin Forgey, "An Overdue Honor for WWII Veterans Once Again Is Unjustly in the Line of Fire," *Washington Post*, May 5, 2001, p. C1.

43. Interview with Margaret Vanderhye, May 30, 2002. Spencer S. Hsu and Linda Wheeler, "WWII Memorial on Mall Gets Final Approval," *Washington Post*, May 23, 2001, p. B1.

44. Linda Wheeler, "House Vote Backs World War II Memorial as Planned," *Washington Post*, May 16, 2001, p. A1. Senator Ted Stevens, Speech in *Congressional Record*, May 21, 2001, p. S5262. Interview with Bob Dole, June 18, 2002.

45. Linda Wheeler, "Panel Not Planning to Vote Again on Memorial Site," *Washington Post*, May 9, 2001, p. B3.

46. S. 580, *Bill to Expedite the Construction of the World War II Memorial in the District of Columbia,* 107th Congress, March 20, 2001. Interview with Senator Tim Hutchinson, December 9, 2002. Tim Dyhouse, "Construction Halted on WWII Memorial," *Veterans of Foreign Wars Magazine*, vol. 88 (May 2001), p. 11.

47. H.R. 1696, *Bill to Expedite the Construction of the World War II Memorial in the District of Columbia,* 107th Congress, May 3, 2001. *Congressional Record*, May 21, 2001, pp. S5260-S5262. *H.R. 1696: Bill Summary and Status for the 107th Congress.*

48. Sciolino, "War Memorial Seems All but Certain on the Mall," p. A14. "Bush Signs WWII Memorial Bill," *Los Angeles Times*, May 29, 2001, p. A12.

49. Public Law 107–11, *To Expedite the Construction of the World War II Memorial in the District of Columbia,* 107th Congress, May 28, 2001.

50. Robert Campbell, "WWII Vets Wait for Monumental Battle to End," *Boston Globe*, April 5, 2001, p. D5. Commission of Fine Arts. Charles H. Atherton, Secretary of the Commission of Fine Arts, Letter to John D. Burnham, Office of Management and Budget, May 9, 2001. Interview with Bob Dole, June 18, 2002. Interview with Frank Moore, May 29, 2003.

51. Interview with Andrea Ferster, May 25, 2002. Elaine Sciolino, "War Memorial Builder Has Link to Nazi Era," *New York Times*, June 13, 2001, p. A31. Spenser S. Hsu, "Memorial Builder's Parent Firm Used Slave Labor During WWII," *Washington Post*, June 14, 2001, p. B4. General Accounting Office, Letter to John Warner and Committee on Armed Services, November 30, 2001. Richard Benedetto, "WWII Memorial's Foes Have New Bullet," *USA Today*, June 13, 2001, p. A11.

52. *National Coalition to Save Our Mall, et al. v. Gale Norton, Secretary of the Interior, et al.*, Motion to Vacate Stay and Dismiss, May 29, 2001.

53. *National Coalition to Save Our Mall, et al. v. Gale Norton, Secretary of the Interior, et al.*, Plaintiffs' Second Application for a Temporary Restraining Order, June 4, 2001, pp. 5, 12–15.

54. Andrea Ferster, The National World War II Memorial, E-mail, October 3, 2003. "Judge Refuses to Block Contracts for War Memorial on the Mall," *New York Times*, June 8, 2001, p. A22. Arthur Santana, "Judge Clears WWII Memorial Plan," *Washington Post*, August 17, 2001, p. B2. Memorandum opinion by Judge Henry H. Kennedy Jr., *National Coalition to Save Our Mall, et al. v. Gale Norton, Secretary of the Interior, et al.*, August 16, 2001, pp. 4, 7. Bill Miller, "Foes of WWII Memorial Site Urge Revival of Lawsuit," *Washington Post*, October 11, 2001, p. B2. Opinion for Court filed by Senior Circuit Judge Stephen F. Williams, in United States Court of Appeals for the District of Columbia in *National Coalition to Save Our Mall, et al. v. Gale Norton, Secretary of the Interior, et al.*, November 6, 2001, pp. 3–4. Bill Miller, "Appeals Court Rejects Suit Over WWII Memorial Site," *Washington Post*, November 7, 2001.

55. National Coalition to Save Our Mall, E-mail on News from U.S. Court of Appeals, February 14, 2002. Andrea Ferster, E-mail on Supreme Court Decision, June 18, 2003. Andrea Ferster, Petition for a Writ of Certiorari in the Supreme Court of the United States for *National Coalition to Save Our Mall, et al. v. Gale Norton Secretary of the Interior, et al.*, May 3, 2002. Opinion of the Supreme Court of the United States, *National Coalition to Save Our Mall, et al. v. Gale Norton, Secretary of the Interior, et al.*, October 7, 2002.

56. J. Carter Brown quoted in "U.S. Commission Approves Design for World War II Memorial on National Mall," *CNN.com, U.S. News*, July 21, 2000.

## Chapter Eight

1. Interview with Ken Terry, December 23, 2001. Ken Terry, E-mail on grandfathers, July 11, 2003.

2. Interview with Victor McCoy, April 4, 2002.

3. Interview with Barry Owenby, July 16, 2003.

4. Interview with Victor McCoy, April 4, 2002. Interview with Barry Owenby, January 6, 2003.

5. National Coalition to Save Our Mall, "Mud Pit," "Eye in the Sky," and "Construction Begins," www.Savethemall.org/wwii/gallery. Interview with Mike Conley, May 31, 2002.

6. Barry Owenby, *National World War II Information*, June 3, 2003. American Battle Monuments Commission, *National World War II Memorial Construction Fact Sheet*. National World War II Memorial, *Construction Fact Sheet*, November 12, 2002. Interview with James Walsh, March 27, 2002. Interview with Wayne Kaiser, June 21, 2002.

7. Interview with James Walsh, March 27, 2002. Christopher A. Thomas, *The Lincoln Memorial and American Life* (Princeton: Princeton University Press, 2002), pp. 104–105.

8. American Battle Monuments Commission, *National World War II Memorial*. American Battle Monuments Commission. Gilbane Building Company, *National World War II Memorial Project Schedule Major Activities*. Interview with Darrell Brown, Barry Owenby, Lawrence Rebel, and Ken Terry, May 29, 2003.

9. Henry Adams, *Mont-St. Michel and Chartres* (New York: Gallery Books, 1980), p. 100. Robert Bellah, "Civil Religion in America," *Daedalus* (Winter 1967), pp. 1–21. Leo Marx, *The Pilot and the Passenger* (New York: Oxford University Press, 1988), pp. 262–263. Interview with James Walsh, March 27, 2002.

10. Interview with Darrell Brown, Barry Owenby, Lawrence Rebel, and Ken Terry, May 29, 2003.

11. Interview with Barry Owenby, June 21, 2002. Interview with Darrell Brown, Barry Owenby, Lawrence Rebel, and Ken Terry, May 29, 2003.

12. Interview with Darrell Brown, Barry Ownby, Lawrence Rebel, and Ken Terry, May 29, 2003. Interview with Barry Owenby, June 21, 2002. Interview with Ken Terry, December 23, 2001. Ken Terry, Building a Slurry Wall, E-mail, June 14 and June 15, 2003.

13. Interview with Darrell Brown, Barry Owenby, Lawrence Rebel, and Ken Terry, May 29, 2003. Barry Owenby, *National World War II Memorial Information*, June 3, 2003. American Battle Monuments Commission, *National World War II Memorial: Interesting Facts*. Ken Terry, Pile Driving, E-mail, July 15, 2003.

14. Interview with Darrell Brown, Barry Owenby, Lawrence Rebel, and Ken Terry, May 29, 2003. Interview with Barry Owenby, August 18, 2003. Barry Owenby, *National World War II Memorial Information*, June 3, 2003.

15. Interview with Darrell Brown, Barry Owenby, Lawrence Rebel, and Ken Terry, May, 29, 2003. Barry Owenby, Answers to Questions, April 15, 2003. Interview with Robert DeFeo, chief horticulturist, National Park Service, National Capital Region, June 25, 2003. Kaskey Studio, *Freedom Wall/Field of Stars Plan and Elevation*, July 15, 2002. Interviews with Nick Benson, August 18, 2003, and September 5, 2003.

16. Thomas, *The Lincoln Memorial and American Life*, p. 107. Helen N. Fagin, "An Imagined Walk Through the National World War II Memorial," unpublished essay, August 31, 1998.

17. National Capital Planning Commission, *Transcript of Commission Meeting*, September 21, 2000, p. 66. Commission of Fine Arts, *Transcript of Meeting*, May 21, 1998, p. 9. American Battle Monument Commission, *National World War II Memorial: Interesting Facts*. American Battle Monuments Commission, *National World War II Memorial Material Information*.

18. American Battle Monuments Commission, *National World War II Memorial Inscriptions Record*, May 19, 2003.

19. American Battle Monuments Commission, "Bas-Relief Panels," *National World War II Memorial: Final Artwork Development CFA Submission*. David Montgomery, "Bronze Star; With WWII Memorial Sculptor Ray Kaskey Is on the Front Lines of Art," *Washington Post*, September 19, 2002, p. C1. Tom Wolfe, *Hooking Up* (New York: Farrar Straus Giroux, 2000), p. 137. Donald Miller, "War and Remembrance," *Pittsburgh Post-Gazette*, October 29, 2000, p. G-3. Interviews with Ray Kaskey, January 9, 2002, and August 18, 2003.

20. Barry Owenby, *National World War II Memorial Information*, June 3, 2003. Barry Owenby, Answers to Questions, April 15, 2003.

21. Alan Borg, *War Memorials: From Antiquity to the Present* (London: Leo Cooper 1991), pp. 58–59. William L. MacDonald, *The Architecture of the Roman Empire*, vol. 2 (New Haven: Yale University Press, 1986), pp. 74–77. H. W. Janson, *History of Art* (New York: Henry N. Abrams, 1982), pp. 169–176. Vincent Scully, *Architecture: The Natural and the Manmade* (New York: St. Martin's Press, 1991), pp. 356–366. Helene Lipstadt, "Learning from Lutyens," *Harvard Design Magazine* (Fall 1999), pp. 65–70.

22. Interviews with Ray Kaskey, January 9, 2002, and August 18, 2003. American Battle Monuments Commission, *National World War II Memorial Inscriptions Record*, May 19, 2003. Commission of Fine Arts, *Transcript of Meeting*, May 20, 1999, p. 7. Barry Owenby, Answers to Questions, April 15, 2003.

23. National Capital Planning Commission, *World War II Memorial: Report to the National Park Service and American Battle Monuments Commission*, September 21, 2000, p. 6. Ken Terry, Freedom Wall Dimensions, E-mail, July 21, 2003. Commission of Fine Arts, *Transcript of Meeting*, November 16, 2000, p. 13. American Battle Monuments Commission, *National World War II Memorial: Interesting Facts*. American Battle Monuments Commission, *National World War II Memorial Material Information*. Interview with Friedrich St.Florian, August 22, 2003.

24. Tom Carhart, "Insulting Vietnam Vets," *New York Times*, October 24, 1981, Section 1, p. 23. John W. Reps, *Monumental Washington: The Planning and Development of the Capital Center* (Princeton: Princeton University Press, 1967), pp. 158–159. Glenn Brown, *Memories, 1860–1930: A Winning Crusade to Revive George Washington's Vision of a Capital City* (Washington, D.C.: W. F. Roberts, 1931), p. 102.

25. Thomas, *The Lincoln Memorial and American Life*, pp. 153–157. David W. Blight, *Race and Reunion* (Cambridge: Harvard University Press, 2001), pp. 384–386. David Brinkley, *Washington Goes to War* (New York: Ballantine Books, 1996), p. 17.

26. For an early observation on the Bernini-St.Florian link, see Benjamin Forgey, "World War II Memorial Design Unveiled," *Washington Post*, January 18, 1997, p. A1.

27. Interview with James van Sweden, March 26, 2002. Commission of Fine Arts, *Transcript of Meeting*, May 20, 1999, p. 14. American Battle Monuments Commission, *National World War II Memorial: Final Architectural CFA/NCPC Submission*, June 30, 2000, p. F2. Barry Owenby, E-mail, October 21, 2003.

28. *Report of the Joint Task Force on Memorials*, August 2001, p. 4. National Capital Planning Commission, *Memorials and Museum Master Plan*, December 2001, p. 7. Elaine Sciolino, "Fighting for Space in Memorial Heaven," *New York Times*, June 28, 2001, p. A24. Elaine Sciolino, "Agencies Limit New Memorials on Coveted Washington Mall," *New York Times*, September 7, 2001, p. A14.

29. Jean Bethke Elshtain, "Spielberg's America," *Tikkun*, vol. 13 (November-December 1998), p. 73. George F. Will, "A Summons to Gratitude," *Newsweek*, August 17, 1998, p. 70. Richard T. Jameson, "History's Eyes: Saving Private Ryan," *Film Comment*, vol. 34 (September-October 1998), pp. 20–23. Nicholas Confessore, "Selling Private Ryan," *American Prospect*, vol. 12 (September 24–October 8, 2001), pp. 21–27. Interview with Friedrich St.Florian, February 18, 2002. Mike Anton, "Strain of Taps," *Los Angeles Times*, November 11, 2002, p. A1. National Center for Veterans Analysis and Statistics, Department of Veterans Affairs, October 24, 2003.

# INDEX